CRIME COUNTS

A Criminal Event Analysis

CRIME COUNTS

A Criminal Event Analysis

edited by

Leslie W. Kennedy
University of Alberta

Vincent F. Sacco
Queen's University

Nelson Canada

I(T)P An International Thomson Publishing Company

Toronto • Albany • Bonn • Boston • Cincinnati • Detroit • London • Madrid • Melbourne
Mexico City • New York • Pacific Grove • Paris • San Francisco • Singapore • Tokyo • Washington

I(T)P

© Nelson Canada
A Division of Thomson Canada Limited, 1996

Published in 1996 by
Nelson Canada,
A Division of Thomson Canada Limited
1120 Birchmount Road
Scarborough, Ontario M1K 5G4

Cover photo: Andrea Sperling—FPG/Masterfile

Canadian Cataloguing in Publication Data

Main entry under title:

　Crime counts

Includes bibliographical references.
ISBN 0-17-604884-7

1. Crime analysis. 2. Crime analysis—Statistics.
3. Criminal statistics. I. Kennedy, Leslie W., 1951– .
II. Sacco, Vincent F., 1948– .

HV7936.C88C75 1996　　364'.042　　　C95-933341-X

Publisher and Team Leader	Michael Young
Acquisitions Editor	Charlotte Forbes
Production Editor	Tracy Bordian
Project Coordinator	Heather Martin
Production Coordinator	Brad Horning
Art Director	Liz Harasymczuk
Cover Design	Julie Greener
Composition Analyst	Nelson Gonzalez

Printed and bound in Canada

1 2 3 4 (BG) 99 99 97 96

CONTENTS

Preface   VII

■ PART I—COUNTING CRIMINAL EVENTS

Chapter 1 Crime Counts and the
Analysis of Crime as a Social Event
LESLIE W. KENNEDY AND VINCENT F. SACCO   3

Chapter 2 Data and Methodology in the Area
of Criminal Justice
BOB GRAINGER   21

■ PART II—OVERALL CRIME TRENDS

Chapter 3 Canadian Crime Trends
MICHAEL MARTIN AND LUCIE ORGRODNIK   43

■ PART III—CRIMES AGAINST PEOPLE

Chapter 4 Homicide
CHRISTINE WRIGHT AND OREST FEDOROWYCZ   63

Chapter 5 Robbery
YVAN CLERMONT   85

Chapter 6 Assault
BOB KINGSLEY   99

Chapter 7 Crimes Against Women and Children in the Family
KAREN RODGERS AND REBECCA KONG   115

Chapter 8 Sexual Assault
HOLLY JOHNSON   133

■ PART IV—PROPERTY CRIME

Chapter 9 Break and Enter
PETER GREENBERG   153

Chapter 10 Fraud
PAUL McPHIE   167

Chapter 11 Theft
DIANNE HENDRICK   181

Chapter 12 Motor-Vehicle Crimes
PETER MORRISON   195

■ PART V—SPECIAL TOPICS—DRUGS AND YOUTH

Chapter 13 Illicit Drugs
LEE WOLFF AND VALERIE POTTIE BUNGE   217

Chapter 14 Youth Crime
GLEN DOHERTY AND PAUL DE SOUZA   231

■ PART VI—OVERVIEW OF CRIMINAL JUSTICE FACTS

Chapter 15 Policing
GAIL YOUNG   255

Chapter 16 The Courts
SANDRA BESSERER AND R. CRAIG GRIMES   271

Chapter 17 The Correctional System
TIM FORAN AND MICHELINE REED   293

References   313
Copyright Acknowledgments   323

PREFACE

When we wrote *The Criminal Event,* it was our intention to offer a new way in which students of criminology could look at crime as a social event. The intention was to focus the study of crime not just on what the offender does but also on the factors that precede crime, the interactions that make it up, and the consequences that crime has. Using this integrated perspective, we apply the different theoretical perspectives developed in criminology to explanations of crime interactions and crime outcomes.

In the last few years, there has been an explosion in information about crime in Canada, but this has often been presented in a fragmented and disjointed fashion. In discussion with Nelson Canada, we suggested that there was a need for a companion book to *The Criminal Event* that applied the integrating perspective of the criminal event to the study of specific types of crime. The book would be strongly empirical and would present arguments about the causes, content, and aftermath of criminal events using contemporary crime data.

The best information about crime in this country is collected and compiled by the Canadian Centre for Justice Statistics, a division of Statistics Canada. We approached its then executive director, Dr. Sangadasa de Silva, and asked him what the best approach would be to incorporate data from the Centre into a book that provided an authoritative survey of crime events in Canada. His suggestion, which we followed, was to ask members of the Centre to write chapters that applied the criminal event perspective to the study of different crime types. By working with Centre staff, we could not only benefit from their professional expertise but also from their access to the microdata files that are not publicly available. The analyses that appear in this book, as a result, provide an authoritative and unique insight into crime in Canada.

We have many people to thank for their help in making this project a reality. Charlotte Forbes, Nelson Canada Acquisitions Editor, had the foresight and courage to sign this book. We thank her, as usual, for her continued support. Heather Martin provided the logistical support for the project and displayed her usual calm and patience when we hit the odd bump on the road to completion. Tracy Bordian and Sarah Robertson made the production process look easy. We would also like to thank the reviewers—Brian Burtch (Simon Fraser University), Larry Comeau (Sheridan College), David Forde (University of Memphis), Chris McCormick (Acadia University), and Scott Nicholls (Humber College)—who provided important feedback to the project, making the product much better than what they first saw.

At Statistics Canada, we thank Sange and have a special thanks for Paul McPhie, who acted as our point man coordinating our contact with authors. This project would have been much more difficult and frustrating without his strong support and encouragement. Thanks to the authors who took the time to prepare the material and to respond to our requests for changes. Mimi Gauthier deserves a special thanks for following up on our requests for papers and making sure that we met some tight deadlines.

Les Kennedy would like to thank his colleagues and support staff at the University of Alberta for their support of this work. Specifically, the constant help from Fran Russell, Kelly McGuirk, and Kerri Calvert is appreciated more than they know. Of course, special thanks go to Ilona, Alexis, and Andrea for providing perspective as well as the moral support that is needed to complete a long, intensive job of editing. This manuscript went everywhere for a time, including a camping trip to the mountains.

Vince Sacco would like to thank his friends and colleagues at Queen's University and elsewhere for their advice and guidance. As always, I extend my deepest gratitude to Tiia, Katherin, and Daniel who stuck with me even though I got them lost in more than one urban high-crime area while this book was in preparation.

Leslie W. Kennedy, University of Alberta
Vincent F. Sacco, Queen's University

The concept of the criminal event assumes that we need to know about more than just the offender when we discuss the nature of crime. Crimes have victims and take place under many different circumstances. The content of crime is also influenced by what occurs before the actual event, be it a change in law or a police decision to actively pursue certain types of criminal behaviour. Of importance, as well, is the aftermath of the event, wherein social and economic costs, criminal justice intervention, and public reactions all combine to enhance prevention and deterrence of future crimes. In Chapter 1, we lay out the theoretical and conceptual bases for defining criminal events. Chapter 2 presents the procedures that are used by official agencies to count crime. This will set the stage for the discussion of different crime types, the focus of later chapters.

COUNTING CRIMINAL
EVENTS

CRIME COUNTS AND THE ANALYSIS OF CRIME AS A SOCIAL EVENT

by Leslie W. Kennedy and Vincent F. Sacco

INTRODUCTION

Throughout most of the history of criminology, researchers have attempted to understand crime in society solely in terms of the actions of criminal offenders (Cohen and Felson, 1979). Explanations of crime have, as a result, tended to focus exclusively on the question of why people are motivated to behave criminally. Such an approach fails to account for the many other factors that operate in defining, controlling, and containing crime. The actions of lawmakers, police, the public, victims, and the criminal justice system must all be included in any overall picture of the extent to which crime occurs in society and the impact that it has on social life. This book seeks to provide an integrated view of crime by examining the many different actors and situations involved in crime, with particular reference to the *criminal event*.[1]

Criminal events take place in particular locations and evolve over time. They are influenced by the definitions of acceptable behaviour that are imposed by the participants in the interaction, and they become criminal when it involves a lawbreaking action that can be attributed to an offender. The consequence, or aftermath, of this action includes apprehension by police, the attribution of guilt and harm to victim(s), and punishment delivered by the criminal justice system.

An integrative perspective on crime is increasingly of interest to policy-makers and police agencies that seek to understand criminal events in their totality. The contributors in this book use the criminal event as a basis for analyzing crime statistics that are routinely collected by police, statistical agencies, courts, and correctional institutions. Such data are traditionally presented with little or no explanation of the context in which crimes occur. These papers go beyond simple description to consider how different types of crime are affected by the relationship of victim to offender, by public opinion about crime, and by changes in the criminal justice system.

WHAT IS THE CRIMINAL EVENT?

While it is impossible to try to understand crime in society without reference to the lawbreaker, it is also true, as we have already pointed out, that there is much more to crime than the offender. Crimes may also involve victims who resist their victimization and in so doing affect the course of action (Kleck and Sayles, 1990; Webb and Marshall, 1989; Ziegenhagen and Brosnan, 1985). They may also involve bystanders and witnesses whose presence may either deter an offender or facilitate the commission of the crime by signalling an apparent tacit approval of the offender's actions (Goodstein and Shotland, 1984). Bystanders or victims may also summon the police, whose appearance at the scene may affect the response of offenders.

The criminal event cannot be separated from the physical and social settings in which it occurs (Miethe and Meier, 1994). Many forms of crime are intricately linked to the routine activities in which both victims and offenders engage and to the places in which these activities occur (Sherman, Gartin, and Buerger, 1989). More generally, criminal events involve the members of the public whose response to perceived increases in crime levels results in pressure on the police to pursue more aggressively some categories of offenders. On an even broader scale, criminal events involve the actions of lawmakers and the social groups to whom they are responsive. The concept of the criminal event encourages us to conceptualize crime in terms that encompass, but also extend beyond, the study of offenders. In other words, rather than "individual" events, crimes are "social events" (Gould, 1989).

When we use the term "event" we acknowledge that incidents occur at particular times in particular places. This is not to say that crime events happen haphazardly, although we often talk about crime victims in terms of "bad luck" or "being in the wrong place at the wrong time." However, if crime events are accidents, they are *systematic* accidents in that they are made more or less likely by the choices people make about how and where they spend their time, energy, and money (Felson, 1987).

The term event also conveys an *episodic* quality. When we use the event as a concept for studying crime, it allows us to see the criminal behaviour in discrete terms. There is a beginning and an end to these social events that facilitates our efforts to count them. By treating the criminal event as a self-contained phenomenon, we can identify it through a set of criteria that goes beyond the simple act of crime commission. Looking at crime in these terms enables us to see that the participants in the event may have had a prior association or that some form of conflict may have predated the event as, for instance, in the case of a homicide (Luckenbill, 1977). But the criminal event has its own distinct dimensions that are related to, but may be understood as distinct from, what went on before it. In a similar way, it is also possible to speak of the aftermath of criminal events in which other social processes are set in motion. This is what occurs in the daily business of the criminal justice system. Offenders are accused and tried, court dispositions are carried out, and victims must learn to cope with the "pains of victimization" (Lurigio and Resick, 1990). As well, members of the public who learn about criminal events through mass-media reports or through conversations with neighbours may become more concerned about their personal safety or about the crime problem and its effect on society.

The *social* character of criminal events derives from the fact that they involve interaction between human beings. Until recently, statistical agencies simply reported the number of offences that were committed. As a result of improvements in their counting procedures, explained in Chapter 2, they now have access to more detailed information about the offence, including the characteristics of the victim and the relationship of the victim to the offender. Data from victimization surveys and self-report studies provide even more information about crime occurrence, including documentation of the circumstances (e.g., time and place of criminal behaviour). By making extensive use of these different types of data, the contributors to this volume help us to learn more about the social character of crime.

The behaviour of any one participant in the criminal event intersects with and influences the behaviour of other participants. This interaction shapes the course of the event by determining the stages through which it will proceed and the extent to which it will be judged a serious one.

OFFENDER CHARACTERISTICS

While statistical studies define who the offenders are, we must be aware that sometimes these definitions are not that clear-cut. Black (1983) argues that much of what is regarded as crime by the criminal justice system is seen as something quite the opposite by those whom the criminal justice system labels as offenders. Those who are judged to be offenders frequently feel victimized by those against whom they offend. Studies of homicide have shown that the eventual victim is often just the first event participant to brandish a weapon or to threaten deadly force (Luckenbill, 1977; Wolfgang, 1958). Similarly, in many cases of assault, offenders may feel that they are merely responding to verbal or physical transgressions on the part of others (Felson, Baccaglini, and Ribner, 1985; Luckenbill, 1984). The wife who shoots her husband after decades of abuse may question a justice system that categorizes her as the offender and her husband as the victim.

Different types of crime may elicit from offenders different self-definitions. White-collar offenders might argue that their crimes are committed out of ignorance or an inattention to detail and, further, that they must be considered in the context of an otherwise law-abiding life. Even contract killers may offer self-definitions that mitigate personal blame. Levi (1981) maintains that organized-crime hit men deny responsibility by emphasizing the need to avoid the potentially fatal penalties that could result from their failure to fulfil a contract.

Offenders may claim that their crime has had positive effects. They might argue, for example, that their actions saved a failing business, thereby preserving much-needed jobs. They may also favourably compare their offences with those of "real" criminals like robbers or rapists (Benson, 1985). People who are guilty of workplace theft or income-tax evasion might defend their actions by arguing that "everyone does it" and "the only real crime is getting caught."

Offender accounts also include an assessment of the harm or lack of harm done to victims. Descriptions of the interaction between offender and victim sometimes include self-blame on the part of the victim, who may feel that he or she forced the offender to act in a criminal way. The rapist may contend that the victim seduced him or that she said no but really meant yes (Scully and Marolla, 1984). Other offenders have argued that they were unfairly targeted by police or that they were victims of an overly zealous court system seeking to make moral statements through punishment. The cultural environment and the historical period, then, partly determine the degree to which an offender account is viewed as plausible.

Offender accounts also alert us to the fact that we apply the label of offender only with relative certainty. Until recently, for instance, our feelings about labelling offenders who are intimately involved with their victims have been ambivalent. In the past, many people argued that a husband who assaulted a wife had somehow committed a less serious act than had a person who assaulted a stranger (Bograd, 1988). Changing interpretations of these events have been reflected in changes in the law as well as in police practices with respect to the pursuit and arrest of offenders.

Our judgments about the suitability of an offender label may also be complicated by the social context in which the offending occurs. A homicide that results from a heated argument between drunken patrons of a bar may not seem as clear-cut as one that occurs in a more sedate environment. When we draw attention to the relationship between offender labels and offender characteristics, the victim–offender relationship, or the social setting, we are suggesting that the study of the offender is inseparable from the study of other dimensions of the criminal event. This makes the job of the researcher difficult. In many cases, crime data are generated by police reports that count offenders and victims on the basis of charges that are laid when, in fact, the court may decide that the charges are not supportable.

Further, the information about the circumstances of the event are provided by the accounts that the police receive from offenders, victims, and bystanders at the time of the event. The police sometimes have difficulty including accurate information about the factors that may have preceded the actual crime transaction. For example, in homicide cases, the relationship of the victim to the offender may be categorized as "stranger" because the two participants appear to have no formal ties one to another. Further investigation might reveal that they were in fact acquaintances (possibly they saw one another at a bar regularly but did not converse). An imprecise measurement of the victim–offender relationship can make it difficult for police to establish the bases for the conflict that ensued. When examining this relationship, however, it is also important to acknowledge that in real life social situations are not always perfectly defined and individuals do not always follow their roles in a predictable fashion.

When considering the offender, we must also take into account those factors that will restrict or curtail criminal behaviour. The contemporary debate about deterrence strategies revolves around differing views about the effects of punishment. According to Williams and Hawkins (1986), individuals are less afraid of punishment per se than of being judged harshly by others for having received it. By contrast, Wilson and Herrnstein (1985) are among those who argue that individuals are deterred only through a punishment scheme that takes into account their innate propensity to offend. This perspective focuses on specific efforts to incarcerate and immobilize rather than on social stigma and the role of community forces in reducing criminality.

VICTIM CHARACTERISTICS

Research demonstrates that involvement in criminal events as a *victim*, like involvement as an offender, is not a random matter. In fact, many of the social characteristics associated with offending are also associated with victimization. This means that we need to understand not only the characteristics of the victims but also the relationship between offenders and victims. Like offenders, victims may be reluctant to define events in which they are involved as crimes. Some events may involve ambiguous or unfamiliar elements that are not readily understood as criminal victimization. In research on mugging, many victims did not immediately define the event as a predatory crime; some even thought the mugger was a neighbour in search of assistance or someone playing a joke (Lejeune and Alex, 1973). The definition of the situation becomes a key factor in the willingness of "victims" to report certain behaviour as crimes in the victim surveys that are used to supplement the crimes "known to the police" that are recorded in the Uniform Crime Reporting (UCR) system.

Willingness to label an event a crime generally depends on the degree of coherence between the victim's definition of a "typical crime" and the characteristics of the event in question (Ruback, Greenberg, and Wescott, 1984). Further, some types of crimes are inherently more ambiguous than others. As discussed in Chapter 8, the meaning of many forms of sexual victimization may be highly problematic with respect to the labels that victims assign to them. A study of 94 women who were sexually assaulted in a number of ways did not define the act as rape unless sexual intercourse was involved (Scheppele and Bart, 1983). Crime definitions are generally less ambiguous when the events contain elements that imply a high degree of legal seriousness, such as murder (Agnew, 1985).

There are other reasons that people give for not reporting criminal action. For example, if someone is victimized during the course of illegal activity, he or she may not want to tell anyone about it. If the event is of minor significance, it may be forgotten by the time the individual is interviewed in a victim survey; this may be a particular problem when the reference period about which the respondent is asked is very long. The opposite problem involves what is called *telescoping* (Skogan, 1986). In this case, crimes the victim regards as significant life events may be reported as having occurred during the reference period when, in fact, they actually occurred at an earlier point in time. Telescoping is most likely to be a problem in the study of serious violent crimes.

Sometimes victims are reluctant to report a criminal event to a researcher. Victims of family violence, for instance, may feel shame or embarrassment, or they may believe that reporting the event will put them at risk. According to a study by Catlin and Murray (1984), sexual assaults and victimizations involving nonstrangers are less likely to be reported to survey interviewers than to the police.

In some cases, people may be victimized but not realize it. Many forms of fraud are intended to accomplish precisely this outcome. Similarly, if a purse is stolen but the victim believes that she has lost it, she will not report it to a researcher who asks her a question about theft. Much of the criminal harm that is perpetrated by corporations and governments is not readily apparent, even to those who are directly affected. As a result, victims may have no idea that they have been victimized (Walklate, 1989).

BYSTANDERS AND WITNESSES

In many cases, criminal events involve individuals other than those who can be described as offenders or victims. Bystanders in many events are more than passive spectators. They may, by their presence, deter an offender from committing a crime or they may prevent an event from escalating. Conversely, they may facilitate the offender's actions. A young male who is insulted by someone in the presence of his peers may be naturally inclined to respond to the insult in an aggressive fashion or else be encouraged to do so by the peer group. In the past, we have known little about the role of third parties in affecting crime outcomes, even though their role often affects the nature of the interaction between victims and offenders. Official crime statistics have recently begun to look at the role of third parties, but the extent of their influence on criminal actions is still not clearly known.

Bystanders may also call the police or offer to act as witnesses (Goodstein and Shotland, 1984). What bystanders do can be affected, as is the case with victims and offenders, by their perception of the event and the participants. Their actions may be influenced, for example, by their view of, or relationship to, the victim and/or offender (Steffensmeier and Steffensmeier, 1977); by how they define the personal costs associated with intervention; and by how much confidence they have in their ability to intervene (Goodstein and Shotland, 1984).

Bystanders are also affected by what they perceive to be transpiring between victim and offender. According to Shotland and Straw (1976), bystanders are less likely to intervene in a violent assault perpetrated by a man against a woman if they believe that they are married rather than strangers. Davis (1991) suggests that when people witness adults physically abusing children in public their concern about intervening in a "private matter" overrides their concern about the welfare of the child. It is frequently documented that people will stand aside and watch while "combatants" (e.g., parents and children or a married couple) sort out their differences, believing that the relationship between them precludes intervention. It has been further observed that the presence of several bystanders tends to reduce the likelihood that any one bystander will take action to assist a victim. This is particularly true if the bystanders are strangers to one another and do not share a common cultural frame of reference (Shotland, 1976). One bystander among many is required to accept only part of the responsibility for not acting; he or she may provide the rationalization that somebody else would take action were something seriously wrong.

Beyond the fact that people make determinations of events based on what they believe to be the relationship between combatants, the actual nature of the conflict can be ambiguous from the standpoint of bystanders. As we do not expect to witness a crime, an event may be well underway before it comes to our attention (Hartman et al., 1972). By the time we make sense of the event and think of a response, it may be too late for us to have taken any action. Further, the fact that we have been slow to register what was occurring, and have missed key information about what precipitated the event and what actually occurred during the event, will tend to make us poor witnesses. The research suggests that eyewitness accounts are quite inaccurate, with bystanders failing to remember even key characteristics of the offender or the event (Loftus, 1979).

Research conducted by Gary Wells raises some serious concerns about the validity of eyewitness accounts. He reports an experiment in which students who witnessed a theft (committed by a confederate of the experimenter) were shown a lineup of potential offenders. When they were assured that the culprit was in the lineup even though he was not, 78 percent of the witnesses identified an innocent person as the culprit. However, when the witnesses were first cautioned that the culprit might not be in the lineup, only 33 percent made a false identification (*Globe and Mail*, January 21, 1995: D8).

Recognizing the limitations of bystander and eyewitness accounts becomes all the more important when we consider that it is third parties and not police who are relied upon to provide "unbiased" observations about crime events. The police often arrive after the event. It is their role to reconstruct the events (with the help of witnesses) in a way that makes sense to the courts. In the final analysis, however, it is the police who provide the official statistics that we use to determine the extent and frequency of crime, and it is the police who can alter these statistics by changing either the ways in which they report crimes or their priorities when it comes to targeting certain crimes over others.

POLICE

POLICE PRACTICE

Police involvement in criminal events may result from either proactive or reactive mobilization. As the police engage in routine patrol work, they may come upon people or situations they define as criminal. Proactive policing is not in any sense a random or arbitrary process. Rather, it is strongly influenced by police priorities, prevailing community concerns, available police resources, and the styles and traditions that characterize police work in particular areas. Ericson (1982) reports that police officers who are engaged in patrol activities use cues that structure their proactive work. For example, their attention may be attracted when certain types of individuals appear in particular places at particular times of the day. Conversely, events that could be defined as crimes are not labelled as such, because the police choose not to stop and question a suspect.

Proactive policing can be offered as a partial explanation for the ways in which police numbers for certain types of crimes rise or fall over time. In recent years, some police forces have decided to reduce the attending of assaults between young males, giving priority instead to violent acts that have women or children as victims. The males who are assaulted are encouraged to report the crime, but this means going to a station rather than having a police officer come to them. Fewer assaults of this nature are reported as victims, instead of taking the trouble to file a complaint, decide to either ignore the event or to resolve the matter themselves (e.g., by "getting even").

This type of priority-based policing can also have interesting effects on the policing of other types of crime. In his study of the policing of a heroin-using community, Stoddart (1991) reports that heroin users who act as police informants are less likely to be pursued by the police than are heroin users who are perceived as interfering with police work. This finding suggests that proactive police activity is influenced not only by what the police do but also by the visibility of the offender's behaviour. Stoddart argues that changes in the nature of the heroin-using community over time have increased the probability of arrest. Members of the heroin-using community today are more apathetic than their predecessors about the fate of their colleagues and less attentive to the risks associated with illegal drug use. Such factors increase the visibility of the behaviour, thereby facilitating police intervention.

The line between reactive and proactive police mobilization is frequently unclear (Ericson, 1982). Citizens may decide to mobilize the police reactively as a result of police-sponsored crime-prevention campaigns that encourage them to do so. On the other hand, widespread public concern about specific crime problems may influence the administrative decisions that are made by police with respect to proactive mobilization. The periodic crackdowns on prostitution or the development of special task forces dealing with sexual assault, armed robbery, or drug-related crime may all serve to increase police activity in these areas, resulting in more reported crime.

POLICE INVOLVEMENT IN DEFINING CRIMINAL EVENTS

The type of mobilization, whether proactive or reactive, does not dictate how the police will intervene in a particular event. As is the case with offenders, victims, and bystanders, the police enter into the criminal event as participants who contribute to its social character and influence its outcome. The police need to be aware of what is happening and to be prepared not only to act but also to react appropriately given the circumstances of the event. The action taken by the police officer may depend on a variety of factors, including the characteristics of the incident, the behaviour of the participants, and the nature of the requests being made of the police (Smith, 1987; Gottfredson and Gottfredson, 1988; Bayley, 1986).

Police tend to respond most emphatically to (i.e., treat officially) events that they perceive as conforming to legal definitions of serious crimes (Black, 1970; Gottfredson and Gottfredson, 1988; Gove, Hughes, and Geerken, 1985). The serious crimes of homicide, aggravated assault, robbery, and sexual assault tend to elicit from the police prescribed responses such as going by the book in terms of the reporting of the crime and ensuring that the rules of evidence are stringently followed. "Less important" crimes may allow for greater discretion, and thus be subject to different reporting by police, depending on particular factors.

One such factor determining police response is the relationship between the victim and the offender. According to Black (1970), the more distant the relationship between a victim and an offender, the more likely the police are to regard the incident as criminal. This observation is consistent with the frequently cited tendency of police officers to process crimes "unofficially" when the disputants are family members (Bell, 1987).

The characteristics of victims and offenders have also been shown to influence police decisions. In a U.S. study of police responses to interpersonal violence, Smith (1987) found that police officers are less likely to employ legal solutions in situations that involve African-American or female victims. In contrast, Boritch (1992) cites Canadian research suggesting that the criminal justice system deals more harshly with women offenders than male offenders, particularly those who deviate from accepted standards of feminine behaviour.

Police decision-making may also be influenced by the demeanour and the preferences of those involved in the event (Smith, 1987). Thus, the police are more likely to label an event as a crime when the complainant is deferential to them or requests that they take official action (Black, 1970; Gove, Hughes, and Geerken, 1985). What this means is that characteristics of the event and its participants can influence whether or not these come to be labelled officially as crimes. If they do, they show up in the Uniform Crime Reporting system, which documents the criminal profile of the country. If not, they are excluded from these records. Is the UCR, then, an accurate reflection of crime?

As Silverman and Kennedy (1993) report, it has been more or less accepted since the 1930s (Sellin, 1938) that police data most accurately represent the criminal event because these data are closest in time to the event, whereas convictions involve such complicating factors as available witnesses, lying participants, and plea bargaining. It is also the case that the rates of index crimes presented in the UCR appear to be reasonably good approximations of true crime rates when the latter are defined as what both citizens and the police view as serious violations of the laws (Gove, Hughes, and Geerken, 1985: 489). Gove et al. conclude that the UCR appears to reflect fairly accurately what citizens and the police view as significant threats to social order, and that the UCR presents a valid indicator of the extent of serious crime that exists.

But what of the "dark figure of crime," that is, crime that goes unreported to the police? According to Gove et al., this dark figure constitutes unreported crime where the harm done is not significant or where the act does not fit the legal definition that the police would use to classify it as a crime even though it might be reported as such in a victim survey. Where there is likely to be substantial underreporting (e.g., in cases of sexual assault and family violence), the changes in proactive policing discussed earlier are having a compensatory effect. Although there are those who believe that the UCR still underestimates the incidence of sexual assault and family violence, Gove et al. contend that the most serious of these crimes are likely to come to the attention of the police.

THE SETTINGS OF CRIMINAL EVENTS

As we stated at the outset, to suggest that there is a relationship between criminal events and the places in which these events occur is to imply that location involves something more than just happenstance. In other words, place matters. There is something about particular types of locations that increases (or decreases) the likelihood that criminal events will unfold. Further, particular types of places are intricately linked to particular types of activities. People who live in the centre of a major city may structure their activities differently than do those who live in the suburban fringe. Those of us who do not live in the downtown core may occasionally journey there in search of "excitement" while seeking rest and relaxation in the countryside. We shop at malls, drink in taverns, perform occupational tasks at work, and read or study at the library. We might ask why some of these places host more criminal events than others. Do certain types of people tend to be attracted to these settings? Does the physical character of a place make criminal events more or less likely? Are the activities associated with a particular setting more or less likely to lead to criminal events?

When we look at the statistical trends relating to these types of factors, we typically examine results that relate to what is happening in particular locations (e.g., in the home or in a bar) and outcomes that vary according to broader categories (e.g., cities or regions of the country). To get valuable information about the former, we have to rely on victim surveys. Generally, we are able to examine variations in the latter through UCR data. In the following chapters, the authors make selective use of locational factors at the individual and collective levels. Place is important and crime varies rather dramatically according to factors that occur in different locations.

What are the characteristics of the locations that host criminal events? In the case of a property crime, settings that offer concealment in the form of poor street lighting, large bushes or shrubs, or hidden alleyways may make a target more attractive to an offender (Goodstein and Shotland, 1984). Similarly, a convenience store that is located near a vacant field may be more vulnerable to robbery than one that is located on a busy city street (Sherman, Gartin, and Buerger, 1989).

In a somewhat different way, patterns of family violence may be related to some elements of physical design. Violence between husbands and wives typically occurs in private settings. The growth of single-family homes not shared with boarders, lodgers, or servants—coupled with the widespread cultural understanding that the home is a private setting closed to neighbours, friends, or even other family members, except by invitation—helps ensure the concealment of such violence (Gelles and Straus, 1988). Within the home, not all locations are equally risky. According to Gelles and Straus (1988), violence most frequently occurs in the kitchen, followed by the living room and the bedroom, although the latter place tends to be the setting for the most violent confrontations. By contrast, the bathroom is relatively free of spousal violence, in part because such rooms are small, have locks, and are understood to be places of individual privacy.

SOCIAL DOMAINS

Just as place matters, so does social context. Crime occurrence can vary by sphere of life, or social domain. In studying criminal events, we can identify three distinct social domains: the family and household, leisure, and work. Each domain is distinguished by particular locations and patterns of activity

(Lynch, 1987). People differ with respect to the amount of time that they spend in each of these domains. For the elderly retired person, the social domain of the household may be of greatest importance. Children spend much of their time at home, but during the teenage years their involvement in this social domain declines while their involvement in the workplace and in leisure activities outside the home increases.

The social domains that we define attract different types of attention from the police and the public in defining acceptable and criminal behaviour. Public leisure settings populated by younger people receive the highest level of police supervision and are generally the locations in which both violent crime and "vice" crimes appear on police ledgers. Victim surveys indicate that people who report that they frequently go out in the evening to bars also report higher rates of victimization (Sacco and Johnson, 1990). Moreover, observations of barroom behaviour (Stoddart, 1991) and police data suggest that taverns are the site of a disproportionate amount of crime (Roncek and Pravatiner, 1989). Although the domains of family and work are also subject to criminal activity, they elicit a different response in terms of the reporting of crimes because, as Chapter 7 illustrates, they involve issues of privacy and cultural definitions of the informal control of behaviour in the private arena.

While we tend to think of private domains as safer places than public domains, there is increasing concern about the prevalence of criminal actions that were previously seen as private acts. The definition of privacy is changing, as are the ways in which the law and the police treat privacy. The criminal event that may once have gone undetected or untreated in the "privacy" of the home is now more likely to attract public attention and strong police action.

For the white-collar or corporate criminal, the offending behaviour may represent little more than a simple extension of his or her legitimate business practices. In other cases, a person's employment may be related to the risk of criminal victimization (Block, Felson, and Block, 1984). People who handle money, who work in an environment that is open to the general public, or who travel from one work site to another are especially vulnerable to many forms of victimization (Collins, Cox, and Langan, 1987). It is partially because of these factors that taxi drivers, police officers, and nurses experience relatively high rates of violence (Block, Felson, and Block, 1984). In still other cases, it is an *absence* of activity that is related to the occurrence of criminal events. With respect to break and enter (see Chapter 9), for instance, households that are unoccupied for long periods of time are at greater risk of victimization than are households that have higher and more regular occupancy rates (Waller and Okihiro, 1978).

STUDYING THE CRIMINAL EVENT

All of the factors discussed in the preceding sections can affect the way in which we report crime. We have seen that crime accounts can be influenced by police practices; by the perceptions of offenders, victims, and bystanders; by legal and cultural factors operating in an environment that defines certain behaviours as acceptable and other behaviours as illegal; and by the physical factors and social dynamics associated with a particular event. But these factors do not operate in a static fashion. The criminal event takes place not only in space but also over time. Beyond the simple definition of the event as a single transaction, which has as its focus a motivated offender and a victim, we see the event as having a beginning, a middle, and an end. Further, the event can be divided into three parts: the precursors of the event, including the locational and situational factors that bring people together in time and space; the event itself, which can be studied in terms of how the interactions among participants define the outcomes of their actions; and the aftermath of the event, including the reporting to the police and the police response, the harm done and the redress required, and the long-term consequences of the event in terms of public reaction and the changing of laws.

PRECURSORS

Studying the precursors of criminal events also allows us to see that behaviour that is defined or evolves into criminality in one situation may not have the same consequences in other situations, depending upon such factors as the relationship between participants, the presence of alcohol or drugs, the interpretation of the harmfulness of the acts, and the anticipated responses to certain behaviour.

We have pointed out that, in order to determine the precursors of crime, we must reconstruct criminal events using information that may be distorted by faulty memories, rationalizations, and so on. But it is exactly this process that the courts use to establish guilt or innocence in the cases that are brought before them. In order to reflect legal as well as social reality, therefore, criminologists must incorporate a similar process in their approaches to crime. First and foremost, we need to know how crime types are defined in law. In the chapters that follow, each author presents, as part of the discussion of precursors, legal definitions of what behaviour constitutes the crime type under discussion.

THE EVENT

When we study the event itself, we move into an assessment of the circumstances and frequency of certain types of crimes. As we will see, different types of data sources (e.g., the UCR survey, victim surveys, and self-report studies) tell us about different aspects of the event, or at least provide different perspectives on such events.

We are interested in the particular groups that are affected by different types of crime. It is in this context that we are able to examine the changes in offender behaviour and the extent of victimization. We are particularly interested in viewing the criminal event not in isolation but rather as it relates to other social events. Discerning trends in criminal events helps us to understand the extent to which we need to respond to them. We are also interested in understanding how trends in crime patterns coincide with trends in social conditions, economic changes, changes in resources for policing, and so on. The explanations that these types of analysis provide throw light on the vulnerability of certain groups to social change and the extent to which legal intervention can work to deter or alter criminal behaviour. This overall pattern is the central focus of the discussion of crime trends in Chapter 3.

Earlier we discussed the problems associated with defining (or not defining) certain events as criminal. Victims may not immediately appreciate that they have been subject to crime, while offenders may rationalize their behaviour as something other than criminal. The strict definition of criminality comes with the actions of the police, who certify criminality through the enactment of legal process, either in naming an event as criminal or arresting an offender.

But what about the events that do not come to the attention of the police but that nevertheless could be defined as criminal? This hidden dimension of crime has important implications for how we define criminal events, as well as for the processes by which the police target certain victims or offenders. Criminal events, then, are dynamic not only in terms of their responsiveness to interactional factors in the environment but also in terms of the claims that are made about them by interested parties. These claims are continuously evolving in response to changing political and cultural values.

THE AFTERMATH

The extent to which we can develop an integrated perspective is very much dependent on the types of information about criminal events to which we have access. We are concerned not only with the actual event but also with the reactions by the police, victims, and others. In considering the aftermath of an event, we are interested in the degree to which the victim has been harmed and in the resources that are needed to facilitate his or her recovery. We are also concerned with whether or not the offender feels that he or she can repeat the offence with impunity. With respect to punishment, has there been sufficient certainty, severity, or celerity to deter a repeat occurrence? These questions frame a great deal of the discussion about how we are managing our crime problems. We need to understand that the responses that we develop to crime are a function of the perspectives that we use in interpreting the reasons for its occurrence. Moreover, these reactions will influence the types of crime that we will experience in the future.

THE PLAN OF THE BOOK

The following chapters examine different types of crime using a criminal event perspective. Using micro-level data sets that connect individual offenders to victims and to situations, the authors have provided a unique picture of the state of crime events in Canada.

The chapters are organized by section. After reviewing the collection procedures that are used to generate data in the next chapter, we turn in Part II to an overview of crime trends in Canada. Part III focuses on violent crime, specifically homicide, assault, robbery, sexual assault, and family violence. Part IV examines property crime, with chapters on theft, fraud, motor vehicle thefts, and break and enter. Illicit drugs and youth crime are the focus of Part V. The concluding section, Part VI, includes chapters on the overall state of Canada's three main criminal justice agencies, namely the police, the courts, and the correctional system.

NOTES

[1]For a more detailed examination of the criminal event, see V. Sacco and L. Kennedy, *The Criminal Event* (Scarborough, Ont.: Nelson Canada, 1994).

DATA AND METHODOLOGY IN THE AREA OF CRIMINAL JUSTICE

by Bob Grainger

Bob Grainger begins this chapter with an analysis of the data and data-collection methods associated with the Uniform Crime Reporting survey. The procedures used by the police agencies to generate UCR data ensure that there is a standard form by which we can compare results over time and across jurisdictions. However, we need more than police-generated data to make sense of crime incidence. To address the "dark figure of crime" (crime that goes unreported to the police), the researcher makes use of victimization studies; Grainger reviews the methodology used in these studies. The examination of crime data provided in this chapter should help the reader to comprehend discussions of methodology in subsequent chapters.

In Chapter 1, Kennedy and Sacco explained the various aspects of the criminal event—the offender, the victim, the witnesses, the location, and the social and cultural milieu within which the action takes place. This chapter will examine the statistical surveys that have been developed in order to illuminate these aspects of criminal events. More specifically, the chapter will provide background information on those surveys that measure the volume and nature of crime, and the flow of offenders through the criminal justice system.

Data collection in the area of criminology is directed at the measurement of two broad aspects—caseload measures and case characteristics measures. *Caseload measures* are concerned with the relative frequency of different events in the system; these "events" include such phenomena as cases, incidents, victims, offences, persons, admissions, charges, and releases. This quantitative component of research is aimed generally at the measurement of the incidence of different units of count—that is, the number of new events occurring in the population. Although different surveys measure the frequency of different entities at different points in the justice system, all are aimed at providing a measure of the flow of "caseload" through the system.

Case characteristics measures describe the qualitative nature of the persons or the events. After ascertaining the relative frequency of an event, the researcher can turn to an examination of the characteristics that are associated with it. When searching for qualitative associations, the researcher typically addresses the following questions: In what circumstances does the phenomenon occur? What are the geographical and temporal patterns of its distribution? What environmental characteristics relate to the occurrence of the phenomenon? Who are the actors (or participants) in this event, and are there consistent patterns with regard to their characteristics? The answers to these types of questions lead the researcher to an understanding of the nature and origin of criminal events.

Data and methods of data collection and analysis are only raw materials and tools to be used by researchers. Without due care, they can be used in the most inappropriate ways to arrive at the most erroneous of conclusions. The following example illustrates the types of problems that can arise when survey data are misinterpreted. In 1995, the Canadian Centre for Justice Statistics (CCJS) released a Juristat entitled "Public Perceptions of Crime." This report examined "official" statistics from the Uniform Crime Reporting (UCR) survey, information from the 1988 and 1993 General Social Survey (GSS), and data from other public opinion surveys in order to determine the relationship between crime statistics and public perceptions of crime. One of the main conclusions of the report was that there had been a significant increase in the national rate (per 100,000 population) of violent crimes being reported to the police between 1988 and 1993. The report went on to say that almost all of this increase was in the area of relatively minor assaults, due, in all probability, to the enactment and implementation, in 1983, of Bill C-127, which made radical changes to the law in the area of assault and sexual assault. Thus increases in the national rate of violent crimes were largely attributable to an increase in reporting, not to an increase in the "real" number of violent crimes in Canada.

A second conclusion of the report was that, on the basis of the results of the 1988 and 1993 General Social Survey, there was no evidence to suggest an increase in violent crime; in other words, the victimization rates for violent crimes were no higher in 1993 than they were in 1988. The report was well received in all parts of the country, with the exception of one city that had experienced several violent crimes in the month prior to the release of the Juristat. When a reporter asked the local police department for an official reaction to the Juristat, a spokesperson stated that the report's findings did not apply to *this* city, which had over the previous five years seen a very dramatic increase in the number of persons contacting the police to report a violent crime. The reporter characterized this response as a major disagreement between Statistics Canada and the police department.

There were three major problems with the reporter's handling of the Juristat data. The first of these was the assumption that local trends must always closely reflect national trends. The national trend is the numeric average of the trends in the various regions, and thus some parts of the country will naturally have crime rates higher than the national average while others will have lower rates.

The second problem stemmed from a confusion between numbers and rates. The Juristat contained information on the rates of crime per 100,000 population, a calculation that standardizes the data for changes (usually increases) in the numbers of people in the population. The spokesperson for the police department used only the absolute numbers of victims who were reporting violent crimes. These data did not reflect the appreciable growth that had taken place in the population of that community. When one calculated the rates of violent crime per 100,000 population for the city, these had actually declined.

The third problem had to do with the differences between the two main surveys, the UCR survey and the GSS. The UCR survey is a census of crimes that come to the attention of the police and that are officially recorded as crimes by them. This count of crime is very dependent on the rate at which crimes are reported to the police by their participants in the incident. Social, cultural, or legislative changes that discourage victims from reporting particular crimes to the police will obviously compromise the authority of these "official" statistics. In contrast, the GSS is a household victimization survey that elicits directly from individuals data about their experiences as victims of crime in the previous year. Because of this style of data collection, the data from the GSS provide a completely different perspective on the phenomenon of crime in Canada than that provided by the UCR survey.

This chapter attempts to clarify some of the confusion surrounding crime data by examining, in a systematic fashion, the fundamental characteristics of both the data and the data-collection methods associated with the major national surveys in the criminal justice field.

An Overview of National Data Sources in Criminal Justice

Surveys providing "official crime statistics" are organized to collect information from administrative systems that have generally been created to assist in the operation and management of a component of the justice system. These components, together with the information systems that accompany them, are the products of a level of government, be it municipal, provincial, or federal.

The population survey, in contrast, is based on direct contact between an investigator and members of the general public. There are no intermediate organizations to filter, distort, or obscure the respondents' interpretations of their experiences with the criminal justice system. The most common manifestation of the population survey is the victimization survey, a data-collection exercise in which members of the general population are interviewed about their personal experiences as victims of crime.

The following sections discuss in more detail national crime surveys as they relate to the primary components of the criminal justice system: the police, the courts, and corrections.

The Police

The Uniform Crime Reporting (UCR) Survey

The UCR survey, which became operational in Canada in 1961, was the product of a joint effort by Statistics Canada and the Canadian Association of Chiefs of Police. The basic objectives of the survey were to provide a consistent methodology for the counting of crimes reported to police (thereby enabling police departments to more effectively allocate resources) and to produce data that could be used as a basis for measuring crime rates across municipalities and provinces. The survey has produced a continuous 32-year record of crime data that has become an essential analytical resource for anyone who is studying the criminal justice system.

In effect, there are *two* UCR surveys: the original UCR survey, which collects aggregate information from police departments once a month; and the Revised UCR survey, in operation for the last eight years, which collects incident-based information in machine-readable form from a number of police departments. These two surveys will be described separately.

The original UCR survey is based on a hard-copy data-collection form that contains ten data elements for each of 108 types of criminal incidents. The variables are divided into three sets: number of incidents, number of incidents cleared (or solved), and number of persons charged in relation to the incidents that were cleared. The original UCR survey is an "aggregate" survey in that the data were collected in such a way that it was not possible to isolate a single incident. This style of data collection was adopted in response to one of the survey's objectives—to measure "police workload," that is, the amount of work undertaken by the police department in a particular month. On any particular offence-specific line on the data-collection form, one will find the total number of incidents of that type that have come to the attention of the department during that month. Also recorded are the number of incidents that have been cleared by the department during that month (whether they occurred during that period or not) and the total number of persons (by age and sex) who were charged in connection with the incidents that were "cleared by charge."

When the police are officially informed of a criminal event, they may attend at the scene, complete an occurrence report of the incident, and undertake a preliminary investigation to establish the existence of the event. This is the process of "founding" the incident. In some cases, it is discovered that no crime actually took place, and thus the original report is deemed "unfounded" and pursued no further. It is tempting to assume that any event that comes to the attention of the police will be recorded by them in their official statistics, but such is not the case. The police exercise some discretion with regard to the formal recognition of a criminal incident, and may decline to see a particular event as a crime.

When a reported criminal incident is found to have been a real crime, two labelling processes take place. First, the event is found to be a "crime" or "criminal incident," and second, the event is labelled as a particular type of crime. The aggregate nature of the data collection means that there is no way to analyze the distribution of persons over the "cleared incidents"; one knows the total number of cleared incidents and the total number of persons charged, but it is not possible to know how they are distributed.

The original UCR survey classifies incidents according to the "most serious offence" that occurred in the incident, generally the offence that carries the longest maximum sentence under the *Criminal Code of Canada*. As a result of this "most serious offence" scoring rule, less serious offences tend to be undercounted by the UCR survey. The survey has slightly different scoring rules for violent incidents and other types of crimes. For violent crime, a separate incident is recorded for each victim. For nonviolent crimes, one incident is counted for each separate and distinct occurrence. (The exception to this rule is robbery, a violent crime that is counted as a property crime.) Thus the total number of incidents recorded by the UCR survey is equal to the number of victims of violent crimes (other than robberies), plus the number of separate occurrences of nonviolent crimes (and robberies).

The original UCR survey is largely a "caseload" survey in that almost all of the statistics produced are related to the volume of cases that are processed; little attention is paid to the qualitative aspects of crime (e.g., characteristics of the incident or the persons involved). Starting in the early 1980s, attempts were made to enhance the utility of the UCR data. The people who used police information and statistics for investigation, management, policy development, and research purposes wanted to have more information about the characteristics of both the perpetrator and the victim as well as the circumstances of the incident.

The Revised UCR survey provides a rich database for researchers, policymakers, and police departments alike. The data elements of the new survey include incident characteristics such as time, location, clearance status, and the presence of weapons. The accused record includes age, sex, and alcohol/drug consumption. For crimes of violence and traffic incidents, the revised survey collects victim characteristics including age, sex, relationship to the accused, alcohol/drug consumption, level of injury, and weapon causing the injury.

For the Revised UCR survey, the aggregate approach of the original survey was rejected in favour of an incident-based approach under which a separate statistical record is created for each criminal incident. The incident-based approach produces a data file with an analytical potential many times greater than that provided by the aggregate survey, because one can create and then progressively subdivide the data file in order to examine different aspects of the records.

The Revised UCR survey was implemented in a "phased" manner; that is, police departments made the transition to the Revised Survey once they had an automated information system in place and once an interface had been created to transform the information in their computer to the standard format accepted by the Canadian Centre for Justice Statistics. The "phased" implementation meant that two versions of the UCR survey would be supported simultaneously by the CCJS and would run concurrently for a number of years in order to produce national statistics.

As of September 1994, approximately 80 police departments from across the country were supplying data on a regular basis to the Revised UCR survey. These departments accounted for about 30% of the volume of national crime data. This proportion will increase steadily as the number of respondents to the survey increases. Although approximately one-half of the volume of the data in the Revised UCR survey comes from respondents in the province of Quebec, this province accounts for about 80% of the respondents to the survey. This discrepancy is explained by the fact that the respondents outside the province of Quebec tend to be larger municipal forces.

THE HOMICIDE SURVEY

Canadian homicide data have been collected by Statistics Canada since 1961. Survey forms are completed manually by a member of the police department in whose jurisdiction the homicide occurs. These forms are then forwarded to the Canadian Centre for Justice Statistics for compilation, analysis, and publication. The data elements and the processing system remained essentially unchanged until 1991, when both were modified.

The term "homicide" includes first- and second-degree murder, manslaughter, and infanticide. Although these crimes are counted in the UCR surveys, information and data on homicides were felt to be so important for public policy purposes that a separate survey was created to allow for a more detailed examination of these offences. Like the Revised UCR survey, the Homicide Survey is "incident-based." For each homicide, incident, victim, and suspect records are created. The incident record contains such information as time, location, and clearance status of the incident, as well as any precipitating crime such as drug trafficking or gang/terrorist activity. The victim and accused records contain standard demographic information such as age, sex, marital status, occupation, accused–victim relationship, weapon used, alcohol/drug consumption, and any history of domestic violence.

When using the Homicide Survey data, it is important to remember that the number of incidents is the number of "events" that were labelled as "homicides" by the police authorities early in the criminal justice process. Changes take place as the case proceeds from the police to the courts and then on to corrections. In 1993, the CCJS completed a longitudinal study of all of the 576 reported homicide incidents that took place in 1988 to find out how the cases were resolved. Of the 228 persons charged by the police with first-degree murder in 1988, 195 faced a trial in adult court, 168 on the original charge. Of them, only 40 were convicted on the original charge. A total of 159 persons (out of the original total of 228) received a penitentiary sentence of more than two years. This explains why there is such a dramatic difference between the number of homicide incidents in a given year and the number of persons admitted to penitentiary for the crime of homicide.

The changes that can occur with respect to the status of an event are not restricted to homicide cases. For example, assume that there is a "break and enter" of a house. The event is duly reported to the police and scored as an actual offence of break and enter. Some hours later, the police encounter someone with the items that were removed from the house. He is arrested but because he cannot be connected to the house in question he is charged with "being in possession of stolen goods." This charge may or may not be changed to "theft" by the prosecutorial authorities. Such changes in case status greatly complicate the process of tracking cases from one sector of the criminal justice system to the next.

THE COURTS

The aftermath of criminal events includes processing by criminal courts. Data about this aspect of the event are included in statistics drawn from court surveys. Under the law, a person charged with an offence may be temporarily held in custody to await an appearance before a justice when the police consider it to be in the public interest or when they do not have the authority to release the accused due to the severity of the offence. For most offences, the accused is brought before the court for a judicial interim hearing. The accused may plead guilty or not guilty, or may refuse to plead. If a guilty plea is entered, the justice may release the accused pending sentencing by the appropriate court. If a "not guilty" or "no plea" is entered, the court is obliged to release the accused unless the Crown prosecution can show cause for detaining the accused.

There are two basic reasons for detaining the accused: to ensure that he or she will appear in court and to protect the public. If the court decides to release the accused, certain conditions may be applied. Such conditions may include an undertaking or a recognizance with or without sureties, deposit (monetary conditions), or other conditions. A surety gives another person responsibility for ensuring that the accused will appear in court. For some offences, the court must detain the accused unless the accused can show why he or she should be released.

The same procedures apply to young offenders; however, there are some additional provisions. All judicial procedures are dealt with in youth court and, in most cases, youths must be held in facilities separate from adults. Finally, rather than detaining the youth in custody, the court may order the youth placed in the care of a responsible person who must ensure that he or she attends court.

With the laying of charges by the police, the focus of attention shifts to the court system, or more precisely to the area of prosecutions, which is closely allied to the courts. In most provinces, it is the police who lay the charges, but in some provinces the police complete a form which recommends to the prosecutorial authority that charges be laid. In this latter case, the Crown prosecutors review the evidence that has been accumulated by the police and make a final decision with regard to the laying of charges and the nature of the charges. In those provinces where the police have the formal authority to lay charges, there is often considerable consultation with the office of the Crown prosecutor to select the most appropriate charges.

The court sector is subdivided according to the age of the person who has been charged, and the procedures differ considerably for young offenders and adults. The different court systems and the data that are obtained through surveys done in these jurisdictions are described in the following sections.

ALTERNATIVE MEASURES

The *Young Offenders Act*, enacted in the mid-1980s, contains provisions for the creation of *alternative measures programs* to which youths are referred when the police, parents, and the court decide that the criminal court proceedings are not in the best interest of either the youth or society. Alternative measures can be applied either before or after a youth has been charged. If the youth has already been charged, the charges are dismissed or withdrawn once the alternative measures agreement has been completed.

Alternative measures may be used only for certain offences—usually property offences—and only under certain conditions. Once a youth has agreed to participate, an alternative measures agreement is negotiated between the youth and the Crown prosecution. If the youth does not comply with the agreement, the case can be referred back to the court.

At present, there is no systematic data collection to monitor the quantitative or qualitative nature of the cases that are referred to alternative measures programs. This means that it is not possible to know which cases are not being heard in youth courts. In addition, the quantity and nature of the cases that are heard in youth courts change over time simply as a result of the changes that are taking place in the screening of cases for alternative measures programs.

YOUTH COURT SURVEY (YCS)

Unlike adults, youths charged with either summary conviction or indictable offences are prosecuted in youth court only. Generally, these proceedings are similar to those applied in summary conviction trials. However, at any time after an information is laid and prior to a decision, the court may order a transfer hearing to determine whether the youth should be transferred to an adult court. A youth may be transferred only if he or she is at least 14 years old and is charged with a serious indictable offence.

The Youth Court Survey (YCS) is intended to be a census of federal statute charges (*Criminal Code*, *Narcotic Control Act*, *Food and Drugs Act*, *Young Offenders Act*, and other federal statutes) heard in youth courts in Canada. The survey excludes appeals, reviews, provincial statutes, and municipal bylaw infractions.

The YCS collects data from all youth courts in Canada. Data are provided through automated systems or by manual extraction. In those provinces with automated information systems, data-quality edits are incorporated to improve the quality of the data for operational purposes. In the manual data-collection process, survey reporting forms for charges laid against young persons are completed by court clerks. While the format of these forms varies across jurisdictions, each form contains a core set of data elements, such as province, charge identification code, date of birth, and court decision and disposition.

The basic input data to the YCS is a file of "charges." This file is transformed into two other files, the *person file* and the *case file*. The person file is created by linking charge records on the basis of an accused identifier code, sex, and date of birth. Subsequently, the case file is created by linking "person" records on the basis of court codes and date of first appearance. The case file serves as an information source for the regular statistical publications (tabulations from the other files are available for special purposes). Because of the nature of the procedures used to create these files, the counts represented in the YCS reports may vary slightly from those available in the jurisdictions' statistical reports.

On an annual basis, the YCS produces summary statistics of the cases that have been disposed of in youth courts. The caseload or volume aspect of these statistics is somewhat suspect because of the unknown effect of the screening procedures in alternative measures programs, and because of the undercounting of charges in some jurisdictions. Nevertheless, the data file is useful in several respects. First, it provides "case characteristics" statistics, including the proportionate distribution of cases by age, sex, and type of offence. Second, it produces statistics on case processing (e.g., number of cases resulting in findings of guilt, number stayed or withdrawn, and number transferred to adult court). And third, it provides insight into the dispositions and sentences associated with these cases; because the survey is incident-based, it is possible to produce a great number of different data tables that can be used to examine different aspects of youth court justice.

ADULT CRIMINAL COURT SURVEY (ACCS)

For adults, the type of trial is determined by the type of offence. Summary conviction cases are usually tried by provincial court judges or justices of the peace in a summary conviction court. The trial procedure for indictable offence depends on the seriousness of the offences. The most serious offences must be tried by a superior court judge and jury, unless both the Crown prosecution and the defence agree to a nonjury trial. For other indictable offences, the defendant may choose to be tried by a provincial court judge or by a judge and jury; relatively less serious indictable offences are tried by a provincial court judge.

For jury trials, a jury is selected from a list of eligible citizens within the jurisdiction of the court. From this list, a subset is drawn and those individuals are requested to attend court for possible jury duty. Twelve people are required to form a jury. The jury is selected by the Crown prosecution and the defence counsel; each side questions potential jurors to determine their suitability. If the trial is by judge alone, the judge can enter a decision of guilty or not guilty. In addition, the judge may find the accused not guilty of the charged offence but guilty of an included offence (i.e., another offence arising out of the same incident). If the trial is by judge and jury, the jury must return with a unanimous decision—guilty or not guilty. The jury may also find the accused guilty of an included offence. If the jury is unable to agree, it may be discharged and a new jury empanelled.

Sentencing options for adults vary depending on how the court proceeds with the charges. The maximum penalty for a summary conviction offence is six months imprisonment and/or a $2,000 fine. Maximum sentences for an offence tried by indictment are more severe, varying from two years to life imprisonment. Young offenders may be sentenced to a maximum of two years in custody for an offence not punishable by life under the *Criminal Code,* three years for those punishable by life, and five years for murder. The maximum fine is $1,000.

Before sentencing, the court may request a presentencing or disposition report that provides information about the offender's support within the community and other relevant information. The court may also hear or receive a victim-impact statement. Most sentencing options can be ordered alone or in combination. The following is a list of the more common dispositions: discharge, fine, forfeiture of proceeds, probation order, suspended sentence, compensation to victim, personal service order/community service order, custody, and treatment. Once the court has passed sentence, the corrections system is responsible for ensuring that the court order is fulfilled.

The Adult Criminal Court Survey (ACCS) is actually made up of two surveys, an aggregate caseload survey and an incident-based case characteristics survey. The ACCS is limited by the absence of national coverage of provincial/territorial courts and by the lack of data from municipal, superior, and appeal courts. Further complicating the situation is the fact that the percentage of "missing data" may change from one year to the next, confounding comparisons across time and space.

The aggregate caseload survey receives data from six jurisdictions (Prince Edward Island, Nova Scotia, Quebec, Ontario, Saskatchewan, and the Yukon) and includes 65% of the national volume of court data. This survey collects data on completed and pending charges, appearances, and cases for federal and provincial statutes and municipal bylaw offences. It also provides information about the changing nature of provincial/territorial court caseloads. The data collected and presented in the published survey include the number of charges and cases initiated, by type of offence; the number of charges and cases disposed of, by type of disposition; and the number of trial and nontrial appearances, by fiscal quarter.

The incident-based case characteristics survey collects data from five jurisdictions (Prince Edward Island, Nova Scotia, Quebec, Saskatchewan, and the Yukon), and accounts for 35% of the national volume. This survey provides detailed information about the characteristics of cases in provincial/territorial criminal courts. The data describe court processes, charge characteristics and outcomes, and basic characteristics of the accused.

CORRECTIONS

The corrections sector is divided into adult and young offender systems, each consisting of two components: custodial and noncustodial (or community services).

ADULT CORRECTIONS SURVEY

The provincial and federal governments share responsibility for administering adult offender dispositions. Generally, the provinces are responsible for noncustodial dispositions and offenders sentenced to less than two years, while the federal government is responsible for those sentenced to two years or more. Parole and mandatory supervision release programs are mainly the responsibility of the federal government, although parole boards have been established in some provinces.

Offenders given noncustodial sentences such as probation must report to a probation officer regularly throughout the period of the order. Other sentence types often attached to probation orders include conditional discharges, compensation to victims, and community service orders. If an offender does not comply with the conditions of the probation order, he or she can be charged with a summary conviction offence.

The Adult Corrections Survey of adult correctional facilities is based upon the completion of aggregate data tables by the thirteen governmental authorities that operate correctional systems: ten provinces, two territories, and the federal correctional service. The survey provides data on the number of admissions by age, sex, ethnic origin, type of offence, and sentence length. The average count of inmates is also provided, for both the facility and the system. Another part of the survey collects data on the number of admissions to the noncustodial portion of the system (i.e., the number of admissions to probation); included here are data on the number of community service admissions and the length of probation orders.

YOUNG OFFENDERS KEY INDICATOR REPORT (Y-KIR)

The provinces are solely responsible for administering young offender dispositions, which differ greatly from those for adults. A mechanism for automatic and optional reviews has been incorporated into the administration of custodial and noncustodial dispositions. Noncustodial sentences for young offenders are handled in a manner similar to that used for adults. Young offenders in custody are kept in secure or open custody facilities, as ordered by the courts. Unlike adults, young offenders are not eligible for parole or mandatory supervision. Instead, transfers between custodial security levels and probation are obtained through a review process.

The Young Offenders Key Indicator Report (Y-KIR) survey provides information on youth corrections. It collects the average daily counts of young offenders in secure and open custody, and on remand. These data are presented monthly, by fiscal year. At the present time, a second survey, the incident-based Youth Custody and Community Services Survey (YCCS) is being implemented across the country. No data are currently available from this new survey.

GENERAL POPULATION AND HOUSEHOLD SURVEYS

General population and household surveys involve contacting members of the general population directly in order to obtain information about their experiences with the criminal justice system. The statistics obtained are used to produce estimates that are accurate for the entire population. Since the data in these surveys are obtained directly from respondents and are not affected by biases in the official criminal justice system, it is not surprising that the statistical picture they present is different from the one painted by the "official" statistics.

Since they are based on samples, these surveys must deal with the issue of sampling error. The sample design and the allocation of the sample determine the size of the sampling error and the extent to which the results can be analyzed geographically. The sample is also stratified to ensure adequate coverage of important sectors of the population. Each member of the sample represents a number of persons in the surveyed population and, as mentioned above, the results of the survey are used to produce estimates for the population as a whole.

Once the sample design and the questionnaire have been developed, the researchers must chose a method of data collection. In recent years, the method of choice has been the telephone survey involving the use of random-digit dialling (RDD) whereby telephone numbers are chosen at random for the process of data collection. This technique has proven to be less costly than face-to-face interviews, and the portion of the population excluded because of the lack of a telephone is quite small.

There are two major surveys to be considered under this heading: the General Social Survey (GSS) and the Violence Against Women (VAW) survey.

General Social Survey (GSS)

The General Social Survey (GSS) was initiated by Statistics Canada to reduce gaps in the statistical information system, particularly in relation to socioeconomic trends. Many of these gaps cannot be filled through existing data sources or survey vehicles because of the range or periodicity of the information required or the lack of capacity of the relevant surveys. The GSS has two principal objectives: (1) to gather data on trends in Canadian society over time, and (2) to provide information about specific policy issues of interest. To meet these objectives, the GSS was established in 1985 as a continuing program with a single survey cycle each year.

The main topics for the "core" content of the GSS include health, education, social environment, and personal risk. The core content of the third and eighth cycles of the GSS, in 1988 and 1993, was personal risk—the risk of accident and criminal victimization. The survey in each of these years concentrated on the measurement of personal risk to criminal victimization as well as on lifestyle factors associated with different rates of victimization. The "focus" content of the surveys related to the use of victim services and perceptions of the criminal justice system.

The target population of the GSS consisted of all persons 15 years and over living in the ten provinces of Canada, with the exception of full-time residents of institutions. The population was sampled using RDD techniques and interviewed by telephone, thus excluding from the sample those persons living in households without telephones (less than 3% of the target population). The sample was allocated to provinces in proportion to the square root of the size of the population and to strata within provinces in proportion to their population.

The total sample size of about 10,000 persons is large enough to allow extensive analysis at the national level and some analysis at a regional level, but only very limited analysis at a provincial level because of the relatively limited extent of victimization. Each person in a probability sample can be considered to represent a number of others in the surveyed population. Each survey record was accordingly assigned a weight that reflected the number of individuals in the population that the record represented. Using these weights, the results of the sample survey were inflated to produce accurate estimates for the population.

Violence Against Women (VAW) Survey

In recent years, the issue of violence against women has reached prominence on the agendas of all levels of governments. In 1993, under the federal government's Family Violence Initiative, Health Canada funded Statistics Canada's first national survey on violence against women. The primary objective of the Violence Against Women (VAW) survey was to provide reliable estimates of the nature and extent of male violence against women in Canada (excluding the Yukon and the Northwest Territories). Whereas most research in this area reflects the experiences of women who report violent incidents to the police or who use the services of shelters or counselling services, the VAW survey went directly to a random sample of women who were asked about their experiences, whether or not these had been reported to the police or anyone else.

Between February and June of 1993, 12,300 women aged 18 and above were interviewed by telephone about their experiences of physical and sexual violence since the age of 16, as well as about their perceptions of their personal safety. The VAW survey investigated a number of different aspects of violence in the lives of women. The questionnaire contained questions about levels of fear about violence, about sexual harassment, about violence and threats of violence by strangers and dates, and about violence and emotional abuse by both current and previous spouses and partners. Data on the respondent's marital history were gathered, and there were classification questions designed to elicit information about the sociodemographic characteristics of the respondent.

The survey defined "violence" as experiences of physical or sexual assault that were consistent with the *Criminal Code* definition of these offences and that could be acted upon by a peace officer. Respondents were asked specific questions about physical and sexual assaults experienced since the age of 16 by strangers, dates, boyfriends, and other men known to them. Physical and sexual assaults by marital partners were defined as "wife assault."

The survey was conducted using the RDD method of contacting households. With this method, every household with telephone service had a chance of being selected. Households without telephones could not participate, nor could women who could not speak English or French. Only 1% of the female population of the ten provinces live in households without telephone service; in approximately 3% of the households contacted, there was a nonresponse due to language.

From the approximately 19,000 eligible households contacted, 12,300 interviews were obtained for a response rate of 64%. Nonresponse occurred for a variety of reasons, including refusals, language, and the unavailability of the woman selected for the interview. Most nonresponse occurred before the respondent was contacted. Among those households where a respondent was contacted (13,500), the response rate was 91%. Estimates of proportions of the female population of Canada 18 years of age and over produced from the VAW survey are expected to be within 1.2% of the true population proportion nineteen times out of twenty. Estimates of proportions of subpopulation will have wider confidence intervals.

SUMMARY AND CONCLUSIONS
■ ■ ■

Victimization surveys were developed in order to address the concern that there was a great deal of crime that was not reflected in official statistics. The reasoning was that there was a knowable "dark number" of crimes and that surveys based on administrative systems were seriously undercounting this number. Indeed, the results of victimization surveys do show that a great deal of crime is not contained within the official statistics of police-reported crime data because, for various reasons, the victim does not inform the police. According to the 1993 General Social Survey, reporting rates for the violent victimizations ranged from 47% for robberies to only 10% for sexual assault; for household victimizations, the rates ranged from 68% for break and enters to 43% for theft of household property.

One of the greatest advantages of the victimization survey is that it enables the researcher to gather from respondents (or victims) not only information about their experiences as victims of crime but also data on salary, housing type, education, drinking habits, and social behaviour. This type of information is invaluable in facilitating the identification of risk factors—those aspects of lifestyle that can be related to victimization rates. It is also possible through the victimization survey to collect information on the after-effects of the victimization. This type of information, which helps researchers to measure the real impact of crime, could never be elicited from a survey based on administrative data.

Population surveys are also more flexible than surveys based on administrative data in that their content can be altered in order to examine an issue from a slightly different perspective. However, the advantage of flexibility that accompanies victimization surveys has to be balanced against the loss of historical comparability when the instrument is changed. A case in point is the GSS of 1988, which produced victimization rates for sexual assault that were too low to meet the criteria for statistical reliability. When the instrument was changed in 1993, the modified instrument "detected" more cases of sexual assault. The 1993 result did not mean that the rate of sexual assault had risen dramatically between 1988 and 1993, but rather that the revised data-collection instrument was much more sensitive to this type of crime. This example clearly demonstrates the strong relationship between the data-collection instrument and the number of cases of crime that are detected in the population. It also indicates the importance of maintaining stability in the questionnaire. Finally, it suggests that it is erroneous to think in terms of a knowable, absolute number of cases of a particular crime in a population; the number of crimes detected is a function of the sensitivity and persistence of the questioning in the instrument.

Victimization surveys are most often compared and contrasted with the survey based on administrative data in the police sector, namely, the Uniform Crime Reporting (UCR) survey. This survey is based ultimately on the hard-copy "incident reports" completed by a police officer at the scene of the crime. The information collected in the incident report can serve several purposes, but the most important of these is to facilitate and track the police investigation. There are real limits to the amount and type of data that can be obtained by the police at the scene of the crime. It is expensive and complicated to collect and store this information, and the (sometimes) emotionally charged nature of the scene restricts the type of questions that can appropriately be posed.

The two types of surveys also differ with regard to the way in which the facts of the case are established. Victimization surveys rely on information from only one of the participants in the incident; they also rely on the victim's understanding of the definitions of the different types of crimes. In contrast, the police officer can obtain information from the victim, from witnesses, and possibly from the offender, and can also draw upon his or her professional experience when assigning a "label" to a particular incident.

The UCR survey has a major advantage over the victimization surveys with respect to coverage and volume. UCR data are currently available on a yearly (or monthly) basis for each of the approximately 1,600 geographic areas of Canada. The UCR survey counts the number of incidents and persons charged for each of 108 types of crime. This large database facilitates analysis of crime data by quite small geographic areas (usually municipalities) for each of the last 32 years. In contrast, the limited sample of respondents on the GSS allows estimates of victimizations for eight types of crime for the provinces and major urban areas.

Whereas the original UCR survey produced only "caseload" information (e.g., number of different types of offences and number of persons charged), the Revised UCR survey also provides "case characteristics" data on the circumstances of the incident and the personal characteristics of both the victim and the accused. Its incident-based approach gives the revised survey considerable analytical potential in terms of its database, since one can create and progressively subdivide smaller files of the incidents in which one is interested. As more police departments are added to the Revised UCR survey, the utility of the database for purposes of analysis will grow as well.

Both UCR and victimization surveys purport to measure the nature and extent of crime in the country, but they achieve this objective in very different ways, with different results, and with different levels of success for different crimes. The UCR survey is the preferred vehicle for measuring serious violent crimes (especially those committed by strangers), crimes against commercial establishments and public property, prostitution and drug offences, and statistically infrequent offences. Victimization surveys contain more data on attempted crimes, and are also the preferred vehicle for collecting data on subtle and sensitive aspects of crime, such as its impact on the victim. These survey types are in fact complementary, giving different perspectives on the same phenomenon. It is clear that the absence of either would greatly impoverish the raw materials available to criminological researchers in Canada.

PART II

The chapter in this section presents an overview of the crime trend in Canada for the period covered by the UCR survey, 1962–1993. The authors follow their examination of the primary measures used to assist researchers in the task of trend analysis with an exploration of the social dynamics underlying changing incident rates for various Criminal Code offences. A brief consideration of the geographic pattern of crime concludes the chapter.

OVERALL CRIME
TRENDS

CANADIAN CRIME TRENDS

by Michael Martin and Lucie Ogrodnik

The picture of the overall pattern of crime provides us with an idea of the extent to which criminal events occur and the conditions that enhance or reduce crime incidence. As we have indicated, the combination of characteristics of offenders and the conditions under which they operate can have a strong impact on what actually occurs. In this chapter, Michael Martin and Lucie Ogrodnik first look at how the different sources of data discussed in Chapter 2 can be used in outlining crime trends. They then discuss the correlates of total crime in Canada. Their review underlines the importance of analyzing crime trend data not in isolation but within the context of social and legislative changes. It also alerts us to the influence that crime trend data have on public perceptions of crime.

Crime can be defined as those acts and behaviours for which society provides formally sanctioned punishments. However, what is considered criminal varies over time and across cultures. In Canada, criminal acts are specified in written law (the *Criminal Code of Canada* and other federal statutes). In analyzing crime trends, one ideally has a measurement instrument that is reliable—that is, the concepts being measured are the same across time periods and are being measured in the same way each time data are collected. Because information about crime is located in different places in society and because conceptions of what crime is and how to measure it differ, the task of trend analysis is difficult and no single measurement tool provides an absolute, unchallenged account of the occurrence of crime in Canada. Furthermore, because the social backdrop against which crime is defined and measured is constantly changing, long-term crime trends are subject to significant interpretation. In Canada, a number of measures have been developed to provide perspective on the national crime-trend picture. In this chapter, crime trends are examined using primarily Uniform Crime Reporting (UCR) statistics.

THE UNIFORM CRIME REPORTING SURVEY (UCR)

As stated in Chapter 2, the most comprehensive and commonly used source of Canadian crime data is the UCR. The UCR counts all *Criminal Code* violations, as well as other federal and provincial statute violations. In order for a crime to be counted by the UCR it must: (1) come to the attention of the police; (2) be verified through police investigation; and (3) be documented by police. The UCR is a census of crime that conforms to all of these conditions. As well, the survey counts the number of crimes that are solved and the number of accused persons implicated. The UCR survey has been in place since 1962. The units of count and the rules used to collect and define the data have remained virtually unchanged over its 33-year history. Consequently, these data represent the most historically consistent source of crime information available in Canada. For the most part, crime trends described in this chapter are drawn from UCR data.

There are inherent difficulties in examining Canadian crime trends using the three decades of UCR data. Societal values and priorities have changed, as has the response of the justice system to criminal behaviour. Under-reporting of such crimes as impaired driving and domestic violence may have occurred in the earlier years as citizens and police were less likely to report or respond to them. Not only do members of the public change their reporting practices in response to changing values about what is or is not considered to be a crime, but it is also reasonable to assume that for a person to report a crime to police, there must be utility in doing so.[1] As discussed in Chapter 1, victimization surveys have clearly demonstrated that a significant proportion of crimes are not reported to police at all and that the reasons given relate to the perceived usefulness of reporting. The 1993 victimization survey indicated that approximately one-half of household victimizations (e.g., theft, break and enter) and even fewer personal victimizations (e.g., 10% of sexual assaults) are reported to police. The reasons given for not reporting a crime to police vary by type of crime (e.g., the crime is too minor, the victim would rather deal with it informally, or the victim believes that the crime will receive no police attention). Changes in police policies and/or practices such as the introduction of the 911 number or the requirement that complainants report thefts in person, change the incentives to reporting crime, thereby affecting overall crime trends. Given the magnitude of unreported crime, even small variances in public-reporting behaviour may have a sizable impact on the number of official crimes documented.

Crime trends are also affected by legislative changes that influence both definitions of crime and the justice response to it. Changes to the assault, sexual-assault, theft, arson, mischief, and prostitution provisions of the *Criminal Code*, the introduction of the *Young Offenders Act*, and the creation of new categories of crime such as criminal harassment all make distinct contributions to the nature of the crime trend.

The recording and statistical reporting of crime does not occur in isolation from the methods police use in responding to and recording criminal events. A considerable source of error in the UCR is *nonsampling error*. This type of error results from such things as technical problems with data capture or data processing and incorrect classification of crime information. UCR crime statistics are taken from police administrative sources and, as such, are influenced by the methods, policies, procedures, and priorities of police. As a by-product of police activity, crime statistics are constrained by the fact that methodologically accurate data capture and classification are not the primary objective of police. The influence of nonsampling error also changes over time. The crime trend over the past 33 years is set against a backdrop of considerable change in the management of police information. Computer-assisted dispatching systems, mobile display terminals, and sophisticated computerized information and records systems have revolutionized the way in which information is recorded and moved around. The application of these technologies and the way in which information flows within a police operation from the time a criminal incident is reported to police by the complainant through to its statistical recording can have a significant impact on the longitudinal picture of crime.

This situation was exemplified by a study conducted by CCJS comparing past police administrative practices in Calgary with those in Edmonton. This study found that approximately 36% of the difference in crime rates between these two cities was attributable to differences in the administration of criminal-occurrence data (CCJS, 1990). It is not unreasonable to expect that movement from a manual to a fully automated occurrence reporting system, complete redevelopment of police information systems, initiatives such as community-based policing, or differential response policies will have an impact on how crime is responded to by police departments. Such factors likely also affect how crime information flows through the system and how these data are ultimately captured as crime statistics.

It is also possible that, during the earlier years of the UCR survey's existence, police-reporting practices were not consistent across the country or over time. It is, for example, not uncommon for rapid increases in numbers to occur for the first few years following the implementation of any new survey or following major survey changes as respondents adapt their systems and practices to those changes. It is also important to note that coverage of the UCR survey was 91.4% of the intended frame of respondents in 1962, increasing to 99.4% in 1968. In this regard, it is notable that during the first eight years following implementation, the amount of crime reported to the UCR survey increased by 115%, a rate of increase not repeated since. Accordingly, high-crime growth periods in the 1960s may be partially due to increased and improved survey coverage.

VICTIMIZATION SURVEYS

As explained in Chapter 2, victimization surveys provide a clearer indication than the official UCR crime statistics of the extent to which people actually experience crime, the nature of their experiences, and their response—what Grainger refers to as the "qualitative aspects of the criminal event." The General Social Survey (GSS) reported in 1993 that a little over one-half (52%) of total victimizations were reported to police.[2] Victimization surveys are able to correct many of the limitations inherent in the UCR survey.

In the United States, crime-victimization data have been collected continuously since 1973 through the National Crime Victimization Survey. Canada's experience with time-series victimization data is much more recent. In 1988, Statistics Canada conducted its first GSS crime-victimization survey. A follow-up study was conducted in 1993, and successive studies are intended every five years. As an indicator of trends in crime victimization in Canada, the GSS currently is limited in that it allows for comparison of only two points in time, with a five-year gap in between.

This is not the only limitation of the GSS victimization surveys. Whereas every crime that occurs has the potential of being captured in the UCR survey and the entire population forms the base of that survey, the victimization survey excludes certain categories of crimes and victims due to the nature of its design. Victimizations of children under 15 are not reported, nor are homicides or occurrences of "victimless" crimes such as prostitution and drug crimes. The GSS also excludes commercial crime such as fraud or business break and enter. Because the GSS is a telephone survey of the Canadian noninstitutional population, victimizations of transients, foreign travellers, residents without telephones, and institutionalized persons (e.g., incarcerates, hospital patients) cannot be captured. Another important consideration in interpreting year-over-year changes in the GSS is the fact that it is a sample survey whereas the UCR is a census survey. As a sample survey, the GSS is subject to sampling error. The impact of sampling error on the researcher's ability to make inferences about crime trends between two time points can be considerable. An examination of the divergence of UCR statistics and National Crime Victimization Survey statistics in the United States shows that a 3 to 4% change in the overall rates must occur before it can be stated with any confidence that the victimization rate has actually changed. For less prevalent crimes, such as robbery or sexual assault, the changes observed must be considerably larger. Of course, the reverse holds true in that the observation of no change from one point in time to the next does not mean that no change actually occurred.

What is important to note from the above discussion is that neither official statistics nor victimization surveys provide an accurate census of all crimes that occur, nor are the counts particularly comparable. Of course, this does not mean that the information contained in these surveys is not useful. Rather, as Grainger concludes, these data tend to complement each other by providing different ways of viewing society's experience with crime.

CANADIAN CRIME TRENDS

Crime in Canada, as measured by the UCR,[3] has increased substantially since 1962. In terms of the absolute number of *Criminal Code* offences, Canadians today are surrounded by considerably more crime than they were in 1962. The number of *Criminal Code* offences (excluding traffic-related ones) reported in 1994 is over five times greater than that reported in 1962. Even adjusting for a 160% increase in population, the crime rate[4] in 1994 was still 3.5 times the 1962 rate. In fact, the crime situation may even be worse than reported by UCR statistics. In counting victimizations rather than the number of distinct crimes, the UCR survey underestimates the actual number of crimes being committed. For example, of the 879,000 incidents reported to the Revised UCR survey in 1994, 8.1% involved more than one crime. The breakdown of actual crime occurrences in 1994 appears in Figure 3-1.

As Figure 3-2 shows, the increase in crime over the past 33 years has hardly been uniform. The third consecutive year showing a decrease in crime rate occurred in 1994. The drop in 1994 (-4.8%) followed a 5.3% decline in 1993 and a 3% decline in 1992. While it is too early to determine whether these figures represent the beginning of a downward trend in UCR reported crime, it is noteworthy that these three years of decrease follow two unusually high years, 1990 (+7%) and 1991 (+9%). The largest rise in the 33-year crime trend occurred between 1962 and 1983, with a rate increase of 205%. Between 1983 and 1994, however, the crime rate increased only 7%.

In 1962, violent crimes constituted 8% of all *Criminal Code* offences reported to the UCR; as Figure 3-3 shows, by 1994 this proportion had increased to almost 12%. Property crimes, the largest category of *Criminal Code* offences, constituted 58% of all reported offences in 1994. In 1962, however, the proportion of property offences was greater at 68%. Other *Criminal Code* offences (e.g., prostitution, arson, mischief) constituted 31% of criminal offences in 1994, an increase from 24% in 1962. What this

Figure 3-1 Criminal Incident Rates, Canada, 1994

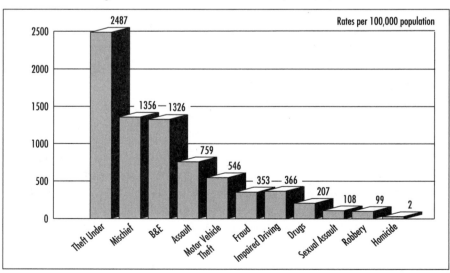

Source: Uniform Crime Reporting survey, Canadian Centre for Justice Statistics, 1994.

Figure 3-2 Canadian Crime Rates, 1962–1994

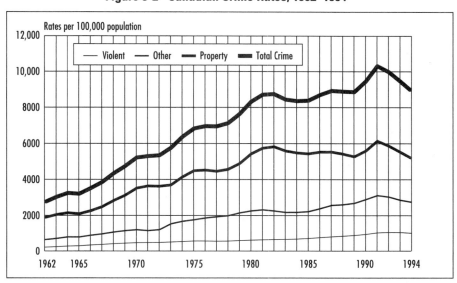

Source: Uniform Crime Reporting survey, Canadian Centre for Justice Statistics, 1994.

analysis obscures is the fact that the proportional distribution of these categories of crime remained essentially unchanged between 1962 and 1983. Although the overall rate of increase in crime has slowed down since 1983, both the other *Criminal Code* categories and in particular the violent crime categories have increased at a faster rate than has property crime.

Figure 3-3 Composition of Crime,* Canada, 1994

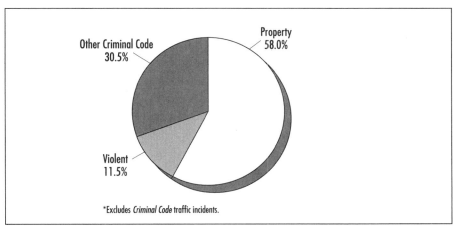

Source: Uniform Crime Reporting survey, Canadian Centre for Justice Statistics, 1994.

Summary crime trends provide an oversimplified view of crime. As stated in Chapter 1, the criminal event can be considered as a social event in the sense that our understanding of crime is enhanced by our knowledge of the social situation in which a crime occurs (i.e., the motives of the offender, the reaction of the victim, the time and place of the crime, and the response of the criminal justice system). Crime trends occur within a broader social context and their characteristics are shaped by a combination of many social factors.

Over time many changes occur that can affect crime numbers. Legislative changes can significantly alter public and official responses to crime. The behaviour being legislated is often not some wrong that has miraculously appeared; rather, it is a behaviour for which the current level of official response is no longer considered satisfactory. (We will examine this issue in detail later in the chapter when we discuss the effects of changes in the assault law, Bill C-127, on crime reporting.)

Social and economic changes also affect crime patterns. Property crime trends, for example, are set against a backdrop of higher per capita availability of targets. There are more cars to steal, more households to burglarize, more businesses from which to steal, and more credit cards to exploit. Because many insurance companies require victims to report thefts to police in order to process claims, the degree to which members of the public are covered by property insurance could influence the reporting of these crimes, particularly during times of economic hardship. This change is evident in the example of UCR reported thefts of expensive bicycles (over $1,000). In 1986, there were approximately 1,500 thefts of bicycles over $1,000; by 1994, the number had increased fourfold to 6,285.

The above explanations are not intended to minimize crime but rather to contextualize the occurrence of crime and thereby permit the reader of crime statistics to more realistically assess whether things have become better or worse. Crime occurs against a broad range of social factors, including demographic change. Young males have consistently been shown to be more active in criminal activity than any other age group. Approximately two-thirds of accused persons identified by police were between the ages of 15 and 34 years (1993 Revised UCR survey). However, while the total population has increased 60% since 1962, the number of persons aged 15 to 34 years has increased 86%. As the Canadian population continues to age into the next century and the proportion of persons in this age group continues to drop, if the relationship between age and crime continues, one can expect to see an overall drop in the crime rate as well.

While persons aged 15 to 34 are most likely to commit crimes, they are also more likely to be the victims of crime. Data from the 1993 Revised UCR survey indicate that 60% of victims of violent crime are between 15 and 34 years, yet this group represents only 30% of the total population. On the other hand, 24% of victims who reported to the survey were 35 years and over, a group that represents 48% of the population. Routine activities theories would suggest that people in younger age groups disproportionately spend their time engaged in activities that put them at greater risk of victimization (Cohen and Felson, 1979). Over the next decade, however, we may see a decline in the pool of available criminals (as well as in the number of suitable victims) as this group changes its lifestyle. This change could also include property-related victimizations. For instance, as the population ages and people retire, they tend to spend more time at home. Consequently, even though there may be households that have a potential for break and enters, these targets will most likely be occupied and therefore less attractive.

UCR crime statistics also show that crime has progressively become less of a "man's game." As Figure 3-4 shows, in 1962, 7.5% of persons charged with *Criminal Code* offences were female. Women's proportion of the total charged has gradually increased to 18% in 1994. This trend is also reflected in incarceration statistics showing that the female proportion of offenders admitted to custody increased from 6% in 1980–81 to 9% in 1992–93. It is

Figure 3-4 Persons Charged by Gender, 1962–1994

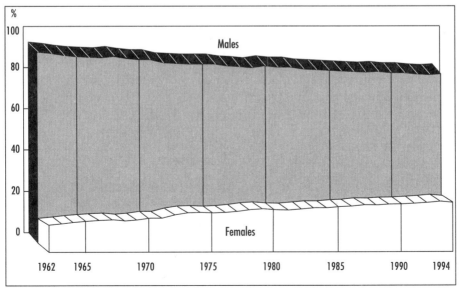

Source: Uniform Crime Reporting survey, Canadian Centre for Justice Statistics, 1994.

not clear to what degree the increase in the female crime rate is due to an increase in female criminality or to changes in the official response to female offenders, which lead to stricter enforcement of the laws.

Although poverty and crime have historically shown a strong association, suggesting that depressed economic conditions and unemployment may affect crime rates, the results of research examining this link have been inconclusive. Some theorists have argued that, rather than unemployment per se, feelings of relative deprivation associated with changes in lifestyle or economic status may be an influencing factor in crime patterns (Hartnagel and Lee, 1990).

VIOLENT INCIDENTS

While violent crime has the greatest personal impact, it represents a relatively small proportion of all crime, averaging under 10% per year over the past 33 years. Since 1962, violent crime has increased sevenfold from 41,026 offences in 1962 to 303,398 in 1994 (nonviolent crimes have witnessed a fourfold increase since 1962). While the violent crime category represented 8% of all *Criminal Code* offences in 1962, it constituted 11.5% of all crimes in 1994. A rapid increase in violent crime commenced in 1983, following the enactment of Bill C-127, which repealed the crime of rape and created three levels of assault and of sexual assault. In addition, prior to Bill C-127, police had either to witness an assault or have evidence of physical injury before they could make an arrest. With the introduction of Bill C-127 these restrictions were removed. The intent (and result) of this legislation has been a dramatic increase in reported assault and sexual-assault crimes. The rise in the incidence of sexual assault and assault may also have been related to a greater willingness on the part of victims to report the offence. Physical assaults[5] have consistently accounted for the majority of violent crime, increasing from 71% in 1962 to 78% in 1994. Thus any change in the number of physical assaults drives the overall rate of violent crime.

PROPERTY INCIDENTS

Property incidents involve unlawful acts by which the offender intends to gain property without the use or threat of violence. In 1994, there were over 4.5 times more property crimes than there were in 1962. Even controlling for the increase in population, the property crime rate increased almost threefold. Crimes against property as a proportion of all *Criminal Code* incidents remained steady at approximately 66%, until 1983 when it began to decline in conjunction with the increase in violent and "other" types of crimes. By 1994, the proportion of property crime had dropped to 58% of *Criminal Code* offences. Nevertheless, being the largest component of total crime, the overall crime trend mirrors the trend in property crime (see Figure 3-2).

The distribution of crimes within the property category has remained stable throughout the history of UCR data collection. Thefts have consistently accounted for two-thirds of property crimes, of which minor theft[6] makes up the majority. Due to the large volume of minor thefts, any change in their number strongly influences not only overall property crime but also the overall crime rate in Canada. Between 1962 and 1994, break and enters have consistently made up one quarter of all property crime committed in Canada. The targets of over one-half of break and enters are private residences. Businesses account for approximately one-third and other miscellaneous locations (e.g., garages, sheds) constitute the remainder. The two other property crime categories are fraud and possession of stolen property.

The above characterization of the property crime trend is incomplete and somewhat misleading because population is not a particularly meaningful base from which to calculate property crime rates. The target of property crime is, in most cases, not persons but property. Measuring the number of potential targets for property crimes is more appropriate for calculating prevalence rates. This view is supported by the results of the most recent international crime victimization survey (van Dijk, 1992), which suggest that international variability in property crime rates is partly determined by different property-related opportunity structures. In other words, countries with high per capita number of bicycles or motorcycles have high rates of thefts of these properties. Similarly, countries with many vehicles have high rates of vehicle theft or theft from vehicles. Changes in the availability of property over time may be an important consideration in relation to UCR property crime trends. UCR break-and-enter statistics, for instance, are based on the number of households broken into. Thus, while the overall population in 1994 was 1.6 times higher than that in 1962, the number of households was more than twice as high[7]. Calculated as a rate per 1,000 households, break and enter has only doubled since 1962, as compared to the 4.5 times increase in the absolute number of break and enters and the tripling in the rate per 100,000 population. Indeed, in recent years, the rate of break-and-enter offences per 1,000 households has decreased from 26.3 offences per 1,000 households in 1980 to 23.4 in 1993.

A similar calculation can be applied to rates of business break and enters. In 1992, the number of incorporated businesses in Canada was three times higher than it was in 1974.[8] The number of business break and enters, however, was only 1.8 times higher. Thus, the rate of business break and enters, controlling for the number of incorporated businesses, actually decreased over this time period. A comparable picture can be seen with respect to motor-vehicle theft. In 1992, the number of motor-vehicle thefts was 1.7 times higher than in 1977. Controlling for the increase in population, the per capita rate of motor-vehicle theft in 1992 was 1.4 times higher than in 1977. When the number of targets (i.e., registered motor vehicles) are taken into account, the picture changes completely. The motor-vehicle theft rate per registered vehicle has remained relatively unchanged between 1977 and 1992, ranging between five and seven vehicles stolen per 1,000 registrations (Statistics Canada, 1992c).

On the basis of the three different property types described above, the availability of property targets has increased at a faster rate than the population as a whole. When one considers the large increases in the number and variety of consumer goods, the increase in the consumer retail sector of the economy, the increase in the number of credit-card transactions,[9] and other opportunities for financial fraud such as debit cards, it is little wonder that property-related crime has increased. However, the risk posed to property itself has not changed as much as the absolute crime number or per capita rates suggest.

OTHER *CRIMINAL CODE* INCIDENTS

Other *Criminal Code* incidents such as mischief, arson, prostitution, and offensive weapons have increased fairly steadily since 1962. In fact, from the mid-1960s through to the mid-1980s, there was a greater percent change in other *Criminal Code* incidents than in either property or violent incidents. Other *Criminal Code* incidents made up 24% of total crime in Canada in 1962, increasing to 30.5% in 1994.[10]

Mischief accounts for one-half of "other" category offences. The majority of mischief offences involve damage to property (e.g., vandalism). In 1985, Bill C-18 changed the way mischief was categorized by adding a value to the property damaged, over and under $1,000. This categorization has caused confusion because sometimes the dollar value of the damage done (say, to a car antenna) is coded while at other times the entire property affected (the car in total) is coded. Combining both the under and over $1,000 groupings, mischief has declined from 54% of all other *Criminal Code* offences in 1977 to 49% in 1994.

Incidents of crime within the other *Criminal Code* category are particularly volatile, fluctuating with changing police-enforcement activity. This is particularly evident with respect to crimes such as counterfeiting and prostitution. Counterfeiting, for example, has increased tenfold since 1983, increasing from 1,267 offences to 20,804 in 1994. Prostitution offences account for less than 1% of other *Criminal Code* incidents. Despite its negligible impact on total crime, prostitution offences are highly sensitive to changes in police policy and enforcement practices, which in turn have been influenced by legislative changes. A 1985 amendment expanded the definition of prostitution to include the act of stopping or attempting to stop a person or communicating for the purpose of solicitation. As a result, the number of prostitution incidents increased sixfold from 1,225 in 1985 to 7,426 in 1986, the year after the amendment.

PROVINCIAL/MUNICIPAL PATTERNS

There is considerable variation in the crime rates between cities and across regions. In 1994, the crime rate ranged from a low of 5,570 in Newfoundland to a high of 24,661 in the Northwest Territories. While municipal and provincial/territorial crime rates have all followed the national crime trend (i.e., rising steadily since 1962), there is considerable variation in the rate of the increase over time (from a 177% increase in Alberta to a 572% increase in Prince Edward Island). It is noteworthy that the variance in the crime rate across Canada is greater than the amount of change in the total Canadian crime rate over the past 33 years. While the Atlantic provinces have traditionally experienced relatively low crime rates, those in the Territories have, however, always been extremely high relative to the rest of Canada. As Figure 3-5 shows, this regional variation has an east-to-west tilt, with the crime rate tending to increase as one progresses westward.

Population density and migration, sociodemographic factors, and differences in police policies and resources are all likely contributors to the geographic pattern of crime. Densely urbanized areas may, for example, create more opportunities for criminal activity. In addition, city living and the relative transience of urban dwellers can leave residents without the same sense of belonging that may be experienced by those who live in smaller communities.

Differences in age structures across the country may also produce varying crime rates. The same factors that help to explain differences in crime rates at the provincial level are also useful predictors at the local municipal level. However, there are many problems associated with making intermunicipal

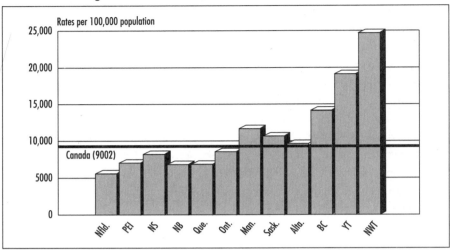

Figure 3-5 Provincial/Territorial Crime Rates, 1994

Rates per 100,000 population

Source: Uniform Crime Reporting survey, Canadian Centre for Justice Statistics, 1994.

comparisons of crime. First, changes in police policies or resources can result in important changes in the number of police-reported incidents. Statistics for prostitution, gambling, and drug crime are particularly sensitive to changes in policing practices. In addition, population figures reflect the resident population of an area. Thus metropolitan areas with many crimes, small resident populations, and large daytime populations will exhibit high crime rates, while suburban areas with large resident populations and few crimes will exhibit low crime rates. The changes in a community's demographic profile over time may cause significant variations in its crime rate.

SUMMARY AND CONCLUSIONS
■ ■ ■

Uniform Crime Reporting was implemented over three decades ago to produce a reliable indicator of the incidence of crime in Canada using a standard survey instrument with standardized concepts and definitions. This survey instrument has shown Canada to be on the crest of a 30-year crime wave, with all categories of crime increasing consistently since its implementation and beginning to decline only in 1992, 1993, and again in 1994. Over the three decades of UCR reporting, however, the social, economic, technological, legislative, and regional context within which the survey operates has changed dramatically. As argued in this chapter, crime-trend data can be properly understood only in terms of this changing environment. For example, increases in property crime have taken place against a backdrop of increased wealth and higher rates of property ownership; increases in the level of assaults have taken place in the wake of specific legislative changes that encouraged an increase in police response and heightened public reaction to the crime of assault; and increases in business break-and-enters have occurred during a period of rapid growth in the number of business establishments.

These various contributing factors should be closely explored by those who analyze crime-trend data if they are to make an informed assessment about whether crime is getting better or worse, and by how much. Rash analysis of the data can easily produce heightened fear of crime among the public; conversely, it can produce unnecessary complacency. Crime data serve an important function in the development of legislation and crime-prevention policies. Caution is therefore necessary on the part of those engaged in identifying and responding to the crime problem. For example, any suggestion that further legislation is needed to curb the large increase in the number of reported assaults since 1983 ignores the fact that this increase is largely the consequence of legislative changes. Understanding the social circumstances that affect the crime trend not only helps to place the crime trend into context, but may also suggest possible crime-prevention strategies.

We have suggested in this chapter that many aspects of crime are related to changing opportunity structures. An increasingly popular approach to crime prevention, therefore, involves reducing the number of criminal opportunities through the use of security systems. Similarly, changing demographics and the associated changes in people's lifestyles alter the risk of victimization.

NOTES

[1] For example, the victim believes that the police will investigate the offence, a report is necessary for insurance purposes, or the citizen is fulfilling his or her social responsibility by making the police aware of a crime.

[2] Results from the 1993 GSS victimization survey illustrate that the decision of whether a crime needs to be reported to police is a complex process. It is also important to note that the definitions within the *Criminal Code* are sufficiently broad that many mundane or trivial activities could be considered crimes and captured in a victimization survey. Consequently, in a large proportion of victimizations, the reason given for not reporting a crime to police was that it was considered by the victim to be too trivial. Thus, at the social policy level, one

must temper the results of victimization surveys with the recognition that many events are counted that may be of negligible concern.

[3] Keep in mind that the UCR measures crime in terms of a unit called an "offence." The UCR scores violent incidents differently from other types of crimes. For violent crimes, a separate incident is recorded for *each victim* (e.g., one person assaulted equals one incident or three persons assaulted equals three separate incidents). For nonviolent crimes, one offence is counted for *each incident* (e.g., one person breaking into five homes translates into five incidents of break and enter). In addition, only the *most serious offence* is counted within an incident. For example, an incident involving both a break and enter and an assault is scored as an assault. As a result of this scoring rule, the less serious offences are consistently undercounted. In simple terms, the *outcome* of the UCR counting rules is that the "offence" is approximately the equivalent of each victimization, where one offence is counted for each victim or complainant irrespective of the number of contributing crimes.

[4] A rate is an approximation of the relative risk of being victimized by a criminal act. It is expressed as a rate per 100,000 population.

[5] Physical assault refers to nonsexual assault, primarily common assault (i.e., assault that does not involve a weapon or serious injury).

[6] The dollar value limits for theft, mischief, and possession of stolen goods have changed three times since the 1970s. In 1972, the *Criminal Code* was amended to increase the dollar value of property stolen from $50 to $200; it was amended again in 1985, increasing the limit to $1,000, and in February 1995 it increased yet again to $5,000.

[7] Statistics Canada, 1961 and 1991 Census.

[8] Revenue Canada reports that there were 307,000 incorporated businesses in 1974 and 930,000 in 1992.

[9] For a discussion of the correspondence between the increase in credit-card fraud and the increase in the number of credit-card transactions, see Canadian Centre for Justice Statistics, "Fraud in Canada," *Juristat Service Bulletin* 12(5). Ottawa: Statistics Canada, 1992.

[10] Statistics Canada, 1992. "Motor Vehicle Theft." *Juristat Bulletin*, vol.12, no.12. Ottawa: Canadian Centre for Justice Statistics.

PART III

This section looks at the more serious crimes of homicide, robbery, assault, wife and child abuse, and sexual assault. As pointed out in Chapter 3, assault is the most common of all violent crimes. Despite their common theme of violence, these crimes have different characteristics and, as such, require different strategies for deterrence and prevention.

CRIMES AGAINST PEOPLE

HOMICIDE

by Christine Wright and Orest Fedorowycz

In this chapter, Christine Wright and Orest Fedorowycz examine the crime of homicide. Important in this discussion are changing definitions of homicide, the nature of the relationship between the offender and the victim, the circumstances under which homicide occurs, incident characteristics, and the aftermath of the event, including the criminal justice response. Wright and Fedorowycz provide an extensive review of the demographic correlates of homicide. They conclude the chapter with an overview of the public response to this crime.

Homicide, the killing of one human being by another, is the most feared and final affront to individual freedom. This chapter will discuss Canadian homicides from the perspective of the criminal event—the precursors, the event, and the aftermath—using data compiled by the Canadian Centre for Justice Statistics (CCJS). These data have been collected by Statistics Canada since 1961 to help police, politicians, criminal justice practitioners, government policymakers, and researchers provide answers about the nature and extent of homicide incidents.

DEFINITIONS

In Canada, criminal homicide is classified as first-degree murder, second-degree murder, manslaughter, or infanticide. Deaths caused by criminal negligence, suicide, and accidental or justifiable homicide are not included in this definition. Homicide is broadly defined as causing the death of a human being under any circumstances, by any means, directly or indirectly. Homicide can be nonculpable (not blameworthy) or culpable (criminal). Homicides that are nonculpable are either justifiable or excusable. A homicide is justifiable if authorized by law, such as when a police officer kills an attacking criminal. Killing a person to protect one's life (self-defence) or someone else's is an excusable homicide that is not a crime. The law allows people to use reasonable force to defend themselves and others when they believe they are in jeopardy. Generally, what constitutes reasonable force depends on the circumstances in each case. Shooting and killing a thief who was in the process of leaving your premises with a television would not constitute justified homicide, since your life was not threatened at the time. The focus of this chapter is culpable homicide, which is killing without legal justification or excuse.

Prior to September 1961, all murder was considered capital and the sentence upon conviction was the death penalty. After September 1961, murder was divided into capital and noncapital murder. Capital murder, still punishable by death, consisted of premeditated murder, murder of a police officer or prison guard, and murder committed in the course of another criminal act. All other types of murder were considered noncapital, and carried a sentence of mandatory life imprisonment. In December 1967, the *Criminal Code* sections dealing with murder were amended again. Under this new amendment, capital murder referred only to murders of police or custodial officers. In 1973, the legal terms "capital murder" and "noncapital murder" were changed to "murder punishable by death" and "murder punishable by life imprisonment," respectively.

In 1976, the *Criminal Code* was again amended; capital punishment was abolished and replaced with a mandatory life sentence for all those offences previously punishable by death. The amendment also reclassified murder from capital and noncapital murder to first- and second-degree murder. Section 232 of the *Criminal Code* defines first-degree murder as:

1. planned or deliberate murder;
2. murder of a police officer or other person employed for the preservation and maintenance of the public peace, acting in the course of his or her duties;
3. murder committed in the course of specified criminal acts (hijacking an aircraft, sexual assault, sexual assault with a weapon, threats to a third

party or causing bodily harm, aggravated sexual assault, or kidnapping and forcible confinement); and

4. murder committed by a person who has previously been convicted of first- or second-degree murder.

First-degree murder and second-degree murder are differentiated by the element of planning and deliberation. Premeditated—planned and deliberate—murder is considered first-degree. There need not be any significant length of time between the forming of intent to kill and carrying out that intent. Killings committed impulsively and without provocation are considered to be second-degree. Firing a gun intentionally into a crowd without regard for human life would be an example of second-degree murder.

Section 234 of the *Criminal Code* defines manslaughter as "culpable homicide that is not murder or infanticide," while Section 232 (1) states, "Culpable homicide that would otherwise be murder may be reduced to manslaughter if the person who committed it did so in the heat of passion caused by sudden provocation." No intent to kill is necessary, only an unlawful act causing the death. If someone dies as a result of wounds inflicted by another during a brawl, for example, then the accused is guilty of manslaughter even though the intent to kill was not formed.

Infanticide, considered the least culpable of all homicide offences, can only be committed by a woman against her newborn child (up to the age of one year). Section 233 states that "a female person commits infanticide when by a wilful act or omission she causes the death of her newly-born child, if at the time of the act or omission she is not fully recovered from the effects of giving birth to the child and by reason thereof or the effect of lactation consequent on the birth of the child her mind is then disturbed." As will be seen, this offence type is rarely charged and may well be eliminated as a *Criminal Code* homicide offence.

These various forms of homicide also differ in terms of sentences allowed by the courts. The punishment for first-degree murder is life imprisonment with no parole for at least 25 years. Those convicted of second-degree murder must serve a minimum of ten years before being eligible for parole. Under Section 745 of the *Criminal Code,* however, an offender who has served fifteen years of his or her sentence may apply for consideration of earlier parole. Though there is no minimum sentence for manslaughter, the maximum sentence is life imprisonment. Infanticide carries with it a maximum penalty of five years' imprisonment.

MOTIVES

Homicide is a complex event and may reflect diverse motivations. During the period of 1983 to 1993, police reported that 32% of homicides were preceded by an argument or quarrel. Over 15% of homicides took place during the commission of another offence, 11% were motivated by revenge, and 7% were the result of jealousy. When females were the victims, jealousy was a factor in 13% of homicides, compared to 4% in male homicides.

ACCUSED–VICTIM RELATIONSHIP

Despite the intense media coverage of murders perpetrated by strangers, the data indicate that homicides are more likely to be committed by persons known to the victim, than by a stranger. Figure 4-1 shows that of the homicides for which an accused was identified, the proportion of homicides committed by strangers remained relatively stable between 1983 and 1993, ranging from a low of 12% in 1983 to a high of 18% in 1986. Almost one-half (48%) of homicide victims were killed by an acquaintance, while over one-third (37%) were killed by an immediate family member or relative.

Figure 4-1 Homicides by Accused–Victim Relationship, Canada, 1983–1993

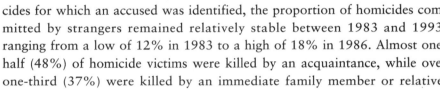

Source: Homicide survey, Policing Services Program, Canadian Centre for Justice Statistics, January 1995.

Since 1983, domestic homicides as a proportion of all homicides have decreased to 33% in 1993, while acquaintance homicides have increased to 51% in 1993. Many domestic homicides are characterized by a history of domestic violence. As of 1991, when collection of information on previous domestic violence was initiated, approximately 40% of family homicides had a history of domestic violence known to police; in 1993, the percentage was 43%.

Family homicides consist of two distinct relationship categories: immediate family (including spouses, parents, children, and siblings) and extended family (including other relatives and in-laws). Since 1983, homicides involving immediate family members have remained relatively stable, accounting for 88% of domestic homicides. In almost 60% of these homicides, the victims were female. In contrast, 72% of victims in homicides involving extended family members were male.

During the 1983–93 period, the largest concentration of immediate family homicides involved spousal relationships (57%), and of these an overwhelming majority were female victims (77%). The second highest category of homicides within immediate family relationships were parents who killed their offspring (24%). The victims of parent–child homicides were almost evenly distributed by gender—53% male and 47% female. Children who kill their parents accounted for 12% of all immediate family homicides during 1983–93. A slightly greater proportion of fathers (53%) than mothers were killed by their children. The least frequent type of immediate family homicide involved siblings. From 1983 through 1993, sibling homicides accounted for over 7% of all immediate family homicides; males were the victims in 89% of these homicides.

SPOUSAL HOMICIDES

In recent years, increasing attention has been given to a subset of family homicides, namely spousal homicides. For this discussion, spousal homicides include persons in both registered marriages and common-law relationships, as well as persons separated and divorced with respect to such unions. From 1983 through 1993, 842 women and 258 men were killed by their spouses. During this period, females have consistently represented the largest proportion of all spousal homicide victims in each year, at a ratio of over three to one. Wilson, Daly, and Wright (1993) found that the probability of a registered married woman being killed by her spouse was nine times greater than that of being killed by a stranger. Even though in 1993 the overall number of homicides was down and the number of spousal homicides (87) was fewer than the average number (100) between 1983 and 1993, spousal homicides continued to account for one out of every six solved homicides.

From 1983 through 1993, females were at a higher risk than males of being killed by a spouse (39% of female homicide victims, 7% of male victims), by another family member (19% of female victims, 18% of male victims), or by someone with whom they shared an intimate nonspousal relationship (6% of female victims, 2% of male victims). In 1993, the proportion of females killed by other family members increased to 21% while the proportion for males decreased sharply to 13%. In the case of intimate nonspousal relationships, the percentages of females and males killed increased to 11% and 4%, respectively. Between 1983 and 1993, males were at a higher risk of being killed by a nonintimate acquaintance (56% of all male victims) or a stranger (18%) than were females (25% killed by a nonintimate acquaintance and 10% by a stranger).

ALCOHOL/DRUG USE[1]

Between 1991 and 1993, police reported that more than one-third (41%) of homicide victims had consumed alcohol, drugs, or both at the time of the offence: 28% consumed alcohol only; 9% consumed both alcohol and drugs; and 4% consumed drugs only. Alcohol/drug use was unknown for 21% of victims. For known cases of alcohol/drug use by victims, male victims (58%) were more likely to have consumed alcohol and/or drugs than were female victims (39%).

For the same period, police reported that more than one-half (53%) of all accused had consumed alcohol, drugs, or both at the time of the offence: 35% had consumed alcohol; 4% had taken drugs; and 14% had taken both alcohol and drugs. There was little difference between male and female accused in terms of alcohol/drug use.

THE EVENT

SOCIAL CHANGE AND TRENDS IN CANADIAN HOMICIDE

In this section, the analysis of general trends in the incidence of homicide will cover a 32-year period beginning in 1961, while the analysis of more specific trends involving circumstances and accused/victim characteristics will cover the period from 1983 to 1993. Since 1961, two trends in the incidence of homicide have been observed (see Figure 4-2). Between 1966 and 1975, the homicide rate increased dramatically from 1.2 per 100,000 population to a peak of 3.0. Though there are no analyses showing a causal relationship between social factors and the homicide rate, as Silverman and Kennedy (1993) point out, Western culture was going through a period of significant change during these years. From 1975 to 1993, the homicide rate, though relatively stable, has demonstrated a slight decline, averaging about 2.5 homicides per 100,000 population. The 1993 homicide rate of 2.2 per 100,000 population was 15% lower than the rate in 1992 and represented the third largest year-to-year decrease since 1961. This latest reported homicide rate is at about the same level as that reported in 1970.

The homicide rate is driven primarily by charges of murder. Since 1961, manslaughter rates have remained relatively stable and infanticide numbers have been almost negligible, representing less than 1% of all homicides in any given year. It must be remembered, however, that these rates are based on the initial classification of homicide incidents made by the police with the information available from their investigation, that is, charges. As will be seen in our discussion of the criminal justice response to homicide, the picture changes when homicide convictions are examined.

Figure 4-2   Homicide Rates,* Canada 1961–1993

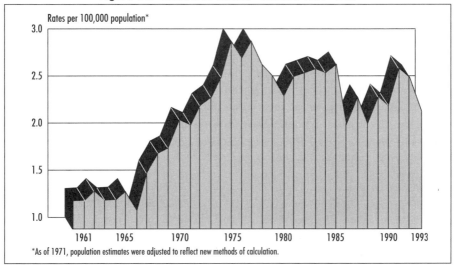

*As of 1971, population estimates were adjusted to reflect new methods of calculation.

Source: Homicide survey, Policing Services Program, Canadian Centre for Justice Statistics, January 1995.

INTERNATIONAL COMPARISONS

When making international comparisons, one must be aware of differing definitions and categorizations. For example, countries may or may not include manslaughter[2] and cases of criminal negligence causing death in their definition of homicide; and some countries may impose age restrictions on the classification of murder. The United States would seem to be a logical choice for such comparisons, as its definition of homicide closely resembles our own; moreover, the United States has collected homicide data over a similar time period.

Although Canadian homicide rates have been consistently three to four times lower than U.S. homicide rates, they appear less impressive when compared with those in other Western countries. In 1991, Adler, Mueller, and Laufer used data from 22 industrialized nations to compare homicide rates for males between the ages of 15 and 24. For this age group, Canada ranked sixteenth highest, with a rate of 2.9 per 100,000 population. The United States had the highest homicide rate at 21.9 per 100,000, followed by Scotland at 5.0 per 100,000. Austria had the lowest rate at 0.3 per 100,000, which is almost ten times lower than Canada's rate. Other countries with lower homicide rates than Canada's were Great Britain, France, Germany, Norway, Sweden, and Japan.

DEMOGRAPHICS

GENDER, AGE, AND MARITAL/EMPLOYMENT STATUS

The gender breakdown for homicide victims shows that since 1983 almost two-thirds (64%) of victims were male and 36% were female. The majority of victims (53%) were between 18 and 39 years of age, the age group representing 36% of the general population. Homicide data indicate that young adult males appear to be the most criminally active. Males accounted for 87% of all those accused of homicide between 1983 and 1993. Almost one-half (48%) of persons accused of homicide were between 18 and 29 years of age, although this age group represented only 18% of the general population. The second highest concentration of homicide accused (24%) was in the 30- to 39-year age group, which represented 18% of the general population.

In the past few years, much publicity has surrounded individuals accused of homicide under the *Young Offenders Act*. From 1983 through 1993, 494 youths aged 12–17 were accused of committing homicide, representing 8% of all accused charged with homicide (see Figure 4-3). In 1993, 35 youths

Figure 4-3 Homicide Victims and Accused by Age Group, Canada, 1983–1993 Average

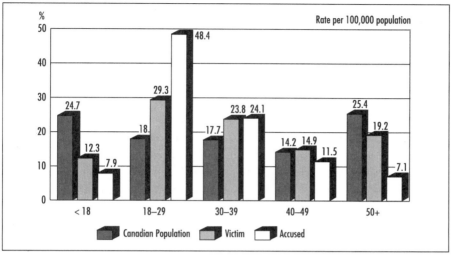

Source: Homicide survey, Policing Services Program, Canadian Centre for Justice Statistics, January 1995.

were accused of homicide, the lowest number since 1984 when 36 youths were charged. Of the 555 homicides between 1983 and 1993 where youths were identified as the accused, 32% of the victims were aged 12 to 24 years, and 16% were 60 years of age or older. Males and females in the 12–17 age group had an equal chance of being killed by other youths.

Almost 60% of homicides involving youths (12–17 years) took place in a private residence, of which 72% were occupied by the victim alone or jointly by the victim and accused. During the period from 1991 to 1993, police reported that 39% of homicides committed by youths involved a precipitating crime. In 1993, this percentage decreased to 33%. Of the 670 youth-perpetrated homicide incidents since 1991, almost three-quarters (72%) occurred at the same time as another violent offence. A further 82 homicides occurred during the commission of a property offence, 46 during a drug offence, and 60 in combination with other types of criminal offences. Some other "motives" for homicides committed by youths were argument/quarrel (21%) and revenge (8%). The most frequent causes of death in youth homicides were beating/strangling (33%) and shooting and stabbing (each 29%). In 84% of cases, the accused was male, and in 70% of cases the victim knew the accused. In cases where the accused were family and relatives, 54% were parents (76% were fathers), 42% were siblings and other family, and 4% were spouses (all husbands in these cases).

During the period 1983 to 1993, 739 elderly persons (60 years or older) were victims of homicide. As a proportion of all homicides, this group accounted for an average of 10% per year. Approximately 62% of these victims were male, which is consistent with the gender breakdown for all homicide victims. Over 76% of elderly homicides occurred in a private residence; 37% of these homicides involved a precipitating crime of which 84% were robbery/theft and break and enter. Almost half (45%) of the victims were beaten or strangled, 25% were stabbed, and 20% were shot. In 88% of elderly homicides, the accused were males; in 26% of these cases, the accused were between the ages of 18 and 24. In 79% of elderly homicides, an accused was identified. Based on these solved homicides, the large majority (68%) of accused were known by the victim. One-third were immediate family members or relatives and 35% were acquaintances. In cases where the accused were family, 46% were spouses, 33% were children, and 21% were siblings and other family.

Between 1983 and 1993, of the 6,600 homicide victims 15 years of age and over, 40% were single at the time of the offence, 36% were married, 17% were separated or divorced, and 4% were widowed. Homicide victims who were either divorced/separated or single at the time of the offence were overrepresented relative to their proportion in the Canadian population. Standardized employment information on victims and accused has been available only since 1991. From 1991 through 1993, 53% of victims were either unemployed or not in the work force (e.g., retired, homemakers, students). For the accused, the percentage was 66%.

PROVINCES AND TERRITORIES

Most of the decrease in the number of homicides at the national level between 1991 and 1993 was a result of large declines in both Ontario and Alberta. Table 4-1 shows that only two jurisdictions—Saskatchewan and the Northwest Territories—reported an increase in the number of homicides between 1991 and 1993. Table 4-2 shows that between 1983 and 1993 the national homicide rate averaged 2.45 per 100,000 population, ranging from a low of 2.14 in 1988 to a high of 2.69 in 1991. Since 1991, the homicide rate of 2.69 has decreased almost 19% to the 1993 rate of 2.19 per 100,000 population. Figure 4-4 shows that there is substantial variation in provincial homicide rates, with the lowest rates in Newfoundland and Prince Edward Island and the highest rates in the western provinces. From 1983 through 1993, the Atlantic provinces still exhibited rates well below the national average. Although the Northwest Territories in 1993 experienced the highest

Table 4-1 Number of Homicides, Canada, 1961–1993

YEAR	NFLD.	PEI	NS	NB	QUE.	ONT.	MAN.	SASK.	ALTA.	BC	YT	NWT	CANADA
1961	1	1	6	2	52	89	15	14	18	34	1	0	233
1962	0	1	10	8	62	76	19	13	18	55	3	0	265
1963	3	0	6	5	69	76	16	8	27	35	3	1	249
1964	5	0	13	5	52	81	16	20	25	32	1	3	253
1965	6	4	10	5	63	77	15	15	20	57	3	2	277
1966	3	1	9	6	56	71	17	12	27	48	0	0	250
1967	1	0	10	5	75	114	15	25	38	47	6	2	338
1968	5	0	9	5	102	104	28	23	25	73	1	0	375
1969	5	1	12	1	126	111	28	33	23	50	0	1	391
1970	1	1	15	8	141	115	29	24	42	78	6	7	467
1971	2	0	16	10	124	151	33	29	45	61	0	2	473
1972	2	2	14	11	157	141	36	28	37	88	3	2	521
1973	3	0	19	17	155	160	38	23	36	87	4	4	546
1974	3	2	8	21	169	160	42	31	44	107	5	8	600
1975	4	0	14	12	226	206	37	36	57	98	6	5	701
1976	6	2	25	14	205	183	31	34	68	88	4	8	668
1977	8	1	14	38	197	192	44	46	70	91	6	4	711
1978	9	4	13	27	180	182	39	32	84	85	2	4	661
1979	5	0	17	11	186	175	44	36	56	90	4	7	631
1980	3	1	12	9	181	158	31	31	55	105	2	4	592
1981	4	1	11	17	186	170	41	29	73	110	1	5	648
1982	6	0	12	13	190	184	35	39	70	109	2	7	667
1983	6	0	13	11	190	202	40	33	75	108	1	3	682
1984	6	0	15	14	198	190	43	30	54	110	2	5	667
1985	5	1	26	14	219	193	26	28	63	113	6	10	704
1986	4	0	15	12	156	139	47	26	64	89	3	14	569
1987	5	0	14	20	174	204	44	30	73	78	0	2	644
1988	7	1	11	8	154	186	31	23	66	80	1	8	576
1989	5	1	16	18	215	175	43	22	67	86	2	7	657
1990	0	1	9	12	184	182	39	36	74	110	1	12	660
1991	11	2	21	17	181	245	43	21	84	128	0	3	756
1992	2	0	21	11	166	242	29	32	92	122	2	13	732
1993	7	2	19	11	159	193	31	30	49	122	0	7	630
AVERAGE	5	1	16	13	181	196	38	28	69	104	2	8	662
TOTAL	143	30	455	398	4,950	5,127	1,065	892	1,719	2,774	81	160	17,794

Source: Homicide survey, Policing Services Program, Canadian Centre for Justice Statistics, January 1995.

rate of 11.13 per 100,000 population, it was 16% lower than the territories 1983–1993 average rate of 13.25%. Among the provinces, British Columbia recorded the highest 1993 homicide rate per 100,000 population (3.45) for the third consecutive year. Newfoundland reported the lowest provincial

Table 4-2 Homicide Rates,[1] Canada, 1961–1993

YEAR	NFLD.	PEI	NS	NB	QUE.	ONT.	MAN.	SASK.	ALTA.	BC	YT	NWT	CANADA
1961	0.22	0.96	0.81	0.33	0.99	1.43	1.63	1.51	1.35	2.09	6.85	0.00	1.28
1962	0.00	0.93	1.38	1.32	1.15	1.20	2.03	1.40	1.31	3.31	20.00	0.00	1.43
1963	0.63	0.00	0.80	0.82	1.26	1.17	1.69	0.86	1.92	2.06	20.00	3.85	1.32
1964	1.04	0.00	1.72	0.82	0.93	1.22	1.67	2.12	1.75	1.83	6.67	11.11	1.31
1965	1.23	3.67	1.32	0.81	1.11	1.13	1.55	1.58	1.38	3.17	21.43	7.41	1.41
1966	0.61	0.92	1.19	0.97	0.97	1.02	1.77	1.26	1.85	2.56	0.00	0.00	1.25
1967	0.20	0.00	1.32	0.81	1.28	1.60	1.56	2.61	2.55	2.42	40.00	6.90	1.66
1968	0.99	0.00	1.17	0.80	1.72	1.43	2.88	2.40	1.64	3.64	6.67	0.00	1.81
1969	0.97	0.90	1.55	0.16	2.11	1.50	2.86	3.44	1.48	2.43	0.00	3.23	1.86
1970	0.19	0.91	1.92	1.28	2.34	1.52	2.95	2.55	2.63	3.67	35.29	21.21	2.19
1971	0.38	0.00	2.00	1.55	2.01	1.92	3.30	3.10	2.69	2.71	0.00	5.45	2.15
1972	0.37	1.76	1.74	1.69	2.53	1.77	3.59	3.03	2.18	3.81	14.78	5.12	2.34
1973	0.55	0.00	2.33	2.58	2.49	1.98	3.76	2.52	2.08	3.66	18.78	9.73	2.42
1974	0.54	1.72	0.98	3.15	2.69	1.95	4.12	3.40	2.50	4.36	23.58	19.32	2.62
1975	0.72	0.00	1.69	1.77	3.56	2.47	3.60	3.91	3.14	3.90	27.27	11.57	3.02
1976	1.06	1.68	2.99	2.02	3.19	2.17	3.00	3.64	3.63	3.46	17.70	17.94	2.84
1977	1.41	0.83	1.66	5.45	3.05	2.25	4.23	4.86	3.58	3.53	26.09	8.89	2.99
1978	1.58	3.28	1.54	3.85	2.78	2.11	3.74	3.35	4.14	3.24	8.37	8.77	2.75
1979	0.88	0.00	2.00	1.56	2.87	2.01	4.23	3.74	2.66	3.36	16.60	15.18	2.60
1980	0.52	0.81	1.40	1.27	2.77	1.80	2.99	3.20	2.50	3.81	8.16	8.57	2.41
1981	0.69	0.81	1.28	2.40	2.83	1.92	3.95	2.96	3.17	3.88	4.15	10.44	2.60
1982	1.04	0.00	1.39	1.83	2.88	2.06	3.34	3.94	2.94	3.78	8.10	14.00	2.65
1983	1.03	0.00	1.49	1.53	2.87	2.23	3.76	3.28	3.13	3.70	4.20	5.83	2.68
1984	1.03	0.00	1.71	1.94	2.98	2.06	4.00	2.95	2.25	3.72	8.30	9.42	2.60
1985	0.86	0.78	2.93	1.93	3.27	2.07	2.40	2.72	2.61	3.78	24.39	18.18	2.71
1986	0.69	0.00	1.68	1.65	2.32	1.47	4.30	2.52	2.62	2.95	12.10	25.27	2.17
1987	0.87	0.00	1.56	2.74	2.56	2.11	4.00	2.89	2.99	2.55	0.00	3.59	2.43
1988	1.21	0.77	1.22	1.09	2.24	1.88	2.81	2.23	2.68	2.56	3.72	14.21	2.14
1989	0.87	0.77	1.76	2.44	3.09	1.72	3.89	2.15	2.68	2.68	7.30	12.17	2.40
1990	0.00	0.76	0.99	1.62	2.62	1.76	3.52	3.56	2.89	3.33	3.57	20.20	2.37
1991	1.90	1.53	2.29	2.27	2.56	2.34	3.86	2.09	3.23	3.79	0.00	4.90	2.69
1992	0.34	0.00	2.28	1.47	2.32	2.28	2.61	3.19	3.49	3.53	6.62	20.87	2.57
1993	1.20	1.52	2.06	1.46	2.21	1.80	2.78	2.99	1.84	3.45	0.00	11.13	2.19
AVERAGE 1983–93	0.91	0.56	1.82	1.83	2.64	1.97	3.45	2.78	2.77	3.28	6.38	13.25	2.45

[1]Rates are calculated on the basis of 100,000 population.

Source: Homicide survey, Policing Services Program, Canadian Centre for Justice Statistics, January 1995.

homicide rate (1.20). With the exception of Alberta, rates generally followed the historical pattern of increasing from east to west, a pattern discussed in the context of overall crime trends in the previous chapter.

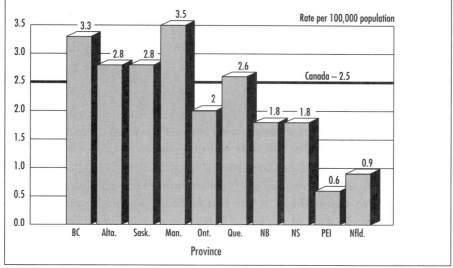

Figure 4-4 Average Homicide Rate by Province, 1983–1993

Rate per 100,000 population

Canada – 2.5

Province	Rate
BC	3.3
Alta.	2.8
Sask.	2.8
Man.	3.5
Ont.	2
Que.	2.6
NB	1.8
NS	1.8
PEI	0.6
Nfld.	0.9

Source: Homicide survey, Policing Services Program, Canadian Centre for Justice Statistics, January 1995.

CENSUS METROPOLITAN AREAS (CMAS)

The Census Metropolitan Area (CMA) refers to an urbanized core of at least 100,000 population, together with adjacent urban and rural areas that exhibit a high degree of economic and social integration with that core. At present, Canada has 25 CMAs.

Table 4-3 divides the 25 CMAs into three population-size categories and shows that the homicide rate for CMAs with a population of 500,000 and over had decreased from 3.1 per 100,000 in 1983 to 2.4 in 1993. The 1983–93 average rate (2.6) for these CMAs was slightly higher than the average national rate of 2.5 homicides per 100,000 population for the same time period. The homicide rate for CMAs with populations of 250,000–499,999 had a 1993 rate (2.1) marginally higher than their 1983–93 average rate (2.0). The third CMA group, with populations of 100,000–249,999, reported a 1993 rate (2.0), slightly lower than their 1983–93 average rate (2.2), which also matched the national figure.

Table 4-3 shows that, from 1983 to 1993, an average of 329 reported homicides per year occurred in CMAs with a population of over 500,000. During this period, homicides in the 25 CMAs represented about 58% of all reported homicides in Canada. With increased migration to large urban areas, CMAs in 1993 constituted 61% of the Canadian population and accounted for 65% of all homicide occurrences.

Table 4-3 Number and Rate[1] of Homicides and Homicide Rates by Census Metropolitan Area, 1983–1993

	1983[2]		1984		1985		1986		1987		1988		1989		1990		1991		1992		1993		1983–1993 Average	
	N	R	N	R	N	R	N	R	N	R	N	R	N	R	N	R	N	R	N	R	N	R	N	R
500,000+ population																								
Toronto	60	1.9	73	2.3	72	2.2	46	1.3	76	2.0	68	1.8	73	1.9	72	1.8	103	2.5	90	2.2	71	1.7	73	2.0
Montreal	116	4.1	114	4.0	105	3.7	87	2.9	88	2.9	71	2.3	125	3.9	105	3.3	104	3.2	105	3.2	105	3.2	102	3.3
Vancouver	44	3.4	44	3.3	66	4.9	44	3.0	44	3.0	35	2.3	45	2.9	54	3.3	63	3.8	61	3.6	63	3.7	51	3.4
Ottawa-Hull	21	2.8	7	0.9	24	3.1	12	1.4	13	1.5	17	1.9	14	1.5	13	1.4	18	1.9	13	1.3	16	1.6	15	1.8
Edmonton	25	3.6	22	3.2	19	2.8	23	2.9	29	3.6	32	4.0	31	3.8	29	3.4	25	2.9	33	3.8	27	3.1	27	3.4
Calgary	18	2.9	11	1.8	16	2.6	13	1.9	22	3.2	13	1.8	10	1.4	15	2.0	19	2.5	35	4.5	10	1.3	17	2.4
Winnipeg	18	3.0	24	4.0	16	2.6	25	3.9	30	4.6	14	2.1	20	3.1	20	3.0	17	2.6	13	2.0	17	2.5	19	3.0
Quebec	16	2.7	7	1.2	17	2.9	7	1.1	10	1.6	10	1.6	14	2.2	15	2.3	12	1.8	6	0.9	13	1.9	12	1.8
Hamilton	22	4.0	13	2.4	14	2.5	12	2.1	7	1.2	13	2.2	9	1.5	10	1.6	16	2.6	12	1.9	8	1.3	12	2.1
Total	340	3.1	315	2.8	349	3.1	269	2.2	319	2.5	273	2.1	341	2.6	333	2.5	377	2.8	368	2.7	330	2.4	329	2.6
250,000–499,999 population																								
London	5	1.7	6	2.1	7	2.4	1	0.3	5	1.4	3	0.8	4	1.1	6	1.5	2	0.5	10	2.5	6	1.5	5	1.4
St. Catharines-Niagara	6	2.0	7	2.3	9	2.9	6	1.7	11	3.1	12	3.3	4	1.1	9	2.4	11	2.9	11	2.9	6	1.6	8	2.4
Kitchener	4	1.4	6	2.0	7	2.3	4	1.2	5	1.5	6	1.8	4	1.1	2	0.5	11	3.0	7	1.9	8	2.1	6	1.7
Halifax	1	0.4	6	2.1	9	3.1	5	1.6	9	2.9	9	2.9	5	1.6	4	1.2	9	2.7	8	2.4	7	2.1	7	2.1
Victoria	7	2.9	8	3.3	2	0.8	6	2.2	2	0.7	7	2.5	4	1.4	8	2.8	2	0.7	5	1.7	7	2.3	5	1.9
Windsor	5	2.0	9	3.7	9	3.6	3	1.1	7	2.6	7	2.6	7	2.6	5	1.8	6	2.2	9	3.3	10	3.6	7	2.7
Oshawa[3]	3	1.9	0	0.0	2	1.2	3	1.4	3	1.4	3	1.3	5	2.1	2	0.8	11	4.4	3	1.2	5	1.9	4	1.7
Total	31	1.7	42	2.3	45	2.4	28	1.3	42	2.0	47	2.2	33	1.5	36	1.6	52	2.3	53	2.3	49	2.1	42	2.0
100,000–249,999 population																								
Saskatoon	7	4.3	4	2.4	2	1.2	2	1.0	5	2.4	1	0.5	2	0.9	9	4.2	7	3.3	7	3.3	6	2.8	5	2.4
Regina	10	5.9	8	4.6	6	3.4	8	4.2	9	4.6	7	3.6	3	1.5	9	4.6	4	2.0	4	2.0	4	2.0	7	3.5
St. John's	2	1.3	0	0.0	2	1.2	1	0.6	2	1.2	2	1.2	0	0.0	0	0.0	3	1.7	1	0.6	4	2.3	2	0.9
Chicoutimi-Jonquière	2	1.5	1	0.7	1	0.7	3	1.8	2	1.2	2	1.2	2	1.2	6	3.7	1	0.6	1	0.6	1	0.6	2	1.3
Sudbury	5	3.4	2	1.4	1	0.7	2	1.3	11	7.2	3	1.9	1	0.6	6	3.7	7	4.3	6	3.6	3	1.8	4	2.8
Sherbrooke[4]	—	—	—	—	—	—	1	0.7	1	0.7	2	1.5	3	2.1	2	1.4	2	1.4	0	0.0	0	0.0	1	0.7
Trois-Rivières	2	1.8	0	0.0	6	5.3	3	2.3	5	3.7	2	1.5	2	1.5	1	0.7	3	2.1	0	0.0	4	2.8	3	2.0
Thunder Bay	3	2.5	7	5.8	4	3.3	1	0.8	6	4.8	3	2.4	1	0.8	1	0.8	3	2.3	7	5.4	5	3.8	4	3.0
Saint John	3	2.6	1	0.9	2	1.8	2	1.6	7	5.6	4	3.2	2	1.6	3	2.3	4	3.1	4	3.1	2	1.5	3	2.5
Total	34	3.0	23	2.0	24	2.1	23	1.6	48	3.4	26	1.8	16	1.1	37	2.6	34	2.3	30	2.1	29	2.0	29	2.2
100,000 population	306	2.8	304	2.8	303	2.8	271	2.6	278	2.6	253	2.4	279	2.6	285	2.6	293	2.7	281	2.5	222	2.0	280	2.6
CANADA	682	2.8	667	2.7	704	2.8	569	2.2	644	2.4	576	2.1	657	2.4	660	2.4	756	2.7	732	2.6	630	2.2	662	2.5

[1]Populations from 1981 to 1985 reflect June 1 census figures; populations from 1986 to 1993 reflect July 1 census figures.
[2]Rates are calculated per 100,000 population.
[3]Prior to 1992, Oshawa fell under the 100,000–249,999 population group.
[4]Prior to 1986, Sherbrooke was not a CMA.

[5]**Source:** Homicide survey, Policing Services Program, Canadian Centre for Justice Statistics, January 1995.

INCIDENT CHARACTERISTICS

MULTIPLE VICTIM/ACCUSED INCIDENTS

A homicide incident refers to a distinct homicide event regardless of the number of victims or suspects/accused. From 1983 to 1993, 94% of homicide incidents involved a single victim. For the same period, at least one accused was involved in 81% of all homicide incidents. Collection of information on precipitating crimes, or the occurrence of a homicide during another crime, became standardized in 1991. During the period from 1991 to 1993, 36% of all homicides were committed in the course of or following another criminal act. Of these 707 homicide incidents since 1991, more than two-thirds (69%) occurred at the same time as another violent offence.

CAUSE OF DEATH AND WEAPON USED

In some homicides, more than one method of killing is used. The Homicide Survey records only the method that caused the death. Figure 4-5 shows that, from 1983 to 1993, shootings and stabbings accounted for 32% and 29% of homicides, respectively, where the cause of death was known. Since 1979, shootings have accounted for approximately one-third (ranging from 29% to 37% annually) of all homicides, while stabbings have represented approximately one-quarter (ranging from 23% to 32%).

Figure 4-6 shows that from 1974 to 1990, the proportion of homicides resulting from the use of handguns remained relatively constant at around 10%. Handgun usage increased to 18% of all homicides in both 1991 and

Figure 4-5   Methods Used to Commit Homicide, Canada, 1983–1993 Average

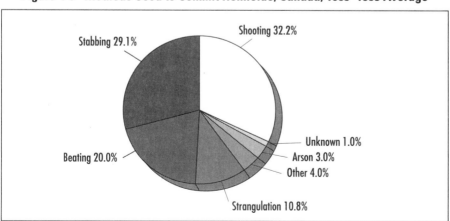

Shooting 32.2%

Stabbing 29.1%

Unknown 1.0%

Arson 3.0%

Other 4.0%

Beating 20.0%

Strangulation 10.8%

Source: Homicide survey, Policing Services Program, Canadian Centre for Justice Statistics, January 1995.

Figure 4-6 Firearm Homicides as a Proportion of All Homicides

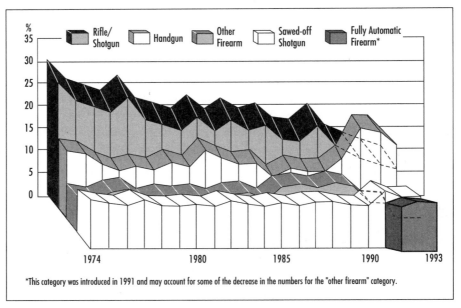

*This category was introduced in 1991 and may account for some of the decrease in the numbers for the "other firearm" category.

Source: Homicide survey, Policing Services Program, Canadian Centre for Justice Statistics, January 1995.

1992 and dropped to 14% in 1993. The use of rifles/shotguns in homicides continued to decrease, from 30% in 1974 to 12% in 1993. The use of sawed-off rifles and shotguns in homicides remained relatively stable between 1974 and 1993, representing 2% of all homicides in 1993. Fully automatic firearms, which have been identified in the Homicide Survey since 1991, also accounted for 2% of all homicides in 1993.

LOCATION OF HOMICIDE INCIDENT

A greater proportion of victims are killed in private residences than in any other type of location. Of the 6,339 known-location homicide incidents that took place between 1983 and 1993, almost 61% occurred in a private residence. Almost one-half (48%) of homicides occurred in a residence occupied solely by the victim or jointly by the victim and the accused. Further detailed breakdowns available since 1991 show that slightly less than one-third (32%) of homicide incidents occurred in a public place. Of these, 23% took place in an open area (such as a parking lot, street, or field), while the rest occurred in commercial areas (e.g., bar, bank, restaurant), public institutions, or vehicles.

THE AFTERMATH

Most of the above information on the victims, suspects, and circumstances of homicide is provided by the various police agencies across Canada. But this is not the end of the homicide incident. Much can happen between the time an offence is recorded by the police and the final outcome is determined. For example, an accused may never be found or, if one is apprehended, charges can be dropped or reduced. Offenders can also be found unfit to stand trial. This section traces the criminal justice response to homicide incidents, from the time an offence is classified by the police or prosecutor to the time an accused is convicted and sentenced, and concludes with a discussion of the public's response to acts of homicide.

CRIMINAL JUSTICE SYSTEM RESPONSE

CLASSIFICATION OF HOMICIDE INCIDENTS BY POLICE

The classification of homicide incidents is based on the initial police investigation, not on the final court disposition. The legal classification of an incident may be changed between the time the police charge the accused and the final disposition of the case in the courts. For example, a homicide initially classified as murder may end up as a manslaughter conviction after the court process.

From 1983 to 1993, the proportion of homicides classified as first-degree murders ranged from a low of 43% in 1983 to a high of 57% in 1991. In 1993, 52% of all homicides were classified as first-degree murder, 35% as second-degree, 12% as manslaughter, and 0.1% as infanticide. While first-degree murders as a proportion of all homicides have been increasing since 1978 (when they accounted for 33%), the proportion of second-degree murders has been declining since 1978 when they accounted for 57% of all homicides; the 1983–93 average was 41%. Manslaughter percentages have remained relatively stable during the same period, fluctuating between 9% of total homicides reported to the police in 1978 to 12% in 1993; the 1983–93 average was 8%. As in previous years, infanticides represented less than 1% of all homicides reported to police.

CLEARANCE OF HOMICIDE INCIDENTS

Homicides are inherently more complex and often take more time to solve than other crimes. It is not surprising, therefore, that some homicides are not solved during the year in which they were recorded. Because of this, data available for a specific year tend to underestimate final police clearance rates. In 81% of the 6,729 reported homicide incidents between 1983 and 1993, the police identified at least one accused. Of those incidents cleared during this period, 90% were cleared by a charge being laid or an accused being identified. In 9% of the cases, the accused committed suicide immediately after the homicide; the remaining cases were cleared by other means, such as the accused being admitted to a mental institution or dying shortly after confessing to the homicide.

We have already noted that since the late 1970s the proportion of homicides classified by the police as first-degree murder has been increasing while those classified as second degree have been decreasing. This trend is in all likelihood a by-product of the introduction, in 1976, of the categories of first- and second-degree murder to replace capital and noncapital murder. Because capital murder was punishable by death, rules for charging under this offence classification were stringent and juries, it has been argued, were less likely to convict given the severity of the penalty. With the abolition of the death penalty, the police seem more inclined to lay or recommend the most serious charge.

As previously outlined, the various offences of homicide have differing penalties associated with a conviction. We have few sources of information in regard to the final court disposition of homicide cases. There are, for example, no national court data at the superior court level, the level at which most charges of homicide are heard.[3] A 1991 study undertaken by the CCJS (Wright, 1993) traced through the justice system those individuals charged with a homicide offence reported in 1988, a year for which most outcomes would be known. Figure 4-7 shows the contrast between the original charge and the final outcome. As is fairly typical, approximately 85% of all homicides reported in 1988 were cleared (i.e., an accused was identified). Of those who were charged, 48% were charged with first-degree murder, 44% with second-degree murder, 7% with manslaughter, and less than 1% with infanticide.

Once those accused of homicide passed through the adult court process, however, the direction changed, with the largest number being convicted of manslaughter (40%), followed by 24% for second-degree murder and only 10% for first-degree murder. A further 3% were convicted of a lesser offence and 23% were acquitted.

The final disposition can be a function of various factors, including original overcharging by the police; lack of evidence for a finding of intent or premeditation; compassion on the part of the jury in cases such as mercy

**Figure 4-7 Initial Charge vs. Disposition* of Accused,
Homicide Offences Reported in 1988**

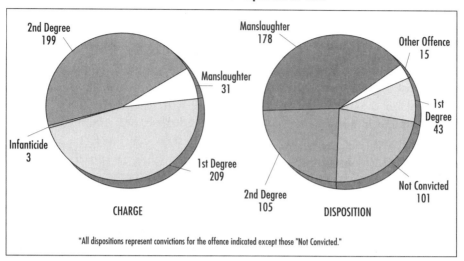

2nd Degree
199

Manslaughter
31

Infanticide
3

1st Degree
209

CHARGE

Manslaughter
178

Other Offence
15

1st Degree
43

Not Convicted
101

2nd Degree
105

DISPOSITION

*All dispositions represent convictions for the offence indicated except those "Not Convicted."

Source: Homicide survey, Policing Services Program, Canadian Centre for Justice Statistics, January 1995.

killings; or a plea bargain resulting from a lack of evidence and/or witnesses. A famous example of plea bargaining is the manslaughter conviction and twelve-year sentence of Karla Homolka, co-accused of Paul Bernardo in particularly gruesome crimes that involved the abduction, sexual assault, and subsequent murders of two teenagers in southern Ontario.[4]

As prescribed by law, all persons convicted of first- and second-degree murder in adult court receive life sentences. For those 178 persons convicted of manslaughter in adult court in 1988, sentences ranged from suspended sentence to life imprisonment. Only 2% received each of the upper and lower extremes, while 10% received a sentence ranging from ten years to life, 42% received a penitentiary sentence between five to ten years, 28% received two to five years, and 16% received a sentence of less than two years to be served at a provincial correctional facility. When there are no prescribed penalties, sentences vary considerably. In any homicide offence, there is at least one victim who has been killed by at least one other person. However, the circumstances surrounding offences differ substantially. For example, the killing of one intoxicated person by another in a barroom brawl where either one could potentially be the victim is a much different event than a group of youths walking into a restaurant and randomly shooting patrons. Malice, intent, state of mind, suffering of the victim, gruesomeness of the offence, likelihood of recidivism, and public outrage are some of the factors judges keep in mind when determining an appropriate sentence.

As previously mentioned, most homicide offences are heard at the superior court level or in youth court. However, manslaughter can be heard at the provincial court level. In 1993, the CCJS (Turner, 1993) undertook a sentencing study at the provincial court level in six jurisdictions in Canada (Prince Edward Island, Nova Scotia, Quebec, Ontario, Alberta, and the Yukon) for the 1991–92 period. Over these two years, there were 73 cases that resulted in a manslaughter conviction. Of these, 66% resulted in a sentence involving incarceration. This figure is in stark contrast to the incarceration rate of 98% for those convicted of manslaughter in superior court for those homicides reported in 1988. The fact that these cases were heard at the provincial court level in the first place, however, may indicate that they were less severe in nature.

Of the 47 persons under the age of 18 who were charged with homicide for an offence that occurred in 1988, 35 were tried in youth court and ten were tried in adult court. Sixty-three percent of those tried in youth court received convictions, with 86% receiving secure-custody sentences. The Youth Court Survey (YCS), discussed in Chapter 2, shows that from 1986/87 to 1993/94, 92 youths were convicted of first- or second-degree murder and a further 49 for manslaughter. Eighty-four percent of those convicted of first- or second-degree murder received sentences involving secure custody, three-quarters of which were for more than two years. For those convicted of manslaughter, 55% received sentences that involved secure custody, half of which were for more than two years.

Nine of the ten youths who were tried in adult court for an offence reported in 1988 were found guilty; the tenth was found not guilty by reason of insanity. Of those convicted, seven were found guilty of murder, resulting in life sentences. These represent 16% of all youths tried for homicide offences, in contrast to about one-third of adults who are tried and sentenced to life imprisonment. Though these data represent only one year, they suggest that if a youth is tried in adult court the conviction rate is high and the repercussions severe.

PUBLIC RESPONSE TO HOMICIDE INCIDENTS

When the savage crimes of a serial killer like Clifford Olson come to light, or when a police officer is murdered in the line of duty, there is generally a call from many sectors of society to reinstate the death penalty. Homicides can also fuel a public demand for improved policies to curb violence. For instance, after Marc Lepine systematically shot 27 women (killing fourteen of them) at a Montreal university, gun control and violence against women resurfaced as major issues. Similarly, murders by young offenders have sparked strong demands for changes to the *Young Offenders Act (YOA)*, including longer and harsher penalties and lower limits on the age at which a child can first be prosecuted for an offence (currently age 12) and before they can be considered adult (currently age 18).

When two or three high-profile homicides occur over a short period of time, the public becomes alarmed, fearing an increase of violence among Canada's youth. Policymakers and legislators face a difficult task in that they must weigh isolated incidents against overall trends to determine which issues must be addressed first and whether new or different measures are required. Certainly, particularly heinous crimes can serve as catalysts for action on the part of governments. In the summer of 1994, the government was spurred into acting quickly on pending gun-control legislation by three separate incidents involving guns: the drive-by shooting of Nicholas Battersby on a street in Ottawa, the murder of an innocent patron in the Toronto restaurant Just Desserts, and the murder of a university student by her estranged boyfriend in London, Ontario.

If fear of crime becomes an issue with the public, then law and order becomes an issue with the government, particularly around election time. Attempts were made to strengthen *Criminal Code* gun-control provisions in 1978 and again in 1995. Among the measures currently being reviewed with respect to the *YOA* is putting the burden on an older youth to show why he or she should not be heard in adult court for certain violent crimes, including murder. Dangerous offender legislation has been enacted to allow for the continued incarceration of particularly violent offenders. Most police departments have enacted policies designed to eliminate police discretion relating to cases of spousal and family violence. Many school boards have implemented zero-tolerance policies to deal with student violence, and have prohibited students from carrying weapons. Bar owners in Edmonton recently banned from their establishments all weapons (including knives) that might be carried by patrons. In most provinces, it is now legally mandated that teachers and health professionals report any incidents of suspected abuse against children. It will be a number of years before researchers will be able to measure the effects of these anti-violence measures on Canada's homicide rate.

SUMMARY AND CONCLUSIONS
■ ■ ■

As the most extreme of all crimes, homicide generates much research data. This crime can be viewed from a criminal-event perspective, with reference to the precursors, the event itself, and the aftermath. As we have seen, the precursors of homicide highlight the importance of social relationship in determining murderous outcomes; despite popular misconceptions, strangers are very unlikely to be the offenders in homicide events. In the event, the most likely offenders and victims are young males. Weapons are often used in homicide incidents; close to one-third of homicides in Canada over the past 32 years have involved shooting. Homicide varies regionally, with levels tending to increase as one progresses westward across Canada. High-profile homicide cases have led to public demands for harsher sentences and stronger gun-control legislation. The realization that homicide is a preventable crime has led to the implementation of measures designed to deter violence in society.

NOTES

[1] Information on these variables has been available only since 1991. It is, therefore, not possible to comment on long-term trends, even though alcohol and drugs were contributing factors in homicides prior to 1991.

[2] Manslaughter was not included in the CCJS Homicide Survey until 1974. However, figures have been supplemented using the Canadian Uniform Crime Reporting (UCR) statistics collected by the CCJS since 1962.

[3] At present, the Adult Criminal Court Survey (ACCS), conducted by the CCJS, collects court data only at the provincial court level.

[4] In exchange for her courtroom testimony against her ex-husband, Homolka received immunity from prosecution for the death of her sister Tammy and for sexual assault against an unknown victim referred to as "Jane Doe."

ROBBERY

by Yvan Clermont

In this chapter, Yvan Clermont examines robbery, a crime that involves theft of property using force. Because of its violent nature, robbery is most often considered a crime against the person. The author reviews how this crime is defined, looks at trends in its occurrence, and compares the Canadian robbery rate with those in other countries, particularly the United States. He also considers robbery in terms of its situational characteristics, its perpetrators, and its circumstances. Attention is given, as well, to variations in robbery across Canada.

Robbery has always attracted our interest and stimulated our imagination. Popular literature, movies, and television respond to the public's fascination with this particular crime. As well, newspapers and media seldom miss an opportunity to bring the most spectacular of robbery incidents to our attention. Once romanticized in tales of daring and even justified with themes of social justice, robbery and its motives have changed over time. To notions about robbery as a means of relief from the grip of poverty must now be added such motives as disbursement of excessive debt, illegal drug purchasing, and ritual initiation into organized-crime groups.

This chapter examines the recent statistical history of robbery in Canada, specifically for the period from 1978 to 1993. The characteristics of this crime, of those who commit it, and of those who are victimized by it will also be addressed. Finally, comparisons with other countries, particularly with the United States, will be made.[1]

DEFINITIONS

As defined in Section 343 of the *Criminal Code*, everyone commits robbery who uses violence or threat of violence against a person or property for the purpose of stealing. In general, robbery is considered to be a violent crime because it is perpetrated in the presence of the victim, in contrast to break and enter or theft in which the victim is rarely present. Normandeau (1968) has suggested that robbery, at least in the United States, has more in common with property crime than with violent crime. Canadian law, however, considers robbery a violent crime because of the presence or the threat of violence against a person, even though robbery often follows the pattern of certain types of property crime. In Canada, robbery is an indictable offence punishable by a maximum penalty of life imprisonment.

PRECURSORS

In 18th-century England, robbery and theft were viewed as evidence of the moral inferiority of the perpetrator, no matter what the circumstances. Such crimes had the effect of separating the offender, as a virtual outcast, from the sympathy (and frequently the shores) of his or her country. In the 19th century, scientists even set off in search, through phrenology, of cranial clues to the criminal disposition.

Today, some view the offender (particularly the young offender) as the product of failed circumstances either within the family itself or in society in general, where too much value is placed upon the pursuit of material well-being and too little upon respect for the rights and property of others. In discussing precursors, one may choose to implicate the absence of parental guidance in the formative years, the demotion of civics in school curricula, or the presence of violence, drugs, and subcultural partitioning in our society.

The total number of incidents of robbery reported to the police in Canada in 1978 was 19,697, or 82 robberies per 100,000 population, expressed as a rate. By 1993, the total number was 29,961, or a rate of 104 (a rate increase between these two years of 27%). During this period, there were fluctuations such that the rate rose and then fell, with the highest robbery rate being recorded, in 1991, at 118. In no subsequent year was the rate lower than that of 1978. For all violent crime, the rate increase was more than double that of robbery at 4.3%.

Without taking into account other possible factors, one may observe in Figure 5-1 and Table 5-1 that, for the last decade and a half, the overall robbery rate for Canada increased along with the unemployment rate of males in the 15–24 age group. Robbery rates went up from 1978 to 1982 while the unemployment rate for 15- to 24-year-old males went up from 1979 to 1983. This period roughly coincided with the recession of 1981. From 1983 to 1989, robbery rates fluctuated up and down with almost no change in the overall rate, while the unemployment rate for 15- to 24-year-old males steadily declined. Then the robbery rate took a big jump in 1990 (7.4%), and an even larger one in 1991 (16.8%). Similarly, the unemployment rate for males in the 15–24 age group went from 14% in 1990 to 18.8% in 1991. Since 1991, the robbery rate has decreased for two consecutive years: nearly 1% in 1992 and 12% in 1993. The young male unemployment rate for these years rose slightly in 1992 and was flat in 1993.

For the cases where the relationship between the accused and the victim was known, 73% of robbers were strangers to the victim, 11% were casual or business acquaintances, and 1% were either close friends or family. The relationship in the remaining 15% was unknown.[2]

Figure 5-1 Total Robbery and Unemployment Rates, Canada, 1978–1993

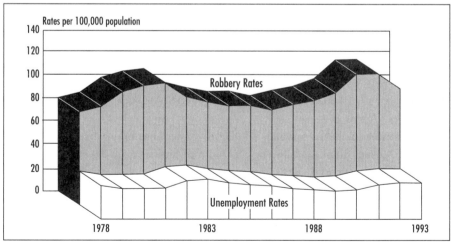

Source: *Historical Labour Force Statistics,* Cat. No. 71-207, annual; and *Canadian Crime Statistics,* Cat. No. 85–205, annual. Ottawa: Statistics Canada, 1993.

Table 5-1 Unemployment Rates (15- to 24-year-old males) and Robbery Rates, Canada, 1978–1993

	Total number of robbery incidents	Rate per 100,000 population	Percentage variation of rate	Unemployment rate, 15- to 24-year-old males	Number of points difference in unemployment rate
1978	19,673	82	—	15.0	—
1979	20,899	86	4.9	13.2	−1.8
1980	34,581	100	16.3	13.7	0.5
1981	26,292	106	6.0	14.1	0.4
1982	27,257	108	1.9	21.1	7.0
1983	24,274	95	−12.0	22.3	1.2
1984	23,310	91	−4.2	19.3	−3.0
1985	22,752	88	−3.3	18.1	−1.2
1986	23,268	89	1.1	16.4	−1.7
1987	22,523	85	−4.5	14.8	−1.6
1988	24,172	90	5.9	12.9	−1.9
1989	25,722	94	4.4	12.4	−0.5
1990	28,109	101	7.4	14.0	1.6
1991	33,236	118	16.8	18.8	4.8
1992	33,201	117	−0.8	20.2	1.4
1993	29,961	104	−11.8	20.2	0.0

Source: *Historical Labour Force Statistics,* Cat. No. 71-207, annual; and *Canadian Crime Statistics,* Cat. No. 85–205, annual. Ottawa: Statistics Canada, 1993.

THE EVENT

CHARACTERISTICS OF ROBBERY AND ITS PERPETRATORS

The Revised UCR survey[3] for 1993 contains information about just over 7,100 persons accused of robbery, that is, for those cases where an accused was identified. Fully 55% of all accused were between the ages of 15 and 24. The average age of the accused, based on this survey, was 24 years. As might be expected, most of the accused were male (91%).

The most attractive targets for robbers are commercial establishments, including stores and small businesses, gas stations, convenience stores, and the like. Of the 14,870 robbery incidents where the target was identified in 1993, 45% fell into this category (convenience stores 11%, gas stations 6%). Surprisingly, noncommercial establishments (government departments, schools, churches, hospitals, etc.) at 24% were higher than banks and financial institutions at 9%. Analysis of the Revised UCR sample also indicates that the more promising the target in terms of money, the more likely firearms were used. Firearms were used in more than half of bank robberies, in 41% of all gas-station robberies and in 35% of all convenience-store robberies (34% of all convenience-store robberies included use of a knife).

Personal victim information is available for over 9,400 robbery incidents on the Revised UCR database for 1993. Ages are not as concentrated for victims as they are for perpetrators. The average age of the robbery victim was 33 years. Women were victims in 37% of the above cases.

ROBBERY CIRCUMSTANCES

Typically, robbery is more likely to occur at night. Over one-half (55%) are committed between 6 p.m. and 3 a.m. The period between midnight and 3 a.m. accounts for only 13% of this total. This is the period when robbers hit taxi drivers, small businesses like restaurants and bars, and transportation and storage facilities (e.g., locker rooms and railcars) (24%). The next most attractive category of targets at this time of night is noncommercial institutions (e.g., hospitals, religious institutions, or shelters) (23%). Convenience stores account for 11% of robberies during the midnight to 3 a.m. period, while gas stations account for 7%.

Interestingly, banks and financial institutions are more likely to be robbed during the month of January (12% of the year's total), while individuals and residences are more vulnerable targets in the summer period. Residences were more likely to be robbed in the month of August (11% of the year's total). Landau and Fridman (1993) explain the occurrence of more robberies in wintertime by noting that in winter the cost of living is higher (clothing, shelter, heating, etc.) than in summer, as is the need or desire for money. During these months, there is also a higher rate of unemployment due to the decrease in seasonal job opportunities.

The aggregated UCR survey distinguishes between robbery using a firearm, robbery using other offensive weapons, and robbery not involving a weapon. In 1993, 41% of robbery incidents did not involve a weapon, while robbery incidents involving a firearm represented 27% of total reported cases. Other offensive weapons (knife, blunt instrument, etc.) accounted for the remaining 32% of cases. Over the fifteen-year period between 1978 and 1993, there was a slight downward trend in the use of firearms in robberies, and a corresponding increase in the use of other offensive weapons (see Table 5-2). Robberies not involving a weapon showed some variation but little overall change in this period. Robbery involving a firearm accounted for 37% of all reported incidents in 1978 and its rate was 30 incidents for 100,000 population.

Table 5-2 Robbery Rates by Type of Weapon Used, Canada, 1978–1993

	Rate of robbery (using a firearm)	Percentage variation	Rate of robbery (other offensive weapon)	Percentage variation	Rate of robbery (no weapon involved)	Percentage variation
1978	30	—	14	—	38	—
1979	31	3.3	16	14.3	40	5.3
1980	35	12.9	19	18.8	46	15.0
1981	36	2.9	22	15.8	47	2.2
1982	36	0.0	24	9.1	48	2.1
1983	29	−19.4	23	−4.2	43	−10.4
1984	27	−6.9	23	0.0	41	−4.7
1985	26	−3.7	22	−4.3	40	−2.4
1986	26	0.0	24	9.1	40	0.0
1987	22	−15.4	22	−8.3	41	2.5
1988	23	4.5	25	13.6	42	2.4
1989	24	4.3	27	8.0	43	2.4
1990	27	12.5	28	3.7	46	7.0
1991	32	18.5	34	21.4	53	15.2
1992	31	−3.1	38	11.8	48	−9.4
1993	28	−9.7	34	−10.52	42	−12.5

Source: *Canadian Crime Statistics*, Cat. No. 85–205, annual. Ottawa: Statistics Canada, 1993.

The impact of Canada's 1978 gun-control legislation is difficult to assess in the above respect. This law included the imposition of stricter controls over the issuance of gun-registration certificates, including the acquisition of handguns, the creation of new types of firearms prohibition orders, new criminal offences concerning firearm use, and more severe penalties for the criminal use of firearms. The steady drop between 1982 and 1988 in the use of firearms in robberies, together with the rise in the use of other offensive weapons since 1988, would suggest that the legislation is having some effect. That offenders are substituting guns with other weapons must, however, be cold comfort for the victims.

REGIONAL VARIATIONS IN ROBBERY

Are there regional variations in robbery across Canada? Crime in Canada usually conforms to a predictable geographic pattern from year to year. The rate at which it takes place is lower in Atlantic Canada and rises as one moves from east to west, with the highest rates occurring in British Columbia and in the two territories. Robbery, however, does not conform perfectly to this pattern.[4]

Atlantic Canada recorded the lowest robbery rate in 1993, at 25 per 100,000 population, well below that of the rest of Canada and less than one-third that of the next closest region, Ontario, which recorded a robbery rate of 82 per 100,000 population. Quebec, whose crime rate is normally below that in those provinces to the west as well as below the national rate overall, recorded the highest robbery rate for all regions in 1993, at 148 per 100,000 population. As Table 5-3 indicates, Quebec has maintained this distinction historically also. The low level of urbanization in the Atlantic region may partially explain the relatively low robbery rate in this region. In order to avoid being apprehended, robbers tend to victimize those unknown to them, and anonymity is more characteristic of large urban areas than rural ones. In 1993, 71% of robberies occurred in cities that had over 250,000 inhabitants and that constituted only 39% of the Canadian population overall; the Atlantic region does not have a city of that size, while Quebec has three. Moreover, the clearance rate for robbery incidents is highest in the Atlantic region, suggesting that smaller population bases offer fewer opportunities to avoid apprehension. The clearance rate is also high in the lightly populated North. As we move toward more urbanized regions, clearance rates are lower.

Quebec has had the highest robbery rates in Canada for many years, despite the fact that overall violent and property crime rates in this province have been well below the national rates over time. As Table 5-3 shows, in 1978 the rate of robbery in Quebec was nearly three times that recorded in the rest of Canada. Over time, however, this difference has shrunk to the point that, in 1993, Quebec's robbery rate was not even double that recorded in the rest of the country.

Gabor et al. (1987) attribute the high incidence of robberies in Quebec to the rapid social and political changes that occurred in the province, beginning in the 1960s. The forces of change, they suggest, may have led to a series of undesired side-effects, nost notably high unemployment resulting from the inability of people to keep pace with rapid technological change.

Table 5-3 Robbery in Quebec vs. the Rest of Canada, 1978, 1988, and 1993

	Number of robberies over 100,000 population	
	Canada without Quebec	*Quebec*
1978	57	149
1988	69	151
1993	90	148

Source: Uniform Crime Reporting survey, Canadian Centre for Justice Statistics, 1978, 1988, 1993.

The authors qualify their observations, however, by pointing out that Quebec's robbery rates also ranked well above the national level in the years preceding Quebec's Quiet Revolution. Others have linked Quebec's traditionally high robbery rate to the longer hours in which commercial establishments such as bars, restaurants, and convenience stores operate—a practice that creates more opportunities for robbery (Calder, 1992).

As Table 5-4 shows, Ontario had a relatively low robbery rate in 1993 (82.2), compared to the national level of 104 per 100,000 population. (Table 5-5 reveals that the lower rates recorded for cities over 250,000 are found in Ontario.) The robbery rate in the Prairies is even higher than the Ontario rate, though still lower than the national level. This may be attributable to the 1993 Manitoba rate, which was startlingly high at 141, as compared with the Saskatchewan and Alberta rates of 51 and 98, respectively. The Manitoba rate is high because of the robbery activity in Winnipeg, home to more than half of the province's population. Table 5-5 shows that the Winnipeg robbery rate in 1993 was 238 per 100,000 population, the third highest city rate in Canada after Vancouver and Montreal.

British Columbia's robbery rate was second only to Quebec's in 1993. DuWors (1992), in comparing robbery rates for Canada's regions from 1974 to 1990, shows that the British Columbia rate has always been high, but never as high as Quebec's. However, while robbery rates started to stabilize and even decline in Quebec from 1989 onward, those in British Columbia continued to rise. In 1993, Vancouver had the highest robbery rate among Canadian cities over 250,000, followed by Montreal.[5] The economic and population "booms" experienced by British Columbia in the past five years may have contributed to its higher robbery rates. British Columbia and the

Table 5-4 Some Indicators for Seven Canadian Regions, 1993

Region	Population	Number of Robberies	Rate	Number Cleared	Percentage Cleared	Adults Charged	Youth Charged
Atlantic	2,386,600	602	25.2	294	49	249	82
Quebec	7,208,800	10,640	147.6	3483	33	2526	579
Ontario	10,746,300	8,829	82.2	3185	36	2297	1137
Prairies	4,781,300	4,701	98.3	1789	38	1270	732
British Columbia	3,535,100	5,126	145.0	1452	28	1070	457
North	94,900	63	100.4	29	46	21	7

Source: Uniform Crime Reporting survey, Canadian Centre for Justice Statistics, 1993.

Table 5-5   Robbery Rates by Municipalities (over 250,000 population), 1993

Municipalities or Police Force	Number of Incidents	Rate per 100,000 Population	% of Robbery Cleared
Vancouver, BC (495,900)	2272	458	23.4
Montreal, Que. (1,753,200)	6644	379	29.9
Winnipeg (Greater), Man. (616,600)	1465	238	32.5
Ottawa, Ont. (326,200)	693	212	38.1
Toronto, Ont. (2,241,100)	4609	206	30.1
Quebec, Que. (265,500)	528	199	33.7
Edmonton, Alta (629,100)	1212	193	32.6
Laval, Que. (326,700)	569	174	27.6
Calgary, Alta (732,300)	1127	154	38.6
Surrey (Dist Mun), BC (270,700)	399	147	27.3
Hamilton-Wentworth Reg. Police, Ont. (453,300)	473	104	29.2
Peel Regional Police, Ont. (747,500)	402	54	53.7
Durham Regional Police, Ont. (419,200)	214	51	42.1
London, Ont. (326,100)	163	50	44.8
Niagara Regional Police, Ont. (401,800)	189	47	37.6
Waterloo Regional Police, Ont. (390,000)	175	45	41.1
York Regional Police, Ont. (551,100)	198	36	36.9
Halton Regional Police, Ont. (326,800)	71	22	52.1

Source: Uniform Crime Reporting survey, Canadian Centre for Justice Statistics, 1993.

cities of the Lower Mainland are also favourite destinations for the younger, more mobile segments of the Canadian population—the group that provides the largest pool of potential offenders.

INTERNATIONAL COMPARISONS

Over the years, the robbery rankings[6] for selected countries have remained fairly stable (see Table 5-6). Spain has experienced the biggest increase in its robbery rate over time, while Northern Ireland is the only country listed in Table 5-6 that has seen a decrease in robberies. Of the fifteen countries covered in the table, only four had a robbery rate that exceeded Canada's in 1990. In that same year, the rates recorded in Spain and the United States were more than twice as high as the rate recorded in France, the next country on the list. Interestingly, Spain has the lowest *reporting* rate (for all crime), which strongly suggests that the problem of robbery in that country is greater than the recorded rate would indicate.

Table 5-6 Robbery Rates, Selected Countries, 1982–1986 and 1990

Countries	Reported robberies per 100,000 persons		Percentage of crimes reported to the police (aggregated ten different types of offence)* (rank)
	Average 1982–1986	1990	
Spain	132	271	31.4 (14)
United States	217	257	52.0 (8)
France	100	106	60.8 (2)
Northern Ireland	126	103	45.8 (11)
Canada	96	101	49.8 (9)
Scotland	85	91	62.3 (1)
Netherlands	54	80	54.7 (7)
Belgium	54	80	58.9 (4)
England and Wales	51	72	58.7 (6)
Sweden	—	69	58.8 (5)
Germany	54+	56	48.0 (10)
Finland	36	56	40.4 (13)
Ireland	—	46	—
Switzerland	22	27	59.0 (3)
Norway	15	24	43.4 (12)

+The average robbery from 1982 to 1986 is only for West Germany.
*The percentage of crime reported to the police is based on different years of survey for each respondent ranging from 1989 to 1992.

Sources: International Crime Statistics, International Criminal Police Organization; INTERPOL for reported incident rates; International Victimization Survey 1993 for reporting rates.

CANADIAN VS. U.S. ROBBERY RATES

According to Ouimet (1993), there is no serious difference in the legal and operational definitions of robbery used in Canada and the United States. As Table 5-7 shows, the U.S. robbery rate per 100,000 population in 1993 was 256, while the Canadian rate for the same year was 104. This result is reflective of the large concentrations of robberies in large urban centres, which are far more pervasive in the United States than in Canada. In 1993, U.S. cities with more than one million population recorded a rate of 955 robbery incidents per 100,000 inhabitants. In Canada, there are only two municipal forces that are policing jurisdictions with more than a million population: Toronto and Montreal. In 1993, these two cities recorded rates of 206 and 379 incidents, respectively. In Canada, 71% of robbery incidents reported in that year occurred in cities with populations over 250,000. Although these cities account for only 39% of the overall Canadian population, they had a combined robbery rate of 190 per 100,000 population. In the United States,

Table 5-7 Rates of Robbery and Homicide, Canada and the United States, 1993

	Robbery	*Homicide*
Canada	104	2.19
United States	256	9.5

Source: Uniform Crime Reporting survey, Canadian Centre for Justice Statistics, 1993.

while the rate recorded for metropolitan areas (populations over 100,000) was 312, it was only 71 for cities outside these metropolitan areas.[7] Other reasons cited for the disparity between the U.S. and Canadian robbery rates include differences in the prevalence and availability of firearms, as well as in the efficacy of policies directed at delinquency, socioeconomic inequality, and racial discrimination.

Although robbery rates in Canada and the United States differ, trends in those rates behave similarly. Between 1978 and 1993, robbery rates rose 27% in Canada and 31% in the United States (see Figure 5-2). For almost every year in which the rate of robbery rose or fell in the United States, the same happened in Canada. The similarity of American and Canadian economic cycles may explain these parallels if one accepts that robbery in both countries is linked to these cycles.

Figure 5-2 Total Robbery Rates in Canada and the United States, 1978–1993

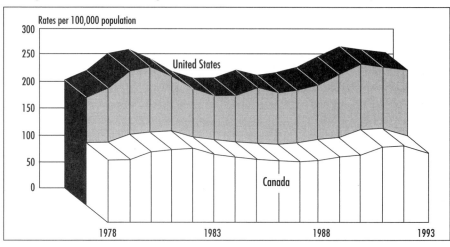

Source: Uniform Crime Reporting survey, Canadian Centre for Justice Statistics, 1993; and *Sourcebook of Criminal Justice Statistics,* U.S. Department of Justice, 1993.

In 1993, the average dollar loss in robberies of less than $100,000 was $1,133; robbers netted less than $215 in half of these robberies. Minor injuries (those requiring no professional treatment or just first aid) were reported by victims in 32% of robbery incidents on the database, while major injuries requiring professional attention were reported in about 9% of these incidents. Fifty percent of victims reported no injuries, and 10% were unknown.

Regarding the sentencing of adults found guilty of robbery, a complete national picture is not yet available. There are, however, comparable data for provincial criminal courts in Nova Scotia, Prince Edward Island, Quebec, Saskatchewan, and the Yukon. Of the 723 cases from these jurisdictions that resulted in conviction in 1993, 83% of the offenders were sentenced to prison. In comparison, in cases of serious assault, the percentage sentenced to prison dropped to 43%. Sixty-five percent of robbery offenders in the above jurisdictions in 1993 were sentenced to prison terms of one year or more, and more than half of these to two years or more. For serious assault and theft over $1,000, only 12% and 14% of prison sentences handed down in these cases respectively were for one year or more.

In 1993, young offenders were the primary suspects in 2,095 cases of robbery heard before the courts. Of these cases, 66% (1,378) resulted in findings of guilt, and secure or open custody were the most serious sentences for 63% of the offenders. For serious assault and theft over $1,000, sentences of secure or open custody were handed down in 38% and 45% of these cases, respectively. Moreover, the median sentence length for young offenders sentenced to secure or open custody in 1993 for robbery was almost double those received by offenders convicted of serious assault and theft over $1,000 (six months compared with three months).

SUMMARY AND CONCLUSIONS
■   ■   ■

While the motivation for robbery may be the theft of other people's property, it is considered a violent crime in Canada because of the presence of the victim and the threat or use of force in the act of stealing. During the fifteen-year period between 1978 and 1993, the robbery rate in Canada has been increasing by about 2% annually. This rate was more than the annual rate of increase for property crime (1.5%), but less than that for violent crime as a whole (4.3%). The robbery rate, however, dropped by 1% in 1992 and 12% in 1993. Weapons were not used in all incidents of robbery in 1993; 41% of cases involved the use or threat of physical force, 27% involved a firearm, and 32% involved another offensive weapon. The data from the Revised UCR survey for 1993 indicate that 55% of persons accused of robbery are in the 15–24 age group, 91% are male, and the average age of these individuals is 24 years. The most attractive targets are small businesses, especially convenience stores and gas stations. Victims tend to be older than offenders (the average age is 33 years), and women are much more likely to be victims (37%) than perpetrators of this crime (9%).

In 1993, the Atlantic region of Canada recorded the lowest robbery rate, at 25 per 100,000 population. Ontario came next with a rate of 82, and Quebec recorded the highest rate, at 148 per 100,000 population, despite its consistently lower-than-average rates for both property and violent crime over the years. Seventy-one percent of robberies occurred in cities with populations of over 250,000; these cities, in turn, contained 39% of Canada's population.

Internationally, Canada's robbery rate is well below that of the United States, but it is still very high when compared to those of many western European countries. The 1990 International Victimization Survey ranked Canada's robbery rate below those of Spain, the United States, France, and Northern Ireland, and well above those of England, Germany, Ireland, Switzerland, and the Nordic countries.

The average dollar loss to robberies under $100,000 recorded on the Revised UCR database was $1,133 in 1993, with half of these netting less than $215. The data sample on the Revised UCR database in 1993 indicated that major injuries were sustained by about 9% of victims of robberies, minor injuries by 32%, and no injuries by 50%.

Sample data from the 1993 Adult Criminal Court Survey suggest that convicted robbers are much more likely than those convicted of serious assault to receive prison sentences; in addition, their sentences are much longer. A similar picture emerges for young offenders convicted of robbery.

NOTES

[1] Data from several surveys were used for this research: the current UCR survey, which contains aggregate data on robbery in Canada; the Revised UCR survey, which covers 32% of the national volume of crime in general and which was used to profile the accused, the incidents, and the victims; the American UCR survey and the Interpol data, used for international

comparisons; the Statistics Canada General Social Survey, used for information on victims; and the Adult Criminal Court Survey and Youth Court Survey, used for sentencing information on robbery offenders.

[2] One of the most complete sources of information on robbery in Canada is *Armed Robbery* (Gabor et al., 1987), which contains the results of several surveys conducted in the early 1980s. Although very small samples were used to establish victims' or robbers' characteristics, some findings are notable. For example, commercial places specializing in retail trade (e.g., convenience stores, grocery stores, and specialized boutiques) seem to constitute the bulk of the targets for armed robbers. Also, 56% of robbery incidents are perpetrated by a single individual and the remainder by teams or groups (39% in groups of two).

[3] The information is based on data collected from 79 police departments across Canada through the Revised UCR survey. These data on the 1993 incident-based research file represented only 32% of the total volume of reported crime in Canada and contained 16,840 robbery incidents. It should be noted that, while the largest urban centres are participating in this survey (Toronto, Montreal, Vancouver, York Region, Peel Region, Windsor, and Laval, to name a few), these data are not representative of any particular region in Canada.

[4] For analytic purposes the country is broken down into six regions. Quebec, Ontario, and British Columbia were considered separately because of their size; Newfoundland, Prince Edward Island, Nova Scotia, and New Brunswick represent the Atlantic region; Manitoba, Saskatchewan, and Alberta represent the Prairie region; and the Yukon and Northwest Territories constitute the Northern region. To supplement regional analysis, cities with more than 250,000 inhabitants were also analyzed.

[5] It should be pointed out that municipal comparisons can be misleading given the differences in police jurisdictions. For example, the Vancouver police force covers only the municipality and not the surrounding suburbs, whereas the Montreal Urban Community police force is a regional force (similar to that in Toronto) that covers less urban territories as well. Forthcoming crime statistics for Census Metropolitan Areas will permit more accurate comparisons for large municipalities.

[6] The reader is cautioned that rules for reporting crime among these countries may differ significantly. Also, the International Victimization Survey notes that the extent of insurance coverage, lack of confidence in policing, or local tradition may play an important part in the results. For example, the extent of insurance coverage (which may have an impact on the reporting of robbery) was noted to be relatively low in Spain. Finally, it is possible that the most common reason for not reporting is the perceived lack of seriousness of the incident. Thus one could interpret the rates of robbery as being the rate of incidents considered serious enough to be reported to the police.

[7] Ouimet (1993) suggests carrying out comparisons at a more disaggregated level, that is, among cities of like size, urbanization, ethnicity, and location. His preliminary findings were that for comparable regions or cities, differences between robbery rates in Canada and the United States are not as distinct.

6
ASSAULT

by Bob Kingsley

In this chapter, Bob Kingsley reviews major trends and characteristics associated with the crime of assault. He begins with an examination of Bill C-127 and its effect on the police response to assault as well as victim reporting of this crime. Changes in assault over time are revealed through UCR and victim surveys. The Revised UCR survey is used to examine the social dynamics of the assault event. A final section looks at the clearance rate for assault cases, in addition to sentencing practices. Of particular interest in this chapter is the finding that, while the results from victim surveys have shown no reported increases in assaults, the official counts of crime have increased. The author is concerned throughout with determining what proportion of the increase in assault rates is due to actual increases in the level of societal violence, and what proportion can be attributed to other factors.

Over the past decade, Canada has experienced a dramatic increase in the rate of police-reported assault offences. This trend is of particular consequence because physical assaults represent more than three-quarters of all violent offences and, as a result, have a major impact on the level of violence within society. Indeed, recent public-opinion surveys report increased concern among Canadians about violent crime. For example, in the 1988 General Social Survey (GSS), respondents indicated that an attack or incidents involving the threat of violence were the type of crime of greatest concern, with 43% of those sampled identifying violent assault as the crime they feared the most. These developments, combined with extensive media coverage of crime issues, have helped to produce a widespread perception among Canadians that crime, and especially violent crime, is on the increase.

The objective of this chapter is to analyze the major trends and characteristics associated with police-reported assaults. In addition to illuminating the circumstances surrounding assault offences, the chapter also explores the factors that might be influencing rising assault offence rates. Of particular interest is the question: What proportion of the increase in assault rates can be attributed to an actual increase in the level of violence within society and what proportion can be attributed to other factors?

DEFINITIONS

A person commits an assault when, without the consent of another person, he or she intentionally applies force, or attempts or threatens to apply force, against another person. While physical violence is not necessary, there must be a threatening act or gesture, as words alone do not constitute an assault. Common assault is distinguished from more serious assaults by the degree of physical injury. The *Criminal Code* establishes three levels of assault: first level or common assault; second level or assault causing bodily harm; and third level or aggravated assault. A threatened assault, or an actual assault that does not produce a serious physical injury, is categorized as a common assault. The more serious second-level assault requires the use or threatened use of a weapon, or the presence of injuries such as broken bones, cuts, and bruises. However, a slap across the face that produces only temporary discolouration does not constitute bodily harm. For an assault to be categorized as level 3 or aggravated, the victim must be wounded, maimed, disfigured, or have his or her life endangered.[1]

BILL C-127 AND SPOUSAL-ASSAULT CHARGING DIRECTIVES

Section 266 of the *Criminal Code* states that everyone who commits an assault is guilty of an indictable offence, or an offence punishable on summary conviction. This new section, introduced in 1983 under Bill C-127, replaces what formerly was known as "common assault." The new section creates a dual-procedure offence (the former section was a summary conviction offence) that allows police to arrest a person when they have "reasonable and probable grounds" to believe an assault was committed. Under the old section, the police could not arrest unless they witnessed the person committing the assault. For example, in domestic-dispute situations involving assault of a wife, they did not have a power of arrest unless they had actually witnessed the assault or the wife had suffered "bodily harm." Under the new section, police are able to arrest the aggressor, thereby avoiding the possibility of further assaults after they leave the scene.

The introduction of Bill C-127 was followed by significant changes in police practices as they related to assaults. Governments at all levels issued formal directives to police agencies to lay charges where there were reasonable and probable grounds to believe an assault had occurred in spousal assault cases. Because the spousal-assault charging directives were introduced intermittently throughout the decade,[2] their impact on police-reported assault data can be expected to be distributed over this extended period.

Bill C-127 redefined assaults, making it easier for police to lay assault charges where there was reasonable and probable grounds to believe that an assault had been committed. This new legislation, combined with the intermittent introduction of mandatory charging directives in spousal-assault cases, helped create and sustain elevated levels of assault rate increases. These elevated rates of increase were at least partially due to changes in police procedures. Prior to the introduction of Bill C-127 and the associated mandatory spousal-assault charging directives, a significant proportion of spousal assaults were not reflected in police or UCR statistics. This happened for three primary reasons. First, as mentioned earlier, it was difficult for police to arrest unless they had actually witnessed the assault. As a result, there were very few domestic situations in which it was possible to lay assault charges. Second, even in cases where police could lay charges, they would often defer to the wishes of the victim, who in many circumstances would decline to have charges laid. In short, there was significant police discretion in the charging decision. Third, prevailing social attitudes at the time were such that spousal conflict was often seen as a private domestic matter. The appropriateness of using the *Criminal Code* and the court system to deal with such matters was not then widely recognized.

The introduction of Bill C-127, and the associated mandatory charging directives in spousal-assault cases, put an immediate end to the above reasons being used as a basis for not laying assault charges. As each province issued mandatory charging directives, and as individual police agencies began to implement them, an entire group of offences that had been previously unreported in police statistics began to show up in large numbers. Thus much of the increase in the reported assault rate during the 1982–90 period may reflect not an increase in actual assault incidents, but rather police reporting of assault incidents that had been previously unreported in official statistics. Further, the fact that the spousal-assault charging directives were issued over a nine-year period helped to ensure that elevated rate increases were spread over the entire decade.

PRECURSORS

Drug and alcohol consumption are important factors to consider in the analysis of assault offences. Incident-based UCR data suggest that more than one-third of all assault victims and accused had consumed alcohol or drugs prior to an assault. In common assaults, 33% of accused and 36% of victims had consumed either alcohol or drugs prior to the assault. A slightly higher consumption pattern emerges for major assaults, where 38% of accused and 35% of victims had consumed alcohol or drugs prior to the assault incident.

The relationship of the accused to the assault victim is illustrated in Table 6-1, which shows that most victims are assaulted by friends and family. The accused is the spouse or ex-spouse of the victim in the largest proportion of common assaults (28%), and another family member in a further 10% of incidents. Strangers are the accused in only 20% of common-assault incidents. In the remaining common assaults, the accused are friends, acquaintances, and business associates. Thus, in 80% of common-assault

Table 6-1 Relationship of Accused to Victim, Percent Distribution, 1993

Relation to Victim	Major Assault	Common Assault
Spouse or ex-spouse	16.9	27.8
Parent	3.5	3.7
Child	1.5	1.9
Other immediate family	3.2	3.0
Extended family	1.3	1.4
Close friend	7.0	8.0
Business relationship	6.2	8.2
Casual acquaintance	28.8	25.7
Stranger	31.6	20.4
Total	100	100

Source: Incident-based Uniform Crime Reporting survey, Canadian Centre for Justice Statistics, 1993.

incidents, the accused are known to victims, and in 38% of cases the accused are family members. Major-assault victimization patterns are comparable to common-assault patterns, with two exceptions. First, spousal assaults represent about 17% of major assaults, eleven percentage points lower than the proportion for common assaults. On the other hand, a much larger proportion (32%) of major assaults are by strangers, twelve percentage points higher than the common-assault proportion.

If we examine the association between the location of common assaults and the relationship of the accused to the victim, we find that common assaults fall into two groups—those involving family and close friends, and those involving business relations, acquaintances, and strangers. Assaults in the first group are far more likely to occur in the home. Indeed, almost 90% of spousal/other family member assaults and 73% of close-friend common assaults occur in private dwellings. Assaults among the second group are more likely to occur at locations outside the home. For example, only 12% of assaults by strangers occur in private dwellings. The same general patterns hold true for major assaults.

THE EVENT

INCIDENCE

According to the GSS, only about 30% of assaults were reported to police in the survey reference years of 1988 and 1993. People do not report assaults to the police for a variety of reasons. The three reasons most frequently reported to the GSS interviewers are (1) victims prefer to deal with the problem in another way, (2) they feel that it is a personal matter, or (3) they consider the incident to be too minor to report. In addition to increasing knowledge on the nature and extent of victimization, information on victim-reporting levels also facilitates the interpretation of UCR data. For example, because the proportion of persons reporting assaults to police did not change between 1988 and 1993, it is much more difficult to interpret increases in UCR assault rates during this period as being caused by increased victim reporting.

Another element of the GSS that can be used in the analysis of UCR data is the assault victimization rate reported by the survey. In 1988, the GSS reported that there were 68 assault victimizations per 1,000 population. In 1993, the survey reported 67 assault victimizations per 1,000 population.

This result, which suggests that there was little or no change in the rate of assault victimizations during this period, does not correspond to UCR data that show a 25% increase in the reported assault rate for the same period. This discrepancy between the two surveys does not mean that one is in error; rather, it helps demonstrate that the two surveys are measuring a similar phenomenon in two different ways.

However, differences in coverage are not large enough to explain the significant variation between the two surveys. A more appropriate explanation relates to the way UCR data are collected, and how they can be affected by changes in legislation and government policy. In the case of assaults, it is clear that the legislative and policy changes produced a large and prolonged effect on the data.

ASSAULT OFFENCES OVER TIME

Before looking at changes in UCR offence rates over time, it is necessary to establish a broad context within which to view the data. Figure 6-1 highlights the status of assault offences within the overall composition of violent offences. It looks at reported actual offences, that is, the number of offences reported to police minus those offences that were investigated and determined to be unfounded. For the purposes of this analysis, these offences will be referred to simply as "reported" offences.

Figure 6-1 Reported Actual Offences, Twenty-Year Averages, 1974–1993

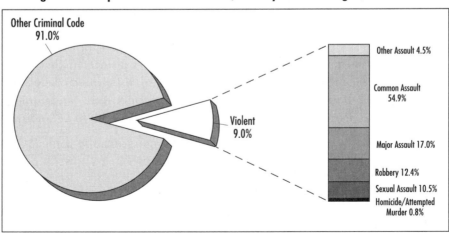

Source: Aggregate Uniform Crime Reporting survey, Canadian Centre for Justice Statistics, 1993.

Figure 6-1 illustrates that over the twenty-year reference period, reported violent offences as a group averaged 196,000 offences per year, or about 9% of an average of 2,170,000 reported *Criminal Code* offences. Within the violent offence group, reported common-assault offences averaged 107,000 offences per year, or about 55% of all violent offences. Reported major-assault offences averaged 33,500 offences per year, or 17% of all violent offences. Physical assaults made up about 77% of all violent offences over the twenty-year reference period. Major assaults declined from 22% of physical assaults in 1974 to 19% in 1993. On the other hand, common assaults rose from 73% of physical assaults in 1974 to 76% in 1993.

Figure 6-2 highlights the percent change in reported offence rates from 1974 to 1993. Over this period, the rate of reported *Criminal Code* offences grew 49% (6,368 to 9,516 per 100,000), the rate of major-assault offences by 67 percent (94 to 156 per 100,000), and the rate of common-assault offences by 100% (308 to 632 per 100,000). Figure 6-2 shows that prior to 1983 the rate of common assaults was increasing at a much slower pace than both the major- assault offence rate and the *Criminal Code* rate. However, in 1984 there was a sharp increase in the rate of police-reported common assaults, at which point the common-assault rate began to grow at a much faster pace than the reported major-assault rate and the overall *Criminal*

Figure 6-2   Reported Offences, 1974–1993

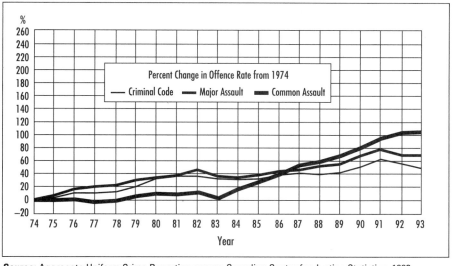

Source: Aggregate Uniform Crime Reporting survey, Canadian Centre for Justice Statistics, 1993.

Code offence rate. These results clearly illustrate that a significant change occurred in the common-assault offence rate after 1983, and that this phenomenon continued to affect the data until 1991, when the rate of increase began to level off.

Figure 6-3 shows that the rate of persons charged with common-assault offences during the 1974 to 1993 reference period increased 255%—a finding that can be compared with the 106% increase in reported common-assault offences illustrated in Figure 6-2. Similarly, Figure 6-2 shows that reported major assaults grew 67% during the twenty-year reference period, while Figure 6-3 shows that the rate of persons charged with major assault increased 134%. In both cases, the pace of growth in the persons-charged rates is increasing much more quickly than the growth in reported offence rates.

Another important fact illustrated by comparing Figures 6-2 and 6-3 is the point in time where change begins to occur. Prior to 1983, the relationship between growth in reported offences and persons charged is virtually identical. It is only after 1983, and the introduction of Bill C-127, that the pace of growth in assault charge rates begins to rapidly exceed growth in the rate of reported offences.

Figure 6-3 Persons Charged, 1974–1993

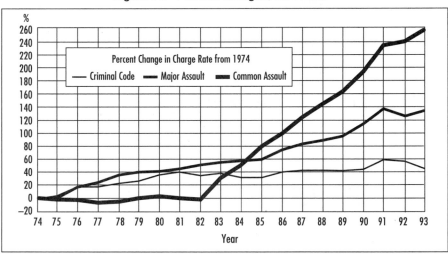

Source: Aggregate Uniform Crime Reporting survey, Canadian Centre for Justice Statistics, 1993.

CHARACTERISTICS OF ASSAULT OFFENCES

The UCR provides data on incident characteristics, victim and accused characteristics, and cross-classified characteristics. The characteristics data presented below are from the 1993 Revised UCR survey.

Table 6-2 outlines assault data by the location of the incident. It shows that the majority of all common assaults (52%) take place in private dwellings. Commercial places (including bars, nightclubs, restaurants, shopping malls, office buildings, etc.) account for 16% of all common assaults, while streets and roads provide a location for 17% of common assaults. Together, these three locations account for 85% of all reported common assaults. The location of major assaults shows a very similar pattern, except that a slightly lower proportion occur in dwellings (45%) and a slightly higher proportion occur on streets and roads (22%).

Table 6-3 displays data on the time of day at which the assault incident occurred. It indicates that common-assault incidents tend to occur relatively infrequently during the early hours of the morning, increase in frequency as the day progresses, and peak during the later part of the evening. Major assaults show a slightly different pattern, with a higher proportion tending to occur later in the day. The majority of major assaults (56.4%) occur between 6 p.m. and 3 a.m., with the 12 a.m. to 3 a.m. period accounting for the highest proportion (21.3%) of these assaults.

The seasonal features of both common and major assault are very similar to each other and fairly evenly distributed. For both offences, a lower proportion of assaults occur in the winter (22%), while a slightly larger proportion

Table 6-2 Location of Assault Incidents, Percent Distribution, 1993

Location	Major Assault	Common Assault
Single home/dwelling unit	44.7	52.0
Commercial/corporate places	17.5	16.1
Parking lots	4.5	3.7
Schools	3.8	4.3
Public institutions	2.3	3.0
Public transportation	1.5	1.6
Streets/roads	22.3	16.6
Open areas	3.5	2.7
Total	100	100

Source: Incident-based Uniform Crime Reporting survey, Canadian Centre for Justice Statistics, 1993.

Table 6-3 Time of Assault Incidents, Percent Distribution, 1993

Time of Incident	Major Assault	Common Assault
6:00 a.m.—8:59 a.m.	4.0	4.4
9:00 a.m.—11:59 a.m.	6.8	9.1
12:00 p.m.—2:59 p.m.	10.2	13.4
3:00 p.m.—5:59 p.m.	14.1	16.9
6:00 p.m.—8:59 p.m.	15.6	18.2
9:00 p.m.—11:59 p.m.	19.5	17.8
12:00 a.m.—2:59 a.m.	21.3	14.9
3:00 a.m.—5:59 a.m.	8.4	5.3
Total	100	100

Source: Incident-based Uniform Crime Reporting survey, Canadian Centre for Justice Statistics, 1993.

occur in the summer (27%). Spring and fall account for 26% and 25% of assaults respectively.

There are distinct gender variations between assault victims and accused. First, males are the victims in 46% of common-assault incidents, but are the accused in 85% of incidents. Conversely, females are the victims in 54% of cases, but are the accused in only 15% of incidents. Major assaults show a different pattern, with higher male victimization and accused rates. Males are the victims in 65% of major-assault incidents, and are the accused in 87% of incidents. Females are the victims in 35% of major-assault cases, but are the accused in only 13% of incidents.

Table 6-4 shows the age ranges of assault victims and accused, and compares them with the age distribution of the Canadian population. It illustrates that the proportion of assault victims and accused are roughly similar within each age range, except for the 1–11 age group. It also highlights that the probability of victimization is greater for younger persons, and then generally declines with age. For example, persons in the 18–39 age range represent about 36% of the total Canadian population but experience 64% of the total assault victimizations. On the other hand, persons 55 and over represent 20% of the population but experience only about 5% of assault victimizations.

Females make up 73% of victims for common assaults occurring in private homes, and are victims in about 34% of common assaults occurring in commercial places, parking lots, streets and roads, and public places. In contrast, males are the victims in only 27% of common assaults occurring in private dwellings, and are the victims in about 66% of common assaults occurring outside the home. In major assaults, males tend to be the victims in

Table 6-4   Age of Victims and Accused, Percent Distribution, 1993

| | | Major Assault | | Common Assault | |
| | Percent of | Victim | Accused | Victim | Accused |
Age	Population	Percent	Percent	Percent	Percent
1–11	16.6	3.6	0.6	4.5	0.6
12–17	8.1	13.2	15.6	13.4	11.4
18–24	9.9	24.8	25.1	21.5	18.6
25–29	8.2	15.9	16.6	16.0	16.4
30–34	9.1	13.7	14.7	14.3	16.8
35–39	8.6	10.1	10.2	10.4	12.2
40–44	7.6	6.8	6.6	7.3	8.5
45–49	6.6	4.7	4.2	5.0	5.6
50–54	5.1	2.6	2.5	3.0	3.6
55+	20.3	4.6	3.9	4.7	6.2
Total	100	100	100	100	100

Source: Incident-based Uniform Crime Reporting survey, Canadian Centre for Justice Statistics, 1993.

a much higher proportion of cases in all locations. They are the victims in about 80% of major assaults occurring outside private dwellings, and are the victims in 46% of incidents occurring inside private dwellings.

THE AFTERMATH

CLEARANCE

Figure 6-4 describes the proportion of assault offences cleared by charge as a proportion of total assault offences cleared. It demonstrates that over the twenty-year reference period there has been a significant increase in the proportion of assault offences cleared by charge, and thus a corresponding decrease in those cleared otherwise. Prior to 1983, the proportion of common-assault offences cleared by charge remained fairly consistent at about 30% of all offences cleared. In 1983, this proportion jumped to 40% and then continued to increase until 1993, when 60% of all common-assault offences cleared were cleared by charge. Major assaults show a similar pattern of change, with just over 60% of offences cleared by charge until 1983, then increasing to 84% in 1993. The proportion of all *Criminal Code* offences cleared by charge remained much more stable, ranging from 61% to 66% during the reference period.

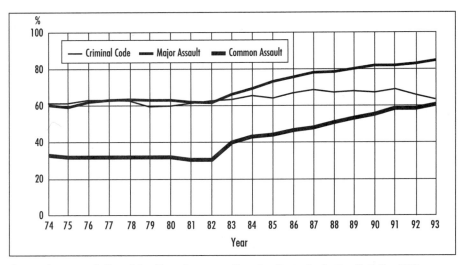

Figure 6-4 Offences Cleared by Charge as a Proportion of Total Offences Cleared, 1974–1993

Source: Aggregate Uniform Crime Reporting survey, Canadian Centre for Justice Statistics, 1993.

Crimes Against People

SENTENCING

Comparable court data for all provinces and levels of court are not yet available in Canada. There are, however, comparable data for provincial criminal courts in Nova Scotia, Prince Edward Island, Quebec, and the Yukon. As one would expect, these data indicate considerable variation between major- and common-assault offences with respect to disposition patterns and the severity of criminal court sentences. For instance, the proportion of common-assault charges resulting in a conviction (50%) is much higher than the proportion of major-assault charges resulting in conviction (25%). In addition, the proportion of major-assault charges transferred to superior court (35%) is much higher than the proportion of common-assault charges transferred to a higher court (16%). Similar variations exist with respect to the most serious sentences received in assault cases. In common-assault cases, 21% of offenders receive a prison term, 57% receive probation, and 18% receive a fine. In major-assault cases, we find that 48% of offenders receive a prison term, 46% receive probation, and only 4% receive a fine.

The more severe sentencing in major-assault cases is reflected in prison and probation sentence lengths, as well as in fine amounts. Table 6-5 highlights these variations by presenting sentence information for assault cases

Table 6-5   Sentencing in Assault Cases, 1993*

Length of Prison and Probation Sentences (Percent Distribution)

	Total	< 3 Mos.	3–6 Mos.	6–12 Mos.	1– 2 Years	> 2 Years
Prison						
Common Assault	100	72.9	19.4	5.8	1.6	0.3
Major Assault	100	40.9	22.1	22.7	10.9	3.4
Probation						
Common Assault	100	2.4	17.9	46.8	27.7	5.2
Major Assault	100	0.8	7.3	38.9	42.7	10.2

Amount of Fine (Percent Distribution)

	Total	Up to $100	$101–$300	$301–$500	$501–$1,000	>$1,000
Common Assault	100	32.2	50.0	14.6	3.1	0.1
Major Assault	100	8.1	39.2	33.9	16.7	2.1

*All ACCS jurisdictions, provincial court.

Source: Adult Criminal Court survey, Canadian Centre for Justice Statistics, 1993.

resulting in prison, probation, or fine. As would be expected, it illustrates that common-assault prison sentences are shorter than those handed down for major-assaults. In fact, almost three-quarters of all common-assault prison sentences are for less than three months, whereas only 41% of major-assault prison sentences are for less than three months. A similar pattern holds for probation sentences, which are generally shorter for common-assaults.

SUMMARY AND CONCLUSIONS
■ ■ ■

The preceding analysis of police-reported assault data showed a significant increase in reported assault offence and charge rates. At the same time, however, it also raised several important questions concerning the interpretation of these data. Of particular concern is the difficulty in determining what proportion of the rate increases is due to actual increases in the level of societal violence, and what proportion is due to other factors.

A significant proportion of the growth in violent offences may be related to the increased reporting of spousal-assault offences that resulted from many factors, including the use of more assertive charging practices in common-assault cases. Spousal assaults represent almost 30% of common-assault offences, and therefore influence considerably the common-assault rate. Because common-assaults constitute a majority of violent offences, increases in common-assaults help to drive growth in the violent offence rate. Thus the introduction of Bill C-127 and related changes in spousal-assault charging practices appear to have had the effect of helping to drive rapid growth in the violent crime rate during the past decade. In turn, rapid increases in the violent offence rate have helped to shape public and media perceptions about the level of violence in Canadian society.

To gain a better understanding of the potential underlying causes of elevated assault reporting rates, a chronology of events related to spousal assault was presented in this chapter. As demonstrated by this chronology, the 1980s saw governments across Canada issue mandatory charging directives aimed at reducing discretion in spousal-assault charging decisions. In response to Bill C-127, and to the intermittent introduction of spousal assault charging directives by various jurisdictions, police began to lay more charges in assault cases. As a result of these more assertive charging practices, the proportion of common-assault offences cleared by charge began to escalate, moving from about 30% prior to 1983 to 60% in 1993. While the rate of reported common-assault offences increased 106% during this reference period, the rate of persons charged increased 255%.

The analysis further suggested that increased police charging in spousal assault cases may also have had the effect of increasing public reporting of common-assaults. Victimization studies show that one of the main reasons victims do not report crimes is that they do not feel that the police can do anything about them. However, if there is evidence that police can respond effectively in spousal-assault cases (i.e., by laying more charges), then victims should be more likely to report such incidents. Visible evidence of increased charging in spousal assaults, then, may have helped to establish a pattern of greater victim reporting in the years immediately following the introduction of Bill C-127.

Examination of the characteristics of common-assault incidents revealed that females are most likely to be assaulted in their own home by someone that they know (most often a spouse), while males are more likely to be assaulted at locations outside of their home by a nonfamily member. The finding that almost 40% of common-assault victims were assaulted by a family member highlights the fact that family violence is a dominant component in assault offences.

We saw that GSS victimization data show no increase in assault victim-izations or in victim reporting to police between 1988 and 1993. These data suggest that increases in police-reported assault rates are not necessarily an indication of increases in the level of violence within society. Even if violence is increasing, a large portion of the increase in police-reported violent crime may be related to the fact that much of the violence that has always been present within society is becoming more visible because of increased report-ing in police statistics. Furthermore, increases in assault reporting rates appear to be a response to public policy initiatives that have sensitized mem-bers of the public—including victims—to the importance of the issue. Increases in reported assaults and higher rates of charging in assault cases may thus be seen as evidence of successful public policy initiatives. Because there have been no new mandatory charging assault directives since 1990, assault rates may stabilize, a process that appears to have already begun.

NOTES

[1] In this study, level 2 and level 3 assaults have been combined with unlawfully causing bod-ily harm offences to form a category called "major-assaults." A small mixed group of "other assaults," representing less than 5% of all assaults, are not included in the analysis.

[2] Directives were introduced in Ontario and Saskatchewan in 1982; Manitoba, Prince Edward Island, and the RCMP in the Northwest Territories and Yukon in 1983; the RCMP in the rest of Canada in 1984; Quebec and Newfoundland in 1987; Nova Scotia in 1988; New Brunswick in 1989; and Alberta in 1990.

CRIMES AGAINST WOMEN AND CHILDREN IN THE FAMILY

by Karen Rodgers and Rebecca Kong

In this chapter, Karen Rodgers and Rebecca Kong examine the physical and sexual abuse of women and children in the family. Until recently, the issue of family violence was obscured by the traditional view that the family home was a place where individuals should be able to set their own rules of behaviour, unconstrained by formal agencies. Drawing extensively upon the Violence Against Women survey, in addition to police and hospital data, the authors explore the risk factors associated with family violence, the characteristics and circumstances of various types of abuse, the physical and emotional consequences for victims, and, finally, formal and informal responses to family violence.

Traditionally, the family has been viewed as a safe haven—a place in which women and children could feel protected from the evils of the outside world. However, the family has also traditionally been a hierarchical unit in which violence has always existed, justified by religious beliefs, moral attitudes, as well as by legal codification (Van Stolk, 1972:103). Under old English common law, husbands were legally permitted to inflict corporal punishment on their wives and children, who were considered their property.

Only within the last few decades have the physical and sexual abuse of wives and children become intolerable, criminal offences. During the 1960s, doctors grew increasingly suspicious of the many small children and infants arriving at hospitals with bruises and fractures, the nature of which were inconsistent with explanations offered by parents. The "battered child syndrome"[1] was born. Shortly thereafter, owing largely to the activities of feminist groups, violence against women in marital relationships began to emerge as a social issue. Around this same period, child sexual abuse was "discovered" and found to be much more extensive than ever imagined.

The growing awareness of family violence was accompanied by legislative changes to improve the criminal justice response to wife assault and child abuse. In 1983, the *Criminal Code* legislation stating that a husband could not be guilty of raping his wife was repealed. During that same period, as discussed in Chapter 6, police forces across Canada were given directives making it mandatory for them to lay charges where reasonable grounds exist to suspect that a woman has been assaulted by her husband. To better protect children, *Criminal Code* legislation was enacted to encompass a wide range of sexual offences against children.

Despite legislative efforts and attempts to change attitudes, family violence continues to be a problem. The dependency of many women and their children, combined with traditional hierarchies in the family, provides an environment that allows those with more power to behave with relative immunity toward those who have less power. In addition, the widespread support for existing authority relations allows those with power to believe that they have a right to expect compliance from those who are less powerful. Violence may be understood as one effective way in which such compliance is gained (Sacco and Kennedy, 1994:190).

Research suggests that many incidents of wife and child abuse remain undetected. This is particularly true of child abuse because the powerlessness of children assures that most incidents remain hidden. At present, our knowledge of child abuse relies on official statistics (e.g., police and hospital reports) that capture information only on those cases that come to the attention of official agencies. No national estimates of the prevalence of child abuse are available. On the other hand, data on the nature and extent of wife assault in Canada is more extensive and is based on police-reported data and findings from Statistics Canada's 1993 Violence Against Women (VAW) survey. Using these sources of information, this chapter will construct the criminal events of wife assault and child abuse.

DEFINITIONS

Violence against women and children within the family is commonly referred to as "wife assault" and "child abuse." Definitions can include all forms of physical, sexual, and psychological abuse, including physical neglect and emotional abuse. Some research includes in its definitions of wife assault and child abuse forms of cruelty that fall outside the social consensus of what is viewed as "violence." This chapter will focus on *Criminal Code* definitions of physical and sexual assault in order to discuss "violence" as it is legally understood. Wife assault and child abuse are defined as violent acts ranging from threats of violence, to threats or use of guns or other weapons, to sexual assault.

PRECURSORS

117

*Crimes
Against
Women and
Children in
the Family*

According to the VAW survey, new partnerships have the highest rates of violence. Women who are currently in a marriage or common-law relationship for two years or less experience higher rates of violence than women in unions of longer duration. Women in partnerships that have lasted more than twenty years are those least likely to have ever been the victim of wife assault. Women living in common-law relationships are also more likely than those who are legally married to experience violence at the hands of their spouse. The risk factor of common-law unions becomes even stronger when combined with age: young women in common-law relationships are by far at the greatest risk of wife assault. Women in common-law relationships also have a disproportionately higher risk of being killed by a marital partner (see Figure 7-1). The number of women killed by men is almost eight times higher in common-law unions than in legal marriages. Rates of abuse for previous relationships are much higher than for current relationships.

One of the strongest risk factors for wife assault is the youth of the couple. Young women aged 18 to 24 are four times as likely as women overall to have experienced wife assault (see Table 7-1). The same pattern exists for violent partners, with the youngest men showing the highest rates of violence. In cases of women killed by their male partners, the greatest risks befell the youngest wives and women's risk declines with age. In addition, homicide data reveal that age disparity in relationships increases women's risk of being killed by their partners, regardless of whether women are much younger or older than their partners (see Figure 7-2).

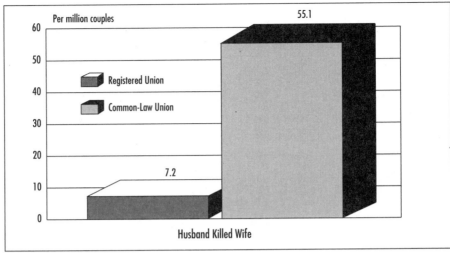

Figure 7-1 Rates of Women Killed by Spouses, by Type of Marital Union, 1974–1992

Source: Homicide survey, Canadian Centre for Justice Statistics, 1993.

Crimes
Against
People

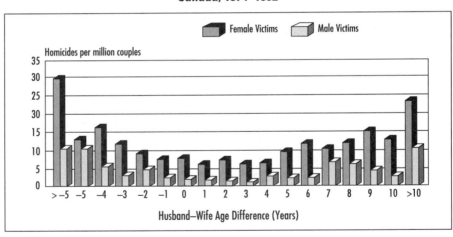

Figure 7-2 Rates of Spousal Homicide by Age Difference, Co-residing Couples, Canada, 1974–1992

Source: Homicide survey, Canadian Centre for Justice Statistics, 1993.

Research suggests that younger children are at greater risk of child abuse than older children (Schlesinger, 1984:13). According to CHIRPP[2] data, the majority of familial child-abuse victims were younger than 6 years old. This may not be surprising given that younger children are much more vulnerable

Table 7-1   Number of Currently Married Women (18 Years +) Who Have Experienced Wife Assault, by Age, Household Income, and Education, Canada, 1993[1]

	Total Currently Married Women (in thousands)	Total Wife-Assault Victims (in thousands)	%
Total	6,690	201[2]	3[3]
Age group			
18–24	334	39	12
25–34	1,641	73	4
35–44	1,761	47	3
45 and over	2,953	41	1
Household income			
Less than $15,000	367	23	6
$15,000–$29,999	1,018	33	3
$30,000–$59,999	2,623	73	3
$60,000 or more	1,728	51	3
Not stated/Don't know	955	21	2
Education			
Less than high-school diploma	1,671	55	3
High-school diploma	1,913	53	3
Some post-secondary education	2,020	56	3
University degree	1,076	37	3

[1] Figures in this table have been weighted to the Canadian adult female population.
[2] Numbers represent incidents of assault that occurred within the twelve months preceding the survey.
[3] Percentages are based on the total currently married female population.

Source: Violence Against Women survey, Statistics Canada, 1993.

and helpless than older children, and that parents and other family members may be less able to understand and cope with the constant and extensive care young children require. In contrast to CHIRPP data, the majority of child physical- and sexual-assault cases captured by the 1993 Revised Uniform Crime Reporting survey involved children aged 11 to 17. This difference between CHIRPP and UCR data can be partially explained by the fact that the CHIRPP study only involved pediatric hospitals, which would tend to be frequented by younger rather than older children. The age of child victims varies, however, between physical and sexual abuse. According to the 1993 Revised UCR survey, the majority of child victims of physical assault (66%) were in the 11–17 age group. However, an opposite pattern appears in cases of child sexual assault, in which a slight majority of victims (56%) were

10 and under. Very young children are also more likely to be killed by a family member than are older children. According to homicide statistics, between 1981 and 1992 the largest percentage of children killed by a family member (48%) were under 3, a finding that is consistent with victims of both sexes.

Contrary to commonly held beliefs, factors such as education level and family income do not have a clear effect on a woman's risk of abuse. According to the VAW survey, a woman's education level has no bearing on her risk of wife assault. On the other hand, the education level of a woman's partner may play a role in her risk of abuse. For instance, of all men who are currently married, those with a university education show the lowest rates of violence, while men with less than a high-school diploma show the highest. Very poor women are also at a greater risk of wife assault. Women with a household income below $15,000 are twice as likely as women with higher incomes to be physically or sexually assaulted by their spouse. In addition, men who are unemployed and facing the frustration and stress of looking for work are twice as likely to be abusive than men who are working.

Few data are available on the economic conditions under which child abuse occurs. However, the CHIRPP study reveals that one-third of abused children treated by the pediatric hospitals involved in the study were living in single-parent families. In contrast, only 13% of families in Canada are headed by a single parent (Statistics Canada, 1992a). It has been observed that the majority of cases coming to the attention of child welfare authorities involve clients who are usually poorly educated, who live in or near poverty, and who are members of single-parent families (Bala, 1991:15). However, it should not be assumed that child abuse is more likely to occur in this socio-economic environment (Frankel-Howard, 1989:25). Rather, this observation may be a reflection of families' lack of access to other support services because of limited resources. Moreover, in some cases the personal or emotional problems that result in a life of poverty may also make it difficult to parent adequately.

Research suggests that persons with disabilities are at a greater risk of physical and sexual abuse. Not only are persons with disabilities more vulnerable to attacks, but depending on the level of disability, family members may be unable to cope with and adequately care for the individual. According to the VAW survey, 39% of ever-married women with a disability or a disabling health problem reported being physically or sexually assaulted by a partner over the course of their married lives, compared to 27% of nondisabled women. Findings are similar in cases of child abuse. In 15% of family-related child-abuse cases that came to the attention of three pediatric hospitals, the injured child had a disability or other medical condition. In comparison, only 7% of children 14 years and under in the general population have a disability (Statistics Canada, 1992a and 1992b).

Research on family violence has suggested that a child who learns violent behaviour patterns at home will be more likely to engage in similar patterns later on. This pattern is known as the "cycle of violence." According to Canadian researcher Peter Jaffe, "The cycle of violence assumption originated in part from the rationale that physical aggression in the home provides both a model for learning aggressive behaviour and a supportive environment that views such behaviour as appropriate" (Jaffe, Wolfe, and Wilson, 1990:57). Research on wife assault has suggested that witnessing violence against one's mother will increase the likelihood that a woman will be involved in an abusive relationship (Walker, 1984). Results from the VAW survey indicate that women whose fathers were violent toward their mothers were twice as likely to be abused by a marital partner than women whose fathers were not violent. Women whose partners' fathers were violent were three times as likely to be assaulted by their partners than women with nonviolent fathers-in-law. Men who as children had witnessed violence against their mothers inflicted more frequent and serious assaults on their partners, who in turn were more likely to fear for their lives than were women in relationships with partners who had not witnessed such violence.

Alcohol appears to play a role in men's use of violence against their partners, although it is not clear how this role should be characterized. The VAW survey shows that while in one-half of marriages involving violence the man was usually drinking at the time of the assault, it is also true that in an equal number of cases he had not been drinking. The rate of wife assault for women currently living with men who drink regularly (at least four times per week) was triple the rate of those whose husbands never drank. Women whose partners drink heavily (those who frequently consume five or more drinks at one time) were six times as likely to be assaulted than those women whose partners never drink.

With respect to child abuse, there are few national statistical data on factors that may increase a parent or family member's risk of abusing children. However, literature suggests that young parents, parents who were themselves abused as children, and those with unreasonable expectations for their children may be more likely than other parents to abuse their children. Young parents, particularly adolescent mothers, have been viewed as high risk for child abuse. However, it is interesting to note that only 4% of abusive mothers identified in the CHIRPP study were under 19 years of age. The largest proportions were between 20 and 30 (45%) and 30 and 40 (40%). Neither the Revised UCR survey nor the CHIRPP study provide data on whether or not parents or other accused family members were themselves abused as children. However, as Phaneuf (1990a) describes the cycle of child abuse, "The vast majority of abusive parents have themselves been abused as children ... [While] previous victimization is not the cause of child abuse, ... it is a significant contributing factor." Also, abusive parents often have unrealistic expectations with respect to their children's developmental ability, even during the child's infancy (Van Stolk, 1972:22). They frequently expect levels of physical, emotional, and mental maturity that exceed their children's limited capacities, and use punishment as a means of enforcing compliance with parental needs and demands. Parents who hold this perception of children's abilities and who equate punishment with good parenting are likely to inflict physical abuse in order to attain an unattainable achievement from children, toddlers, and infants.

THE EVENT

PREVALENCE

According to the 1993 VAW survey, 29% of women who had ever been married or lived in a common-law relationship have been physically or sexually assaulted by their partner at some point during their relationship. Of currently married women, 3% experienced violence within the twelve months prior to the survey. During 1993, 17% of physical assaults reported to the police were against children under 18 years of age; 20% of these assaults were perpetrated by a family member. A very high proportion (60%) of all sexual assaults reported to the police in 1993 were against children; more than one-third of these assaults occurred within the family. In 65% of family-related physical assaults against children and 45% of sexual assaults, the accused was a parent (see Table 7-2).

Family violence often becomes lethal. In fact, women and children are more likely to be killed by a family member than by a stranger. For example, the probability that a registered-married woman would be killed by her spouse is nine times greater than the probability that she would be killed by a stranger (Wilson, Daly, and Wright, 1993). Between 1974 and 1992, an average of 76 women were slain by their husbands each year. This represents

Table 7-2 Percentage Distribution of Child Victims[1] of Family-Related Physical and Sexual Assault by Victim/Accused Relationship and Type of Abuse, 1993

Relationship of Accused to Victim	Total Assaults %	Type of Abuse Physical Assault %	Sexual Assault %
Total[2]	100	100	100
Parent	57	65	45
Spouse/ex-spouse	6	9	1
Other immediate family	23	20	27
Extended family	15	6	27

[1] Children are defined as victims aged 0 to 17 years.

[2] Based on incidents reported by 79 police agencies to the Revised UCR database, representing 32% of the national volume of reported crime in Canada.

Source: Revised Uniform Crime Reporting survey, Canadian Centre for Justice Statistics, 1993.

123

*Crimes
Against
Women and
Children in
the Family*

1,435 women in Canada, or just over one-third of all adult female homicide victims. Between 1981 and 1992, over one-half (52%) of all child homicides were committed by a family member. Of these, approximately eight in ten were committed by a parent, slightly more than half of whom were fathers or stepfathers (58%). Children killed by a family member were most often beaten to death (see Figure 7-3).

TYPE OF ABUSE

Among women who are assaulted by their spouses, pushing/grabbing/shoving is the most commonly reported type of violence, followed by threats, slapping, throwing objects and kicking, biting and hitting with fists (see Table 7-3). Although pushing, grabbing, or shoving were the most frequently reported forms of violence, only 5% of abused women said that these were the only types of abuse that they had suffered. Similarly, just 4% of women reported having been only threatened by their partner. This suggests an escalation in seriousness, with threats of violence almost always followed by more serious acts. In addition, almost one-half of abused women have had a weapon[3] used against them. Considering only the *most serious* acts of violence, 16% of ever-married women were kicked, hit, beaten up, choked, threatened with or had a gun or knife used against them, or were sexually assaulted; 11% were pushed, grabbed, shoved, or slapped; and 2% experi-

Figure 7-3 Percentage of Family-Related Child Homicides by Method of Killing, 1981–1992

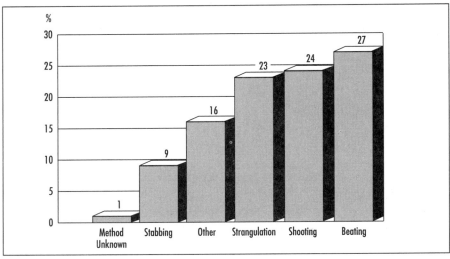

Source: Homicide survey, Canadian Centre for Justice Statistics, 1993.

enced nonphysical assaults, including being threatened or having something thrown at them.

Research has suggested that wife assault is cyclical, each cycle having three phases (Walker, 1984). In the first stage, tension builds and leads to the second phase, which is the act of violence. The third phase is one of loving and kind behaviour displayed by the batterer toward the woman. This final phase provides reinforcement to the marital relationship and is what keeps many women hopeful that the violence will not happen again. Rarely is this the case. According to the VAW survey, for almost two-thirds of women who live with a violent partner, the violence happens on more than one occasion; for 41% of women, the violence occurs more than ten times.

Not only is the violence repeated and ongoing, it can also occur at any time during a relationship. Sixteen percent of women in violent relationships stated that the violence had occurred before they were married. Common-law relationships are also different in this regard: rates of violence before marriage were lower among legally married women than among those living common law.

The violence in some marriages continues or begins even during pregnancy. Pregnancy has often been seen as an event in a marital relationship that may trigger violence. MacLeod (1980) suggests that wife assault is

Table 7-3 Number and Percentage of Marital Partnerships with Violence, Women 18 Years and Over, by Type of Violence, Canada, 1993 [1]

Type of Violence	All Partners (in thousands)	%	Marital Partnerships Current Partner (in thousands)	%	Previous Partner (in thousands)	%
Total[2]	2,652	29	1,020	15	1,781	48
Threatened to hit her with something	1,688	19	461	7	1,292	35
Threw something that could hurt her	1,018	11	237	4	804	21
Pushed, grabbed, or shoved	2,221	25	819	12	1,500	40
Slapped	1,359	15	295	4	1,103	30
Kicked, bit, or hit her with his fist	955	11	154	2	819	22
Hit her with something that could hurt her	508	6	80	1	434	12
Beat her up	794	9	94	1	716	19
Choked her	607	7	76	1	540	14
Threatened or used a gun or knife	417	5	44	1	379	10
Sexual assault	729	8	108	2	629	17

[1] Figures in this table have been weighted to the Canadian adult female population.
[2] Figures will not add to totals because of multiple responses.

Source: Violence Against Women survey, Statistics Canada, 1993.

125

*Crimes
Against
Women and
Children in
the Family*

rooted in patriarchy and argues that "the increased dependence and power-lessness of the woman in the family combined with her isolation from people outside her immediate family during many pregnancies triggers a response that makes the pregnant woman an appropriate victim—a response that is rooted in our deepest understanding of the role of the family, and the woman's place in it." Results from the VAW survey show that 21% of abused women were assaulted during pregnancy; 40% of these women stated that the abuse began during their pregnancy.

Many believe that the pattern of violence cannot be broken until the relationship is terminated (Loseke and Cahill, 1984). When a woman tries to leave an abusive relationship, however, she may be met with more violence—violence that is more frequent and severe. In fact, approximately one-fifth of women who experienced violence by a previous partner reported that the abuse occurred following or during separation; in 35% of these cases, the violence increased in severity at the time of separation. This increase in violence is consistent with theories of power and control: if a male authority figure feels threatened by his partner's increasing freedom, he may become increasingly violent to regain his sense of control.

Although there is little information on the extent to which child abuse is ongoing, doctors are able to tell from medical examinations whether the violence was a one-time incident or repetitive in nature. The "battered child syndrome" came into recognition when X-rays of children revealed old bone fractures in various stages of healing, which indicated that abuse had been repetitive (Kempe et al., 1962).

Child abuse is expressed in several different forms. Data from the CHIRPP study show that one-half of all family-related child-abuse cases that came to the attention of three pediatric hospitals were sexual abuse, about one-third were physical abuse, 5% were neglect, and 10% were combined types of abuse. In comparison, findings from the 1993 Revised UCR survey indicate that of all child-abuse cases captured by the survey, 59% involved physical assault while the remaining 41% involved sexual assault. Moreover, in 29% of physical-assault cases and 25% of sexual-assault cases, a weapon was used. In slightly over half of physical and sexual assaults, physical force (as opposed to an inanimate weapon) was used against the child.

Unlike many other types of crimes, incidents of wife assault or child abuse are rarely witnessed by bystanders other than family members. According to the VAW survey, 39% of women in abusive marriages reported that their children saw them being assaulted. This, however, may be an underestimate because clinical research has shown that many parents tend to "minimize or deny the presence of children during incidents of wife assault by suggesting that the children were asleep or playing outside" (Jaffe et al., 1990). In addition, Jaffe et al. reveal that children who witness violence against their mothers may witness a range of abuse, from listening to the violence to being forced to watch their mother being abused by their father as a lesson in fear and control. The VAW survey shows that children in fact see very serious forms of violence. In one-half of the abusive relationships in which children witnessed the violence, women feared for their lives. Furthermore, in 61% of violent marriages in which children witnessed the abuse, the violence was serious enough to result in the women being injured. Having children witness the violence influences a woman's decision to seek help. Women whose children had witnessed the assault were twice as likely to use a social service and three times as likely to report their partner to the police than those not in this situation.

Violence within the family can have serious consequences. This is not surprising given the repetitive nature of family violence and the "relative inability of victims to escape violent encounters that occur in the context of the
family" (Sacco and Kennedy, 1994:195). Victims of wife assault and child
abuse often suffer both physical injury and lasting emotional trauma.

According to the VAW survey, one-half of women assaulted by their
spouse suffered a physical injury. Many of these injuries resulted in the
woman requiring professional medical attention (40%), having to take time
off from her everyday activities (50%), and fearing for her life (33%).
Among those who were injured, the most frequent types of injury reported
were bruises, followed by cuts, scratches, and burns; broken bones; and fractures (see Figure 7-4). In addition, 9% of injured women stated that they suffered internal injuries or miscarriages.

Similar to cases of wife assault, incidents of child abuse frequently lead
to injury. According to data from the 1993 Revised UCR survey, six in ten

127
*Crimes
Against
Women and
Children in
the Family*

**Figure 7-4   Percent of Ever-Married Women (18 years +) Who Reported Violence
by a Marital Partner, by Type of Injury, Canada, 1993**

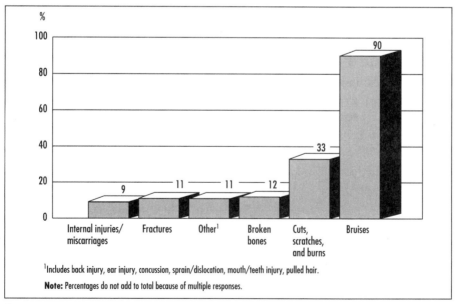

[1]Includes back injury, ear injury, concussion, sprain/dislocation, mouth/teeth injury, pulled hair.

Note: Percentages do not add to total because of multiple responses.

Source: Violence Against Women survey, Statistics Canada, 1993.

child victims of physical assault experienced some form of injury that was apparent to the attending police officer: 57% suffered minor injuries and 3% major injuries[4]; in 9% of cases, it was unknown whether or not there was an injury. On the other hand, two-thirds of children who were sexually assaulted reportedly suffered no apparent physical injury. This may be explained by the very nature of sexual assault: children may not immediately report the incident because of shame, embarrassment, or fear, and less violent forms of sexual assault, such as sexual touching, may not result in physical injury.

Although the type of injury cannot be determined through the Revised UCR survey, other sources of official data such as hospital records suggest that injuries can range in severity from bruises or abrasions to death. Eight cases of child abuse out of the 951 cases captured by the CHIRPP study resulted in the death of the child. The perpetrator was a family member in all but one case. Results from this study show that children who had been physically abused had the highest rates of physical injury. The majority of all injured children suffered minor soft-tissue damage, while smaller proportions sustained fractures, burns, cuts and bites, and serious hemorrhage. Injury sustained by sexually abused children was primarily the result of penetration. The body part most often injured in physical-abuse cases was the child's head and brain, followed by lower extremities, and trunk/abdomen and upper extremities. Victims of sexual abuse who were injured sustained injuries primarily to sexual organs. The small number of neglected children who were injured sustained head injuries and injuries to extremities.

Wife abuse and child abuse have other serious consequences to the victims beyond physical injury. Women and children may also suffer emotionally from family violence, harbouring feelings of anger, mistrust, and fear. Studies and reports reveal that "battered women, after prolonged abuse, suffer from low self-esteem, they stop taking care of their appearance and health, they frequently blame themselves ... and they feel overwhelming guilt" (MacLeod, 1987:31). Consistent with these findings, the VAW survey found that almost nine in ten women who were abused by their partners indicated that they experienced some type of emotional effect. The most commonly reported consequences were anger, fear, becoming more cautious or less trusting, and lowered self-esteem. Large numbers of women reported being depressed or anxious, feeling ashamed or guilty, and having problems relating to men. Although no national data are available on the emotional consequences of child abuse, several interview or clinical studies have found that abused children can be severely traumatized, feel low self-esteem and

Crimes
Against
People

mistrust, and have difficulty adjusting socially (Jaffe, Wolfe, and Wilson, 1990; Canada, 1980:41).

Women may use a variety of ways to cope with the physical and emotional consequences of wife assault. According to the VAW survey, approximately one-quarter of abused women reported using alcohol, drugs, or medication to help them deal with the situation. Women who sustained an injury were more likely to use alcohol or drugs. Alcohol use by women who previously lived with a violent partner was almost twice the rate of those currently living with violence.

Given the serious physical and emotional consequences of wife assault, it is not surprising that about one-half of women who were abused had left their partners. Many factors can influence a woman's decision to leave. Clinical research has found that the physical danger to children is identified by most women as the main reason for leaving, with life-threatening attacks being another important reason (Hilton, 1992). The VAW survey found similar results. Women who had reported to the police, who had feared for their lives, or whose children had witnessed the violence were the women most likely to leave their abusive partners either permanently or for a short while. The majority of women who had left their partners stayed with friends or relatives, followed by transition homes or shelters.

Unlike situations in which the violence is perpetrated by strangers, it is difficult in cases of family violence for victims to disassociate themselves from their attackers. According to the VAW survey, almost three-quarters of women who left their abusive partners eventually returned home—a decision that may be very difficult for the woman to make and for society to comprehend. Victimization surveys offer some insight into why women decide to return. The most common reasons stated were (1) for the sake of the children; (2) to give the relationship another chance; (3) the partner promising to change; and (4) lack of money or housing. In addition, women whose partners received counselling for the abuse were more likely to return home than those whose partners did not get professional help.

Until recently, cases of family violence came to the attention of the police only infrequently. Moreover, when family violence cases were reported, police were reluctant to lay charges against the suspects. This shows that family violence, although illegal, was not seen as a situation in which the state should be involved. Until the early 1980s, when mandatory charging policies were implemented, police considered that "their primary role in domestic disputes was to restore order: that is, once the officers were able to separate and calm the partners, they believed their jobs were done" (Jaffe,

1993:63). As a result, it is not surprising that the VAW survey found that only one-quarter of wife-assault victims reported their abuse to the police. Among the reasons women cite for not reporting to the police are (1) they felt that the incident was too minor; (2) they wanted to keep the incident private; or (3) they did not want help. Not only do women infrequently report to the police, but many have never told anyone about their abuse (22%). A number of the women who had never disclosed their violence to anyone suffered severe and frequent forms of abuse: 18% of them had suffered injury, 11% had been abused on more than ten occasions, and 10% had at some point feared for their lives. These women have a variety of reasons for not telling anyone about their abuse, including a feeling of shame or embarrassment, being afraid of their spouse, or not having anyone to turn to.

Women who do turn to the police for help are often in desperate and potentially life-threatening situations. Results from the VAW survey show that women whose children had witnessed the violence, women who were injured, women who had a weapon used against them, or women who had been abused more than ten times were more likely than women not in these situations to have reported to police. One-half of women who contacted the police were satisfied with the way the police handled the case. Although in 84% of cases reported to police, the police responded to the woman by seeing her, in only 28% of these cases was a charge laid. However, 79% of charges laid by the police resulted in the offender appearing in court.

Police involvement does not necessarily stop the violence. While the violence decreased or ended in almost one-half of the cases in which police intervened, in 40% of the reported cases there was no change in the man's behaviour. In the remaining 10% of cases, the violence actually increased.

Whether or not a case of wife assault or child abuse comes to the attention of the police, victims of family violence may seek refuge or support from family, friends, or formal helping agencies. This has not always been the case. Until recently, women and children who disclosed the violence were often not believed by family or friends; nor were they always considered credible witnesses within the criminal justice system.

As the issues of wife assault and child abuse became more visible, and as women began to organize and advocate on behalf of women and children suffering from family violence, shelters for abused women and their children began to emerge across Canada. The first shelter opened its doors in the early 1970s. By 1975, only eighteen shelters existed, while an additional 57 began operation between 1975 and 1979. Since that time, as issues of family violence gained the attention of federal and provincial governments, the number of shelters has grown rapidly. Currently, there are between 350 and 400 residential facilities in Canada according to a 1993 Statistics Canada survey of transition homes.

In the fiscal year 1992–93, there were 86,499 admissions to 303 residential facilities.[5] According to the VAW survey, only 6% of abused women stay in a shelter. These women are often in desperate situations. Over 80% of women who used shelters had suffered an injury at some time during the abusive relationship, and eight in ten women who went to a shelter had feared for their lives. Women cite a number of reasons for not seeking refuge: they did not want or need help; the violence was not serious enough; they were unaware of any shelters; or there were no services available. The majority of women who did use a shelter found it to be beneficial. This finding is consistent with a study of 270 abused women who reported that transition-home workers were among the most helpful of those who provided professional services (Hamilton and Coates, 1993).

Overall, according to the VAW survey, women from abusive marriages relied most heavily on their family, friends, and neighbours when they needed help. Many women say that these personal sources of support are the most helpful in dealing with violence.

SUMMARY AND CONCLUSIONS
■ ■ ■

Physical and sexual assaults against women and children in the family have only recently come to the attention of the Canadian public. Although child abuse was "discovered" in the 1960s and wife assault did not emerge as a social issue until the 1970s, much more is currently known about the nature and extent of wife assault than of child abuse. At present, we know that 29% of ever-married women have been assaulted by their partners and that some women are at greater risk of abuse, particularly if they are young, in common-law or new marriages, or if their partners are facing the stress of looking for work. The abuse suffered by women can range in severity, as can the emotional and physical consequences; it seems that women are more likely to seek help when the abuse results in injury, is repetitive, and is witnessed by children.

To date, our knowledge of the incidents of child abuse largely relies on police and hospital data. It remains difficult to measure child abuse in Canada because of the ethical and methodological issues that arise when children and parents are randomly surveyed about violence in the home.

However, we do know that in one-quarter of the child physical- and sexual-assault cases brought to the attention of the police in 1993, the suspect was a family member, most often a parent.

Family violence is a crime that is difficult to combat. Powerlessness, fear, shame, and social attitudes make it difficult for victims to seek help. Without intervention, the cycle of violence may repeat itself. Recently, federal and provincial governments have implemented many legislative and policy changes to deal with family violence. However, family violence is dealt with not only by formal institutions but also by informal ones such as family and friends. It is to these informal institutions that victims of family violence most often turn. This fact underlines the importance of developing multifaceted approaches to the problem. As Touchette (1994) observes, "The criminal justice system, on its own, cannot deal effectively with all impacts of family violence."

NOTES

[1] A term coined by Dr. C.H. Kempe in 1962 to describe the pattern of repetitive, suspicious injury suffered by young children, which often led to death.

[2] Between 1991 and 1992, the CHIRPP (Canadian Hospital Injury Research and Prevention Programme) at the Laboratory Centre for Disease Control at Health Canada conducted a survey focusing on intentional injuries of children who were brought to the attention of three pediatric hospitals across Canada. Data were collected retrospectively from records and charts beginning January 1991 and extending up to 24 months. Information from the survey is limited to descriptions of episodes of intentional injuries that occurred during the study period.

[3] Weapons include having something thrown at them that could hurt them, being hit with something that could hurt them, and having a gun or knife used against them.

[4] The Revised UCR survey defines "minor injury" as physical injury that required no professional medical treatment or only some first aid (Band-Aid, ice, etc.). "Major injury" is defined as physical injury that is more than "trifling" or "transient" in nature and that requires professional medical attention at the scene or transportation to a medical facility.

[5] While Statistics Canada identified 371 facilities in operation at the time of the 1992–93 Transition Home Survey, not all responded to the survey. We can assume, therefore, that the total number of admissions is higher than that indicated.

SEXUAL ASSAULT

by Holly Johnson

Holly Johnson begins this chapter with a discussion of sexual-assault laws and the effects that recent changes in the legal definition of this crime have had on the response of the criminal justice system for both victims and perpetrators. After looking at sexual assault from the perspective of sex-role theory, the author uses data provided by the Violence Against Women survey to examine the offence in terms of characteristics, trends, and reporting rates. Explanations for the sharp increase in reported sexual assault following the recent legal reforms are provided, along with reasons for the unwillingness of victims to report this crime to the police.

Interest in the crime of sexual assault has been growing over the past decade among governments, academics and other researchers, the media, the medical profession, victim-support groups, and the general public. This interest has been accompanied by a groundswell of research into the incidence, effects, and consequences of sexual violence. Most recent research estimates the prevalence of sexual violence among women and children to be much higher than previously thought. A great deal of this research paints a picture of victims who, because of shame, embarrassment, and mistrust of the justice system, never report their experience to the police.

Drawing upon data from a national telephone survey, as well as on police and court statistics, this chapter examines the extent and the nature of sexual assault as it is experienced by Canadian women, and how incidents of sexual assault that are reported to the police are processed through the criminal justice system. Theoretical explanations for why sexual assault occurs are also offered.

DEFINITIONS

Sexual assault is defined very broadly under Canadian law. It ranges in severity from relatively minor acts of unwanted sexual touching to very serious sexual attacks resulting in injury or disfigurement to the victim. Victims can include both males and females, and both children and adults. Rape (or forced penetration) is not a necessary component of sexual assault, although it falls within this definition. The crimes of rape and indecent assault were removed from the Canadian legal books in 1983 and replaced with three new offences of sexual assault:

(i) Sexual assault (maximum 10 years' imprisonment)
(ii) Sexual assault with a weapon, threats to a third party, or causing bodily harm (maximum 14 years' imprisonment)
(iii) Aggravated sexual assault resulting in wounding, maiming, disfiguring, or endangering the life of the victim (maximum life imprisonment).

The crime of sexual assault was undefined by the lawmakers at the time of implementation. However, in the 1987 case *R. v. Chase*, the Supreme Court ruled that a sexual assault is differentiated from an assault by the part of the body touched, the nature of the contact, the situation in which it occurred, the words or gestures accompanying the act, and all other circumstances surrounding the contact.

In addition, the following offences of child sexual abuse were created in 1988:

(i) Sexual interference—sexual touching of a child under 14 years of age (maximum 10 years imprisonment)
(ii) Invitation to sexual touching—inviting or counselling a child under 14 to be involved in sexual touching (maximum 10 years imprisonment)
(iii) Sexual exploitation—a person who is in a position of trust or authority or with whom the child is in a position of dependency and who is involved in sexual interference or invitation to sexual touching (child is between 14 and 18 years of age; maximum 5 years imprisonment)

(iv) Incest—sexual intercourse with a person who is related by blood and who is a parent, child, brother, sister, grandparent, or grandchild (maximum 14 years imprisonment).

These legal reforms were implemented in response to growing criticisms from researchers and women's groups that the way the criminal justice system dealt with complaints of rape and indecent assault amounted to a "secondary victimization" of the victim. She was assaulted first by her attacker and then again by the police, the Crown, defence attorneys, and the judge as her credibility was questioned and her reputation demeaned. The aims of these legislative changes were to downplay the sexual nature and emphasize the assaultive nature of these crimes, to encourage victims to report them to the police, and to improve police and court handling of cases, thereby reducing the trauma to victims and increasing the number of convictions (Roberts and Gebotys, 1992). The scope of the new law was also broadened to allow prosecution of men who committed sexual assault against their wives, who had enjoyed a "spousal exemption" under the previous law.

In 1991, further changes were made to sexual-assault laws when, in the case of *R. v. Seaboyer and Gayme*, the Supreme Court of Canada struck down the section of the *Criminal Code* that limited the questioning of victims in sexual-assault trials about their sexual history. It was successfully argued that the "rape shield" law, designed to protect women from unnecessary intrusion into their past sexual conduct, violated the rights of the accused to a fair trial. In 1992, Parliament established guidelines to assist judges in determining when it would be permissible to admit evidence about a victim's sexual history. It also provided a definition of the concept of "consent" as it applies to sexual assault, and restricted the conditions under which the defence of "mistaken belief" could be used. For example, consent is not obtained when

- it is given by someone other than the victim;
- the victim is incapable of consenting due to intoxication or some other condition;
- it is induced by abusing a position of trust, power, or authority;
- the victim indicates by word or conduct her lack of consent; or
- the victim indicates by word or conduct that she has withdrawn her consent.

The last two conditions, specifying either *word* or *conduct*, were included in recognition of the unique vulnerability of disabled women to sexual assault and the fact that some disabilities prevent the articulation of lack of consent.

The law also states that "nothing in [the above list] shall be construed as limiting the circumstances in which no consent is obtained." In other words, the list is not exhaustive and the prosecution may present other conditions to indicate absence of consent. With this change in the law, the focus shifts from determining whether the perpetrator used force or caused injury to determining whether the complainant articulated *consent* to engage in sexual activity.

This legislation also restricted the conditions under which the accused could say he "mistakenly believed" that the victim was consenting. The accused person's mistaken belief that the victim was consenting cannot be used as a defence if the belief stems from the accused's drunkenness, recklessness, or willful blindness, or if the accused did not take adequate steps to determine whether she was in fact consenting. In 1994, however, in the case of *R. v. Daviault*, the Supreme Court allowed the defence of severe drunkenness and overthrew the conviction of a man who had been found guilty of sexually assaulting an elderly woman. One justification of the Court in granting this defence was that the degree of intoxication required is so extreme that the situation would rarely arise again. Since then, the same defence has been used successfully in several acquittals of intoxicated men who had assaulted women. In 1995, Parliament passed amendments to the *Criminal Code* that disallow the drunkenness defence in violent offences requiring "general intent," such as assault and sexual assault.

PRECURSORS

Sexual violence is different from most other offences (with the exception of violence in the family) in that women and children are by far the most vulnerable targets. Several explanations for sexual violence have been offered. Some men who commit very violent acts of sexual aggression with extreme forms of cruelty have been found to be suffering from serious psychiatric problems or mental illness. However, sexual violence is much too common to be accounted for by mental illness in all but the most serious forms of sexual assault. Researchers have instead been looking at societal factors, particularly traditional male–female relations and social institutions, in an attempt to explain the occurrence of sexual assault.

According to sex-role theory, notions of proper masculine and feminine behaviour are learned through a process of socialization. Masculine qualities of toughness, power, and dominance over women are cultural messages that predominate in the rearing of boys in North America. Girls, on the other hand, grow up learning submissive, ladylike behaviour and accept that their responsibilities will be to maintain relationships and to serve others. Cultural messages of relationships between men and women commonly present images of men as sexually dominant. Sexual assault has been described by some researchers as an extreme manifestation of these gender dynamics (Clark and Lewis, 1977; Brownmiller, 1975; Russell, 1984).

Stereotypes and attitudes about rape victims that blame victims them- selves for assaults against them have been found to coexist with a tolerance for rape, and a greater likelihood of committing rape. These myths and stereotypes have been damaging to female victims and have helped minimize both the seriousness and extent of the problem. For example, many people continue to believe that only certain types of women get raped, that any woman who doesn't want sex can resist it if she wants to, that women ask to be raped by the way they behave or the way they dress, and that once he is sexually aroused, a man cannot control himself and it is the woman's respon- sibility to avoid rape. These attitudes about women and rape are especially strong among people who hold stereotypical beliefs about male–female rela- tionships in general, including the belief that violence and coercion in inti- mate relationships are acceptable (Burt, 1991). Controlled experiments with college students revealed that young men who accept these myths about rape were more likely to say that they would rape or force a woman into unwanted sex (Check and Malamuth, 1985).

Some research has presented evidence of a connection between the viewing of pornographic material and the acceptance of rape myths. Pornographic images often present coercion and violence in sexual relation- ships as normal and suggest that the victim desires and derives pleasure from the abuse and violence inflicted on her (Malamuth and Briere, 1986). The viewer receives positive messages about the willingness of women to be sub- jected to such abuse, and thus about the appropriateness of assaulting and degrading women. Studies have linked long-term exposure to depictions of sexual violence in which women are shown enjoying rape to increases in the acceptance of rape myths, in aggressive behaviour toward women, and in reported willingness to commit rape (Linz, 1989; Check and Guloien, 1989; Check and Malamuth, 1985). Those who don't actually commit sexual assault as a result of viewing pornography nevertheless may develop beliefs that women are legitimate victims of violence and then provide support to their peers who behave aggressively toward women. The fact that attitudes toward sexual violence can be learned through exposure to it lends support to the sex-role theory.

Even in the absence of pornography, men who relate strongly to extreme ideals of masculine toughness and dominance over women may be more likely to accept it as their right to take what they want from women sexually. They may demand obedience and submission from the women in their lives and use threats or violence to achieve it. Rape has been described as a method through which the perpetrator can overcompensate for underlying feelings of inadequacy and can express his insecurities about his own power, authority, and identity (Groth and Birnbaum, 1979). Sexual violence enables him to exhibit dominance over someone less powerful than himself and to re-establish his masculinity at the same time. Through sexual violence he proves to himself, his victim, and the world that he is a real man.

Sexual assaults often occur in the context of alcohol. Alcohol itself cannot be said to be a direct cause of sexual aggression, because there are many other social and personality factors that precede the drinking occasion. However, alcohol can contribute directly to a woman's risk of sexual violence by diminishing a potential offender's inhibitions with respect to violent behaviour and by giving him a socially approved excuse (drunkenness) to use in the aftermath of the assault. At the same time, intoxication may cause a blurring of perceptions and communication skills that may increase the possibility that expectations about sexual activity will be misinterpreted and forced sex will result. If the woman is intoxicated, she may appear more sexually available and easier to seduce (Benson, Charlton, and Goodhart, 1992). In a practical sense, being intoxicated also decreases the woman's control over the situation and impairs her ability to flee or to defend herself.

THE EVENT

How widespread is sexual assault in Canada? Through random anonymous surveys of the population, we can make reasonably reliable estimates of the prevalence of certain crimes in the population. Victimization surveys are not subject to the same measurement problems as police statistics, which count only those incidents that police detect themselves or have brought to their attention by victims, bystanders, or other witnesses. In victimization surveys, usually conducted by telephone, a sample of the population is randomly selected and asked about their experiences of crime and violence—whether they reported criminal incidents to the police, reasons for not calling on the police for help, the impact of the experience on them, and their perceptions of their personal safety. Random selection helps ensure that the responses of the sample are representative of the population at large and that generalizations can be made about the extent and the nature of crime.

Statistics Canada's Violence Against Women (VAW) survey was designed to provide reliable estimates about the extent and the nature of sexual and physical violence against women in Canada. Respondents were interviewed about their experiences of violence at the hands of strangers, husbands and common-law partners, dates and boyfriends, and other men. Women were asked to report on any incident of violence they had experienced since the age of 16. According to the VAW survey, a total of 39% of Canadian women have had at least one experience of sexual assault in their adult lifetime. (See Table 8-1).

As Table 8-1 indicates, over four million Canadian women have been sexually assaulted in one or both of the ways measured by the VAW survey. One-quarter of all women have received unwanted sexual touching from a man, and the same proportion have been sexually attacked in a way that included violence or the threat of violence. As the percentage who reported each type of assault does not add to the total of 39%, it is evident that a great many women have been sexually assaulted more than once. In fact, almost 60% of all women who have been sexually assaulted have been assaulted more than once, and 26% were assaulted *four times or more*.

THE VIOLENCE AGAINST WOMEN SURVEY

In 1993, Statistics Canada interviewed 12,300 women aged 18 and over across the country by telephone about their experiences of sexual and physical violence. Definitions of violent offences used in this survey followed legal definitions. The following questions were used to make estimates about the prevalence and the nature of sexual assault:

Unwanted sexual touching
Has a [male stranger, known to you other than a spouse, date, or boyfriend] ever touched you against your will in any sexual way, such as unwanted touching, grabbing, kissing, or fondling?

Sexual attack
Has a [male stranger, date or boyfriend, spouse, or other man known to you] ever forced you or attempted to force you into any sexual activity by threatening you, holding you down, or hurting you in some way?

The question about unwanted sexual touching was not asked for spouses, dates, or boyfriends.

**Table 8-1 Number and Percentage of Canadian Women (18 years +) Who Have
Experienced Sexual Assault, 1993**

Type of Sexual Assault	Number (in millions)	Percentage
Total women	**10.5**	**100**
Total sexual assault	4.1	39
Unwanted sexual touching	2.6	25
Sexual attack	2.5	24

Note: Figures do not add to totals because many women had experienced more than one type of sexual assault.

Source: Violence Against Women survey, Statistics Canada, 1993.

The VAW survey collected data on both victims and the incident itself. These data describe which individuals are at greatest risk of sexual assault and which settings present the greatest risk. By far the highest rates of sexual violence are found among young women aged 18 to 24. In the one-year period preceding the survey, 18% of young women experienced a sexual assault, over three times the national rate of 5%. The percentages drop off sharply for older women (see Figure 8-1).

Persons known to the woman pose the greatest threat of sexual assault. Altogether, women were more likely to have been sexually assaulted by men

Figure 8-1 Twelve-Month Rates of Sexual Assault by Age of Victim, 1993

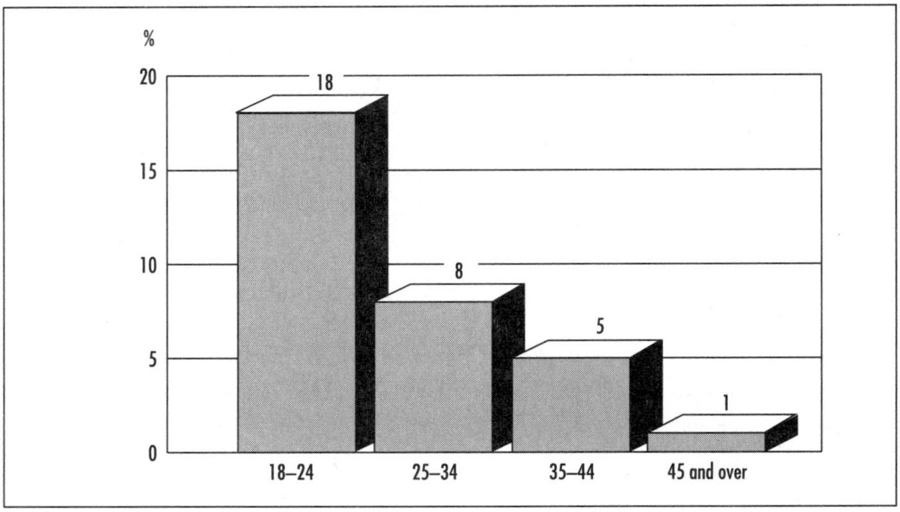

Source: Violence Against Women survey, Statistics Canada, 1993.

known to them than by strangers. Twelve percent of women have been sexually assaulted by a date or boyfriend, 8% by a husband or common-law partner, and 21% by another man known to them as compared to 19% who were assaulted by a stranger (see Figure 8-2). Altogether, 31% of women have been sexually assaulted by men known to them.

A private home is the most common location for sexual assault. Altogether, 35% of sexual assaults took place in a private home, either the woman's (15%), her attacker's (11%), or the home of someone else (9%). One in ten occurred in a car, and a similar proportion at the woman's place of work (see Figure 8-3). About four in ten took place in public places such as bars, the street, and public buildings. For some, sexual violence is an occupational hazard, while for others it is not an uncommon risk associated with being on the street, at a bar or dance, or using public buildings.

Eleven percent of women were physically injured in some way during the assault. This figure was considerably higher in the case of the more serious sexual attacks (22%) than in cases of unwanted sexual touching (4%). The type of sexual attack that was most likely to result in injury was that perpetrated by a stranger (27%). In most cases, injuries were described as bruises (82%), internal injuries (13%), or cuts, scratches, or burns (27%).[1] In one in five cases, the injuries were serious enough to warrant medical attention.

Figure 8-2 Relationship of Perpetrator to Victim in Cases of Sexual Assault, 1993

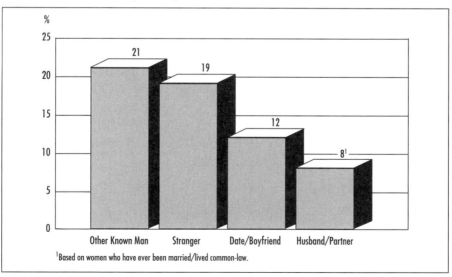

¹Based on women who have ever been married/lived common-law.

Source: Violence Against Women survey, Statistics Canada, 1993.

Figure 8-3   Location of Sexual Assaults, Percent Distribution, 1993

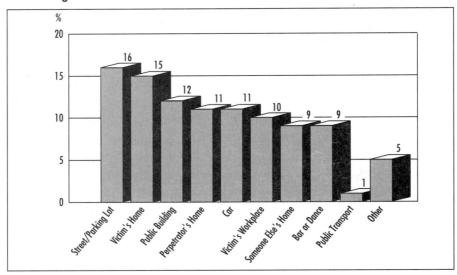

Source: Violence Against Women survey, Statistics Canada, 1993.

Weapons were rarely used by sexual attackers. In only 3% of all incidents of sexual assault was a weapon present; almost one-half of these sexual assaults were committed by men who were strangers to the victim, a finding that helps explain the higher rate of injury among stranger assaults. Knives and other sharp instruments were the type of weapons most often used (half of all incidents with weapons). The number of guns used in sexual assaults was too small for statistically reliable estimates to be made.

Four in ten (43%) of incidents of sexual assault involved a man who, in the opinion of the victim, had been drinking at the time of the incident. Perpetrators were more likely to have been drinking at the time of the more serious sexual attacks (47%) than at the time of unwanted sexual touching (39%). The situation most likely to occur within the context of drinking was sexual attacks by dates and boyfriends (50%).

THE AFTERMATH

Since the 1970s, support services for victims of sexual assault have been increasing at a steady pace. With their genesis in grassroots community groups, rape-crisis centres (known more recently as sexual-assault support centres) began to spring up across North America. These centres aim to provide counselling and support for women who have been assaulted, to increase public awareness about sexual violence, to break down stereotypes, to eliminate biases among criminal justice and other helping professionals, and to lobby for legislative reform. The centres have been effective in changing the way the helping systems respond to cases of sexual assault. Most police departments across the country now have special programs to train officers in the appropriate handling of sexual-assault cases. Many hospitals have specialized treatment teams that have been trained to deal sensitively with victims and to gather evidence for use by the courts. Some communities have instituted protocols and agreements among various agencies to ensure a coordinated, sensitive response.

Despite these activities, very few cases of sexual assault are reported to the police. According to the VAW survey, only 6% of all sexual assaults were reported (11% of sexual attacks and 4% of incidents of unwanted sexual touching). Women were more likely to talk to friends (51%) or family (38%) about the experience. Small proportions also sought help from doctors (6%) or social services (6%). One-quarter of sexual-assault victims had told no one at all about the experience before disclosing it to an interviewer, a finding that demonstrates the very hidden nature of this offence.

Women declined to report crimes of sexual assault to the police for a variety of reasons. Some believed that the incident was too minor to report (more common in unwanted sexual touching), or that the police couldn't do anything about it; others wished to keep the incident private, or chose to deal with it in some other way (see Table 8-2). Shame, embarrassment, and a wish to avoid contact with the police and the courts were reasons cited more frequently by victims of sexual attack than victims of unwanted sexual touching.

The VAW survey is a snapshot survey and cannot trace changes in reporting trends over time, but police statistics suggest that rates of reported sexual assault have increased dramatically over the past decade. There has been a clear increase in the rate of sexual assault since the passage of the reform legislation in 1983. In 1993, a total of 34,764 incidents of sexual assault were reported to the police in Canada. This figure can be calculated as 121 incidents for every 100,000 people in the population, up from 11,932 incidents reported in 1983, or 48 per 100,000 population (see Table 8-3). Thus there has been a 152% increase in the rate of sexual assault reported to the police over the ten-year period. Upon closer scrutiny, it appears that the increase occurred exclusively in offences coded by the police at the first level

**Table 8-2   Victims' Reasons for Not Reporting Sexual Assault to Police,
Percent Distribution, 1993**

Reasons	Total Sexual Assault	Sexual Attack	Unwanted Sexual Touching
Too minor	44	28	53
Didn't think the police could do anything	12	14	11
Wanted to keep the incident private	12	17	8
Dealt with through other channels	12	12	12
Shame or embarrassment	9	15	6
Didn't want involvement with police or courts	9	12	7
Wouldn't be believed	6	8	5
Fear of the perpetrator	3	6	2
Didn't want him arrested or jailed	3	3	2
Didn't want or need help	2	—*	3

* not statistically reliable.

Note: Columns do not total 100% because more than one reason could be given.

Source: J.V. Roberts, "Criminal Justice Processing of Sexual Assault Cases," *Juristat Service Bulletin* 14 (7). Ottawa: Canadian Centre for Justice Statistics, 1994.

of seriousness. Rates of sexual-assault level 1 increased from 43 to 117 per 100,000 population, an increase of 172%. Rates of sexual-assault levels 2 and 3 have remained constant at about 4 per 100,000 and 2 per 100,000, respectively, over the same ten-year period (see Figure 8-4).

In the five years prior to law reform, rates of rape and indecent assault increased only 18%, from 38 to 45 per 100,000. How can we explain the dramatic increase in the rate of sexual assault—and level 1 sexual assault in particular—since 1983? It is unlikely that the passage of the new legislation would have coincided with a real increase in acts of sexual aggression (Johnson, 1996). It would appear on the surface that the legal reforms, and the publicity surrounding their introduction, have had the desired effect of encouraging victims of assault to seek redress through the criminal justice system. An alternative explanation is that both victims and the police have interpreted the new law to include a wider range of behaviours that were not included under the previous offences of rape and indecent assault. For example, under the new legislation, charges can be laid against men who sexually

Table 8-3   Number and Rate of Incidents of Sexual Assault[1] Reported to Police, Canada, 1978–1993

Year	Number	Rate per 100,000 population
1978	8,961	38
1979	9,754	42
1980	10,164	42
1981	10,550	44
1982	10,990	45
1983	11,932	48
1984	14,793	59
1985	18,248	73
1986	20,530	82
1987	22,369	88
1988	24,898	96
1989	26,795	101
1990	27,843	104
1991	30,351	113
1992	34,355	121
1993	34,764	121

[1] Includes rape and indecent assault in the years 1978 to 1982, and sexual assault levels 1, 2, and 3 in the years 1983 to 1993.

Source: Uniform Crime Reporting survey, Canadian Centre for Justice Statistics, 1993.

Figure 8-4   Rates of Sexual Assault Reported to Police per 100,000 Population, 1978–1993

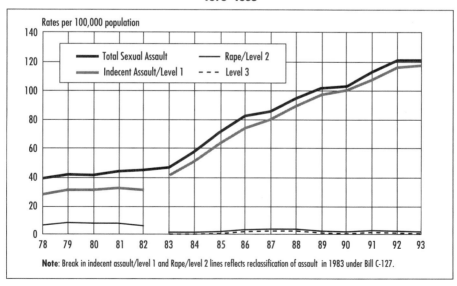

Note: Break in indecent assault/level 1 and Rape/level 2 lines reflects reclassification of assault in 1983 under Bill C-127.

Source: Violence Against Women survey, Statistics Canada, 1993.

assault their wives, and, in some cases, male as well as female victims. Since almost two-thirds of sexual assaults reported to the police involve victims under the age of 18, there may have been a dramatic increase in the reporting of sexual assaults against children (Roberts and Gebotys, 1992; Roberts and Grossman, 1994).

Investigations undertaken by the Department of Justice in the evaluation of the reform legislation suggest that these factors alone are not sufficient to have caused the sharp increase in reported cases of sexual assault. Research suggests that incidents now recorded as sexual assaults by the police do not differ greatly from the kinds of incidents formerly recorded as rape or indecent assault. The number of cases in which the suspect was the husband of the victim, or the victim was male, remain very small (5% or less in both cases). Data on the characteristics of victims were not compiled prior to the implementation of the new legislation, so it is impossible to confirm or refute the hypothesis that the increase is due to a significant rise in reports of child sexual abuse. However, research findings suggest that the increase in child victims has been relatively small and cannot explain the dramatic increase in overall reports of sexual assault (Roberts and Gebotys, 1992; Roberts and Grossman, 1994; Department of Justice, 1985).

Given the lack of an obvious direct cause for the sharp increase in reported sexual assault, and given the fact that the increase took place simultaneously with the implementation of a legal change, it is tempting to conclude that the new law is directly responsible for changing the attitudes of the public toward both the nature of the offence and the law as a means of achieving redress. An alternative explanation, however, appears more plausible. Legal reform tends not to precede public opinion, but rather to be an expression of it. It generally comes about as a result of widespread dissatisfaction with existing legal codes, intensive lobbying on the part of interest groups, and lengthy public debate. Clark and Hepworth (1994:117) cite a number of historical factors that coincided with or preceded the change in the law, and that must be taken into account when evaluating the impact of legal reform:

1. the changing social, economic, and political status of women;
2. increased media scrutiny of the treatment of women in the courts;
3. heightened awareness of and focus on victims of crime, particularly female victims, accompanied by government initiatives and services;
4. the growth in police departments across the country of investigation units specially trained in the investigation of complaints, the gathering of evidence, and the treatment of victims;

5. the expansion of sexual-assault support centres;
6. the growth in hospitals of specialized treatment teams trained to deal sensitively with victims of sexual assault; and
7. intensive lobbying by women's groups, which preceded the passage of the rape reform legislation.

In view of these important social changes, it would be erroneous to attribute the dramatic and steady increase in the reporting of sexual assaults exclusively to the success of law reform. While important changes were brought about by the law, analysis of sexual assault statistics cannot be divorced from the context in which the legal reform took place. Significant social changes, of which legal reform was but one, have brought about growing efforts to eradicate the biases that have confronted sexual assault complainants in the justice system and to provide better treatment and services in all the helping systems. All of these factors may have had an effect on victims' willingness to report sexual assault, even in the absence of law reform.

According to the VAW survey, charges were laid against a perpetrator in 34% of all cases of sexual assault reported to the police. Incidents were more likely to result in charges if the perpetrator was known to the woman (53%) than if he was a stranger (24%). This difference is no doubt due to the fact that in stranger assaults police are least able to make a positive identification that could lead to an arrest.

A perpetrator appeared in court in 46% of all cases in which charges were laid. Scant information on sentencing patterns is available in Canada. According to a study of provincial courts in six provinces conducted by the Canadian Centre for Justice Statistics, a majority of convictions for sexual assault result in the offender serving a prison sentence (Roberts, 1994). Approximately nine in ten of the more serious level 2 and 3 offences and 60% of level 1 offences resulted in incarceration (see Table 8-4). Probation was the most common sentence for level 1 offences, but this disposition frequently accompanied a jail term. A substantial proportion of all sexual assault convictions resulted in a prohibition order pertaining to such factors as possession of a firearm or a peace bond. Other community sanctions were rare for sexual offences with the exception of suspended sentences which frequently accompany probation orders. The median prison sentence was five years for level 3 offences, two years for level 2 offences, and six months for level 1 offences.

Historically, victims of sexual assault have been critical of police handling of these cases. According to the VAW survey, 56% of women who reported an incident of sexual assault to the police were satisfied with the police response while 44% were dissatisfied. Among the latter group, the

Table 8-4 Court Disposition for Sexual Assault Cases Heard in Provincial Court, Percent Distribution, 1991–1992

Disposition	Sexual Assault Level 1	Sexual Assault Level 2	Sexual Assault Level 3[1]
Prison	60	94	89
Probation	73	35	33
Prohibition	19	26	33
Community service order	2	—	—
Fine	15	2	6
Suspended sentence	20	2	—
Conditional discharge	3	—	—
Absolute discharge	1	—	—

[1] Figures are based on small counts and should be interpreted cautiously.

Note: Columns do not total 100% because of multiple sentences.

Source: J.V. Roberts, "Criminal Justice Processing of Sexual Assault Cases," *Juristat Service Bulletin* 14 (7). Ottawa: Canadian Centre for Justice Statistics, 1994.

most common complaint was that the police were not supportive enough (55%). Again, it should be pointed out that police performance in the VAW survey was evaluated on the basis of earlier, as well as recent cases, and, as such, may not reflect with complete accuracy police performance as it stands today.

SUMMARY AND CONCLUSIONS
■ ■ ■

In seeking to explain sexual violence, researchers and theorists have focused primarily on societal factors and sex-role stereotyping. Sex-role theory suggests that the impetus for sexual violence is to be found in the acceptance of certain rape myths and in the extreme acting out of certain masculine qualities such as toughness, power, and dominance over women. According to Statistics Canada's national Violence Against Women survey, sexual assault affects a significant proportion of the female population, with young women being at greatest risk. Sexual assaults often occur in private homes, and a majority of incidents involve men known to the victims.

Over four million women have had at least one experience of sexual assault since turning 16; of these women, 2.5 million of these have suffered a sexual attack that included outright violence or the threat of violence. The majority of sexual assaults never come to the attention of the police. Some women may feel that the incident was too minor or that the police won't be able to do anything about it, while others may be reluctant to deal with the police or courts. Many women never tell anyone at all. Despite the apparent lack of confidence in the justice system on the part of women who have been sexually assaulted, an increasing number of sexual-assault incidents are being reported to the police every year. The majority of those who are convicted of sexual assault receive prison sentences, often in conjunction with probation orders.

NOTES

[1] Figures add to more than 100% because women respondents in the VAW survey were able to report more than one kind of injury.

PART IV

Property crime accounts for about 60% of the total crime that occurs in Canada each year. While less serious than violent crime in terms of its consequences for the victim, property crime creates fear and highlights individual vulnerability. In this section, we will examine the different types of property crime—namely, break and enter, fraud, theft, and auto crime. Particular emphasis will be given to the characteristics of these crimes, their overall impact, and strategies for preventing them.

PROPERTY CRIME

BREAK AND ENTER

by Peter Greenberg

Of all of the property crimes, break and enter is considered the most serious. After reviewing legal definitions of this crime, Peter Greenberg considers the different offender types and the criteria that professional burglars use when determining whether to hit a specific target. Characteristics of the event, its impact on the victim, and the problem of nonreporting to police are also examined. Greenberg concludes with a discussion of the steps that can be taken to reduce the chances that this crime will occur.

The incidence of crime and the ability of the justice system to respond to increasing levels is at the forefront of the current political agenda. Indeed, the effectiveness of existing legislation in dealing with crime is being debated with an urgency similar to that associated with the national debt. As Figure 9-1 shows, the crime of break and enter (B&E) constitutes a significant proportion of reported crime in Canada. The following discussion of B&E will focus on the location of incidents, the parties involved, the extent of damage and victimization, current perceptions of public safety, and recommended approaches to crime prevention.

Figure 9-1 Percent Distribution of Reported Crime by Most Serious Offences in Canada, 1993

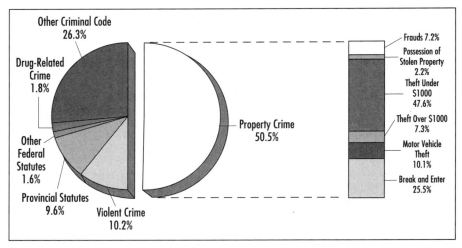

Other Criminal Code 26.3%

Drug-Related Crime 1.8%

Other Federal Statutes 1.6%

Provincial Statutes 9.6%

Violent Crime 10.2%

Property Crime 50.5%

Frauds 7.2%

Possession of Stolen Property 2.2%

Theft Under $1000 47.6%

Theft Over $1000 7.3%

Motor Vehicle Theft 10.1%

Break and Enter 25.5%

Source: Uniform Crime Reporting survey, Canadian Centre for Justice Statistics, 1993.

154

Property Crime

DEFINITIONS

An individual commits B&E when he or she gains forcible entry into any private or commercial dwelling, or any other building, motor vehicle, or trailer, with the possible intention of committing another offence. The following are examples of B&E:

1. entering a private home by smashing a window; assaulting the occupant; and proceeding to steal jewellery, credit cards, and some cash;
2. gaining entry to an office building by destroying the front lock, and then going on to burn down the building;
3. gaining entry to an apartment building's garage, then breaking a car window and stealing the vehicle's stereo;
4. entering a school through an open window on a weekend, then destroying the audiovisual equipment and spraying the walls with graffiti; and
5. breaking the front lock and door chain of a private dwelling and killing the occupant.

In each of the above examples, B&E is essential to the commencement and completion of the criminal event, although the offence of B&E itself may not be the most serious violation. In most cases, however, the criminal event is one of "burglary."

The *Criminal Code* identifies B&E as an indictable offence, indicating that the crime is deemed a serious crime and that the penalties attached to it are severe. An individual who unlawfully breaks into another person's home, assaults the occupant causing serious physical injury, and steals all cash and jewellery is liable to life imprisonment for the crime of B&E itself. The other violations call for their own penalties. If the location is not a private dwelling, the penalty for the same crime may be fourteen years' imprisonment. Further, any individual who simply enters a private home with the intent to commit an indictable offence is liable to imprisonment for ten years whether the intended offence was completed or not. In its analysis of B&E as a criminal event, this chapter will consider two types of offenders: those who commit B&E in order to engage in burglary or another nonviolent crime, and those who use B&E as a stepping stone to a more serious offence such as assault causing bodily harm, sexual assault, or murder.

PRECURSORS

OFFENDER TYPES

Is there a typical burglar? Many researchers have classified offenders as "occasional" versus "persistent" burglars (Waller and Weiler, 1984). Persistent offenders, who appear to have been disadvantaged in several areas of their lives, tend to begin their criminal careers at an early age. Most offenders in this category are males who are aggressive, possibly predatory, and willing to take risks. They are thus more likely to confront another person during the commission of their crimes. For Cromwell, Olson, and Avary (1991), the potential offender is either "rational" or "opportunistic." The rational burglar plans in advance all aspects of the crime, whereas the opportunistic burglar hits a specific target on the spur of the moment because the target is clearly vulnerable at that time.

Burglars can be placed into one of three categories (Cromwell, Olson, and Avary, 1991). The *novice* is usually a younger burglar who seizes an immediate opportunity when committing the crime. This offender is often inexperienced or relatively new to the trade and may require assistance from someone else in order to fence the stolen goods. The *journeyman* is a seasoned thief who searches for vulnerable locations, thereby creating his or her own opportunities. This individual has developed strong contacts for fencing the stolen property. Finally, the *professional* is a rational burglar who uses superior technical and organizational skills to commit the crime. The professional's contacts for fencing are well established and reliable. In addition, this burglar is likely known in the law-enforcement community and considered to be a "professional."

TIMING AND MOTIVATION

It is generally accepted that residential burglary is profitable and requires little real technical skill. Further, police clearance rates (i.e., cases solved by police with the possible laying of a criminal charge) are relatively low (Waller and Okihiro, 1978, Statistics Canada, 1994). While it is difficult to pinpoint the timing of burglaries, research results indicate that these events can occur at almost any time and are a function of occupancy. In other words, the immediate concern is whether the place is occupied or not, because most burglars do not wish to confront anyone while in the dwelling.

Burglary is generally committed for the purpose of obtaining either money or portable goods that can be easily fenced to obtain money. The proceeds of a burglary are often used to purchase drugs or alcohol, which may themselves be precipitating factors in the event. Other strong motivations include the need for the approval of one's peers or fellow gang members or simply the thrill and excitement of participating in the activity.

THE DECISION TO ENTER

Cromwell, Olson, and Avary (1991) outline several factors that may contribute to a burglar's decision to enter or avoid a specific dwelling. First, the vast majority of burglars would not knowingly break into an occupied residence. There are many methods that can be used to probe for occupancy. If someone answers the door of the potential target, the would-be burglar might pose as someone lost and in need of directions or possibly ask for a nonexistent person. Should entry be obtained, the burglar will evaluate the contents of the residence and return later when it is unoccupied.

The technique of gaining entry may be determined by the burglar's capacities and level of experience. For example, a desperate drug addict might only be able to smash a window and take whatever can be taken quickly, while an experienced burglar can break in without leaving signs of forced entry. Further, the skilled burglar might remove small articles, the loss of which might not be detected for some time following the break-in.

The decision-making process might also be informed by insider knowledge relating to, for instance, the schedule of a location's occupants and its level of security. For example, a burglar might decide that a home protected by alarms or sophisticated locks is not worth the risk. According to Cromwell et al., the variation in security systems and hardware may be an issue only for the opportunistic burglar, whose decision to break and enter is a function of the apparent vulnerability of the location. The rational burglar, in contrast, will take steps to counteract the level of "target hardening" and will actively seek methods to overcome better security. Regardless, most burglars are said to be opportunistic and, as such, their decision to enter will be affected by a location's perceived vulnerability. Research suggests that the decision to hit a specific target is based more on risk assessment as to the level of vulnerability than on the potential value of the stolen goods. Most burglars assume that something worth stealing exists in almost all locations.

According to Cromwell et al., there are three considerations in assessing the risk of a specific location. *Surveillability* is the extent to which a location is observable by neighbours and others expected to be in the neighbourhood at the time the crime is to be committed. Professional burglars may strive to demonstrate that they "fit into" the neighbourhood (e.g., by posing as a person who inspects meters), or they may choose to conceal their presence (e.g., by taking advantage of natural coverage such as shrubs). The extent to which a would-be target accommodates such strategies will enter into the burglar's decision making. *Occupancy* is the second consideration. Most burglars will assess the presence of vehicles, noises from within the location, and any other signs indicating the presence of occupants. As noted earlier, the majority of burglars seek to avoid confrontation. Finally, *accessibility* is important to the decision to enter. The potential target will thus be considered in terms of such factors as level of target hardening and location with respect to the street and other houses. If any of these factors are unfavourable, the burglar will likely decide to pass on the specific location.

THE EVENT

In 1993, there were approximately 406,000 incidents reported by police to Statistics Canada in which B&E was the most serious offence. As expected, the majority of these (59%) consisted of residential break-ins and a further 28% consisted of business-establishment break-ins. While high, the officially reported national rate has fallen almost 9% since 1991. Nonetheless, this crime accounts for 15% of all *Criminal Code* incidents reported to police.

According to data reported by police in 1993, the majority of B&Es (95%) are committed by males; of these offenders, almost 60% are in the 18–34 age group while a further 28% are between 12 and 17. B&Es involving violence are committed mostly by adult males (82%) between the ages of 18 and 49, followed by adult females (7%), males aged 12 to 17 (7%), adults over 50 (3%), and females under 17 (1%). Adult males in the 18–49 age group also make up the majority of accused persons in nonviolent incidents (66%), followed by males 12 to 17 (27%), adult females (3%), and females under 17/offenders over 50 or under 11 (4%).

Police statistics record the presence of a victim(s) only if the event involves violence. In 1993, 55% of victims were females. Females (32%) and males (27%) in the 25–34 age group are the most often victimized. In 1993, almost 60% of victims in B&E incidents knew their attackers. The extent of personal recognition ranged from being a casual acquaintance (28%), a spouse or ex-spouse (17%), a close friend (8%), other family members, including parents and children (5%), and business acquaintances (2%). The accused was unknown to 40% of the victims.

Break and enter is generally a nonviolent crime. As noted earlier, burglars tend to want to avoid confrontation, concerning themselves first with whether or not a dwelling is occupied (Waller and Okihiro, 1978). In 1993, only 1% of B&Es involved violence. Of these incidents, the majority (54%) were classed as common assault, a less serious violent crime involving threats, shoving, and other types of physical force that do not result in significant physical injury to the victim (see Figure 9-2). A further 19% involved aggravated assault/assault with a weapon while 15% involved robbery. The most serious violent incidents, including sexual assault and sexual assault with a weapon, occurred in approximately 7% of cases.

In 1993, the General Social Survey (GSS) reported that almost 20% of all Canadian households (more than 2 million) had been subjected to some form of household victimization. The majority (29% or almost 600,000 households) identified vandalism as the form of victimization, while 26% (546,000 households) were victims of B&E. B&E rates in urban and rural settings are roughly proportional to the number of households in these areas. According to sample results, urban households accounted for 74% of B&E victimizations. Of the 1.4 million households that were not identified as either rural or urban in setting, 12% were victimized and the majority of these victimizations were not classified.

The 1993 Revised UCR survey provides data on 154,159 incidents involving at least one B&E violation. Of these incidents, 126,488 are single violations of B&E and 27,671 are multiple violations. These data indicate

Figure 9-2   Percent Distribution of Violent Crime Events in Break and Enters,[1] by Type of Violence, 1993

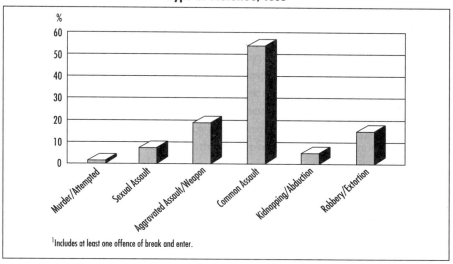

[1] Includes at least one offence of break and enter.

Source: Revised Uniform Crime Reporting survey, Canadian Centre for Justice Statistics, 1993.

that B&E is the most serious violation in almost 99% of incidents. Equally significant is the fact that B&E is the only violation in almost 82% of these events. With respect to the multiple-violation incidents, 95% are nonviolent and occur in conjunction with theft over $1,000 (43%), theft under $1,000 (40%), and mischief (9%). It should be noted that even though B&E is the only crime reported for many situations, this does not mean that nothing was taken or damaged.

The largest number of all B&E incidents (47%) occur in private residences, specifically single homes, while another 19% occur under the general classification of dwelling unit (see Figure 9-3). Commercial (e.g., stores) break-ins account for approximately 26% of incidents. The remaining 8% occur at other commercial dwellings (e.g., hotels, motels), schools, public institutions, and unknown locations.

In 1993, during events within which weapons were identified, approximately 4% of victims were faced with the threat of firearms. Knives were the weapon faced by 9% of victims, while 6% of victims were faced with clubs or similar instruments. The vast majority of victims (69%) were subjected to actual or threat of physical force. While it is true that the actual presence of serious weapons was reported to be low, almost 90% of victims of violent B&E incidents were classified as being a victim of a weapon, force, or the threat of force.

Figure 9-3 Location of Break and Enter Events, Percent Distribution, 1993

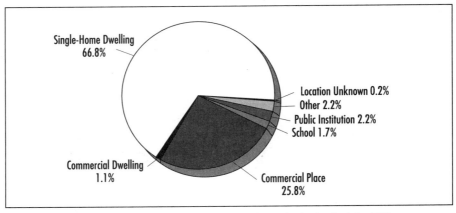

Single-Home Dwelling
66.8%

Location Unknown 0.2%
Other 2.2%
Public Institution 2.2%
School 1.7%

Commercial Dwelling
1.1%

Commercial Place
25.8%

Source: Revised Uniform Crime Reporting survey, Canadian Centre for Justice Statistics, 1993.

It is also interesting to note that only 6% of all B&E incidents and 13% of violent incidents included positive identification of the existence of alcohol and/or drugs. Approximately 70% of violent occurrences were associated with incidents of assault or aggravated assault. A small percentage of victims (4%) were involved, to some degree, with drugs and/or alcohol. It is important to note that the determination of drug and/or alcohol involvement on the part of the accused is often difficult to assess, especially if significant time has elapsed between the actual event and the suspect's arrest. Accordingly, statistics attempting to measure this dimension must be considered with caution.

To summarize, B&E events are generally nonviolent burglaries that for the most part occur in residential locations and result in theft, mischief, and/or damage. While weapons are present in most violent incidents, the majority of victims are subjected to the threat or actual use of less serious physical force such as pushing or shoving. In addition, police statistics indicate very low usage of drugs and/or alcohol during the commission of these crimes, with the rate increasing slightly if the event becomes violent.

THE AFTERMATH

There is a huge financial burden associated with property crime. Statistics Canada data indicate that the $2.6 billion reported for losses due to B&E in 1993 accounted for approximately 38% of all property crime loss and was

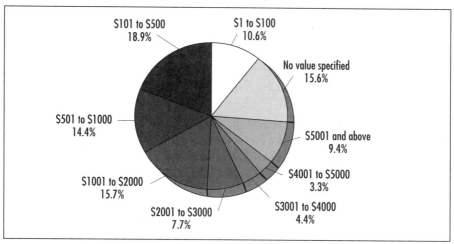

Figure 9-4 Value of Goods Stolen During Break and Enter Events, Percent Distribution, 1993

$101 to $500
18.9%

$1 to $100
10.6%

No value specified
15.6%

$501 to $1000
14.4%

$5001 and above
9.4%

$4001 to $5000
3.3%

$1001 to $2000
15.7%

$3001 to $4000
4.4%

$2001 to $3000
7.7%

Source: Revised Uniform Crime Reporting survey, Canadian Centre for Justice Statistics, 1993.

second. only to the $3.1 billion reported for theft. According to police-reported data, the dollar value of stolen property was zero in 15.6% of all B&E incidents (see Figure 9-4). Almost 44% of incidents recorded a monetary loss of between $1 and $1,000, while 15.7% of incidents recorded losses between $1,000 and $2,000 and 7.7% recorded losses between $2,000 and $3,000. In total, more than 75% reported monetary losses of less than $2,000, while more than 9% reported losses of greater than $5,000.

Excluding incidents with no dollar loss due to theft, the average value of property losses due to B&E was approximately $2,600. However, almost 90% of all incidents reported $5,000 or less in losses due to stolen property. Of these incidents the average dollar value of losses was approximately $1,225. For the most part, items stolen during these events included radios or televisions and stereo players (27%), Canadian currency (11%), jewellery (9%), machinery and tools (8%), and other unclassified property (6%). The most valuable property stolen was not known in 10% of the cases.

B&E might also result in structural or other property damage during the commission of the crime. Sample data indicate that, where structural or other property damage was recorded in 1993, the average amount of losses sustained was approximately $310. The majority of these incidents (72%) reported damages between $1 and $1,000; for this group, the average amount of damages was approximately $180. Of all reported incidents,

27.6% either did not report or reported no monetary loss resulting from damages.

IMPACT ON THE VICTIM

Regarding physical injury, detailed police statistics refer only to victimization incidents during which the individual victim was present. The detailed statistics provide an indication as to the level of injury in B&E incidents. The majority of victims (54%) received no injuries (or the extent of their injuries was not known), while 40% received only minor injuries. Approximately 6% of the victims received injuries classified as major; a very small percentage (less than 0.5%) resulted in death.

While it appears that the extent of physical injury is generally minor or negligible, it is nonetheless insufficient to label these events as nonviolent simply because of the absence of physical injury. The emotional trauma and personal stress resulting from B&E crimes can be devastating both to the victim and the victim's family. Continuing fear on the part of victims can lead to diminished mobility and/or a complete change in lifestyle. Some victims, fearful of another incident, develop an unhealthy preoccupation with security. Not just victims but family and friends as well may experience heightened feelings of suspicion, fear, and vulnerability.

NONREPORTING OF INCIDENTS

As noted earlier, the 1993 GSS reported that just under 550,000 households in Canada were victimized by B&E. Equally significant, however, is the finding that 32% of these incidents (representing approximately 175,000 households) were not reported to police. This figure seems alarmingly high given the current elevated placement of crime prevention in most federal, provincial, and municipal political agendas. Even more alarming is the fact that, at 32% nonreporting, all the other categorizations of victimization had a higher rate of nonreporting.

The reasons for nonreporting are varied. Those who do not report crime incidents to the police generally feel that the losses due to the victimization are likely to be outweighed by the burden of resolving these incidents through the normal channels available in the justice system. Figure 9-5 shows that the most common reason for the nonreporting of B&E is the feeling that an incident is too minor to warrant police involvement. The next most prevalent reasons were (1) the wish to deal with the event in another way, (2) the

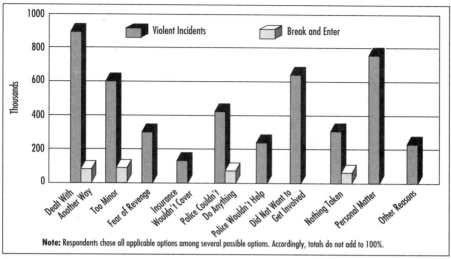

Figure 9-5 Number of Criminal Victimizations Not Reported to Police, 1993

Violent Incidents   Break and Enter

Thousands

Note: Respondents chose all applicable options among several possible options. Accordingly, totals do not add to 100%.

Source: Canadian General Social Survey, 1993.

sense that the police would be unable to resolve the situation in a satisfactory manner, and (3) the attitude that since nothing was taken in the course of the incident there was no point in pursuing the matter.

PREVENTION

There are several measures that can be utilized to lessen the likelihood that a home, business, or public building will be victimized by B&E. Most Canadian police services offer practical advice to local communities on improving security, particularly by lessening the opportunity for victimization to occur. Burglars assess situations quickly and avoid targets that present difficulty or high risk.

Making one's home less inviting by reducing the opportunity for B&E is often referred to as "target hardening." The extent to which private residents secure their homes is based on needs, budget, general lifestyle, and relative feelings of insecurity. Businesses obviously have different and more extensive security requirements. Preventive measures range from expensive electronic home or business security systems to window bars, upgraded locks, visible window or door braces, and motion-sensing external lights.

Other less obvious measures can be employed to send a message that the house is occupied or could become occupied at any time. For example, light timers raise the possibility that someone is in the house (continued newspaper delivery will, if left unattended, have the opposite effect). Regular snow removal suggests that there is ongoing activity around the house. The presence of garden hoses or inexpensive lawn equipment by the garage, by the side of the house, or even in the yard itself also suggests occupancy.

Some communities have implemented Neighbourhood Watch programs in which participants are encouraged to be aware of likely targets (vacationing neighbours, homes that are unoccupied most of the day) and to ask questions immediately whenever they detect suspicious persons or events. Finally, the police promote Operation Identification programs, which involve engraving on valuable items specific identification numbers (driver's licence numbers are recommended because they can be quickly accessed and traced). An Operation Identification sticker, like its Neighbourhood Watch counterpart, might deter a burglar from breaking and entering, due to the many problems associated with "unloading" goods that have been identified as stolen.

The above measures, while not guaranteed, are steps that will decrease the likelihood that a specific dwelling or set of dwellings will become a target for burglary. In a larger sense, of course, these measures will tend to displace crime rather than prevent it.

SUMMARY AND CONCLUSIONS
■ ■ ■

Criminal events that commence with B&E generally do not extend in level of seriousness beyond theft or mischief. Yet while these events are for the most part nonviolent, they can have devastating effects on the victimized household or business not only in terms of financial losses but also in terms of emotional stress and trauma.

In most cases, breaking and entering is a means of committing theft, mischief, or other damage. The majority of persons accused in these events are males between the ages of 18 and 34. Most burglars are opportunistic in that they act immediately upon assessing a location as vulnerable and unoccupied. Drugs and/or alcohol are generally not significant factors, although there is evidence of some drug/alcohol use in violent B&E incidents. In addition, the majority of the violent events are common assaults or less serious violent crimes involving the use of physical force rather than weapons.

Most victims in violent B&E events know their attackers to some degree. While many victims are spouses, ex-spouses, or family members, almost as many are casual acquaintances. With respect to the level of injury reported in

B&E incidents, the majority of victims receive either no injuries or minor ones.

A significant proportion of criminal incidents are not reported to the police—a finding that raises questions about public confidence in the ability of the criminal justice system to effectively deal with these incidents. Despite the existence of measures that can be used to decrease the likelihood of victimization, fears about personal safety among the general public appear to be on the rise. Clearly, restoring public faith in the justice system should be at or near the top of the Canadian political agenda.

FRAUD

by Paul McPhie

Fraud is a crime that involves the acquisition of property through deceit or falsehood. In this chapter, Paul McPhie focuses on the types of fraud "that pose the greatest threat of financial loss to the largest numbers of targets." Particular attention is given to those types of fraud that are on the increase, including credit-card fraud, computer/telecommunications fraud, and telemarketing fraud. UCR data are used as a basis for discussion of target groups, dollar losses, and police clearance rates, among other topics.

The media-reported dollar value of losses through fraud committed by individuals and organized crime is beginning to compete with stories and dollar values normally associated with drug crimes. Collective annual losses, depending on the type of fraud, are not infrequently in the hundreds of millions of dollars, and have given rise to specialized crime and security units dealing solely with certain types of fraud. Most fraud, however, is still practised by individuals or small groups who pass bad cheques; use found, stolen, or altered credit or bank cards; or who misrepresent themselves in some manner during financial transactions. Being nonviolent in nature, fraud offences attract media attention only when dollar amounts are very large and when the modus operandi and/or the plight of victims are deemed newsworthy. Nonetheless, fraud can be personally devastating for many victims, some of whom do not report their losses.

DEFINITIONS

Fraud may be defined as any attempt to obtain goods, services, or financial gain through deceit or falsehood. The Uniform Crime Reporting (UCR) survey focuses mainly on data on and characteristics of three types of fraud: cheque fraud, credit-card fraud, and "other" fraud. Cheque fraud involves the fraudulent use of a promissory note (cheque), traveller's cheque, money order, postal order, or any facsimile of a cheque. Credit-card fraud involves the fraudulent use of plastic cards, plates or coupon books issued to obtain on credit money, goods, or services, either upon the direct presentation of the card or through an automated teller machine. "Other" fraud encompasses such crimes as breach of trust, false pretenses, forgery, destroying or falsifying books and documents, trademark forgery, unauthorized use of computers, mail fraud, telemarketing fraud, insurance fraud, and fraudulent manipulation of the stock exchange.

It is not possible here to catalogue or address all the types of fraud that beset Canadians. Attention will focus, rather, upon those types of fraud that pose the greatest threat of financial loss to the largest number of targets, those that preoccupy the police and other investigators to the greatest degree, and those that involve a high social cost in their aftermath.

PRECURSORS

Unlike the motivation behind many forms of violent crime, most property crime, including fraud, is motivated by the simple desire for personal gain. Ideally, from the offender's viewpoint, the returns should outweigh the risk and effort expended on the crime. There may be additional, more subtle factors that lead one to commit property crime, including the adrenalin rush brought on by the planning and successful execution of the crime, and even the follow-up honours accorded by the offender's subculture.

A good deal of fraud, such as the one-time use of a found credit card or the "padding" of an otherwise legitimate insurance claim, is opportunistic. This is not to excuse such practices, because the accumulated losses from them are enormous. But clearly the antecedent conditions that create these lapses of character are different from those that create the unrepentant, career fraud artist. While it is beyond the bounds of this chapter to explore these issues in detail, an examination of the event itself may give clues to its attraction for those who practise its many forms.

THE EVENT

How prevalent is fraud in Canada? There were just over 113,000 cases of fraud reported by Canadian police to the UCR in 1993, a rate of 393 per 100,000 population. This is the lowest actual number reported since 1981 and the lowest rate per population since 1979. Over the past ten years, the number of reported cases ranged from 113,000 in 1993 to the decade peak of 137,000 in 1991, with a ten-year average of 125,600 cases.

An examination of each type of fraud as a percentage of the reported annual totals reveals an interesting pattern for the period 1979 to 1993. Cheque fraud, still the highest category of all reported frauds, accounted for 68% of all reported frauds in 1979 (see Figure 10-1). This category then declined steadily to 57% by 1990 and to 50% by 1993. The credit-card

Figure 10-1 Percentage Distribution of Fraud Crimes by Type of Fraud, Canada, 1979–1993

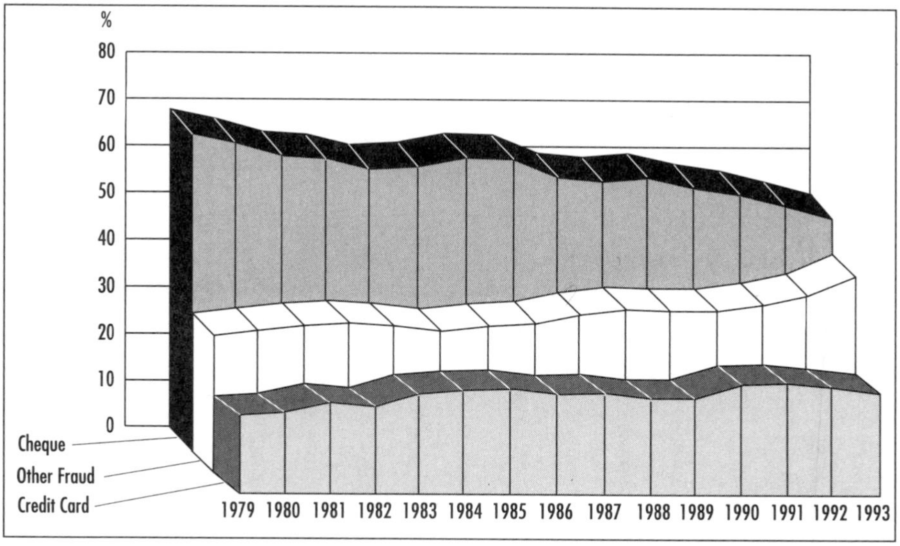

Source: Uniform Crime Reporting survey, Canadian Centre for Justice Statistics, 1993.

fraud ratio to total fraud doubled in the four years between 1979 and 1983 from 7% to 14%, and settled within three percentage points of this peak for the next ten years. The category "other fraud" complements the declines in cheque fraud, increasing from 25% in 1979 to 38% by 1993.

For the four years from 1990 to 1993, the Yukon and the Northwest Territories had the highest combined average fraud rate at 620 per 100,000 population (see Figure 10-2). Saskatchewan and Alberta had the next highest rates at 576 and 553 respectively, compared with the national four-year average rate of 448 per 100,000 population. Ontario's four-year rate was 477, with Quebec and Newfoundland coming second lowest (335) and lowest (291) per 100,000 population, respectively.

Remembering that cheque fraud was the most popular form of fraud in 1993 at 50% of the total, with credit cards at 12% and other fraud at 38%, some provincial variations are noteworthy. In Newfoundland, other fraud made up 80% of all its reported fraud in 1993. The proportion of credit-card fraud was less than 3% in Newfoundland, and about 6% in the remaining Atlantic provinces. Other fraud was also high in the two territories. Cheque fraud was highest proportionally in Nova Scotia (66%), and credit-card fraud was highest in British Columbia (20%).

Who practises fraud? As with most other crimes, both violent and property, males are the main culprits. But because fraud does not normally include contests of physical strength with victims as do many other types of

Figure 10-2 Fraud Rates by Province/Territory, 1990–1993

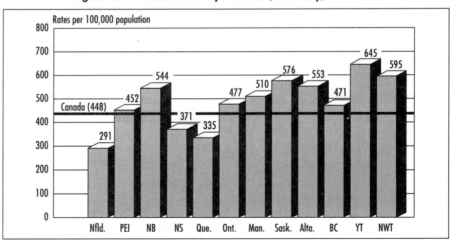

Source: Uniform Crime Reporting survey, Canadian Centre for Justice Statistics, 1993.

crime, one might expect to find a degree of female involvement. Indeed, adult women were charged in 30% of all cases of fraud when an adult accused was identified in 1993, compared to 23% for all property crime. In that year, adult women showed a greater propensity for cheque fraud (or for getting caught at it), comprising 33% of all those accused of this form of fraud.

Youths are normally charged in a much smaller proportion of fraud offences than other *Criminal Code* offences. While young persons aged 12 to 17 accounted for 14% of persons accused of violent incidents and 25% of those accused of property crimes in 1993, youths were charged with only 7% of the total fraud charges laid by police. Young females made up 30% of all youths accused.

What are the distinguishing characteristics of fraud? Based upon an examination of 32,472 fraud incidents reported by 79 police agencies across Canada to the Revised UCR survey in 1993, much can be said about the number of frauds committed per fraudulent act, the targets of fraud artists, and the types of property obtained.

The theft or finding of a credit card or a book of cheques may result in their use in multiple frauds. In 1993, 84% of all fraud incidents sampled involved a single fraudulent action. A further 11% involved between two and five actions, and the remaining 5% involved six or more actions. Credit cards involved multiple actions more frequently than other reported fraud in 1993. Eight percent of credit-card incidents involved more than ten fraudulent actions, compared with less than 2% for cheques and less than 5% for other fraud.

Table 10-1 shows that most fraud (70% of the sample) was committed against commercial/corporate establishments such as department stores, hardware stores, restaurants, and service stores (43%), and banks (21%). The second largest targets of fraud (16%) were nonprofit organizations such as religious institutions, government departments, penal institutions, and private social service agencies. The third largest group of identifiable targets was people in their homes (6%).

Concerning the types of property obtained, Canadian currency was the most frequent property stolen (42%) in the almost 17,000 incidents reported to the Revised UCR survey in 1993 where fraud was the most serious offence (see Figure 10-3). Other securities such as government securities and bank drafts came next at 8%, followed by identification property such as credit cards (7%). All other property, including items like cigarettes, liquor, appliances, clothing, money orders, jewellery, sporting goods, and musical or photograph equipment, collectively made up 39% of property types obtained through fraud.

Table 10-1   Percentage Distribution of Fraud by Target of Incident, 1993[1]

Target of Incident	%
Residence	6
Banks/other financial institutions	21
Convenience store/gas station	4
Car dealers/other motor vehicle	2
Commercial/corporate establishment	43
Noncommercial enterprise	16
Other[2]	8
Total Fraud Incidents	100

[1] Sample includes 32,472 incidents.
[2] Includes other targets such as individuals.

Source: Uniform Crime Reporting survey, Canadian Centre for Justice Statistics, 1993.

**Figure 10-3   Percentage Distribution of Type of Property Obtained
through Fraud, 1993**

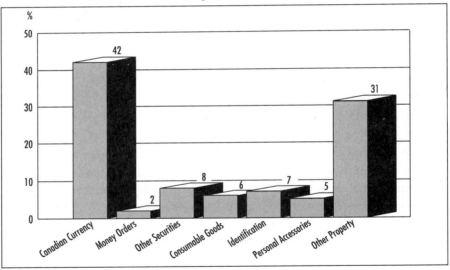

Source: Revised Uniform Crime Reporting survey, Canadian Centre for Justice Statistics, 1993.

Fraud can take on an organized character, as is the case in telemarketing fraud. According to the Phone Busters Unit of the Ontario Provincial Police, telemarketing fraud is basically a confidence crime, netting thieves an estimated $80–$100 million annually in Canada and from $3 billion to $40 billion in the United States, depending on estimation techniques. Typically, the illegal telemarketer exploits the trust of a large number of small victims by offering tantalizing deals or prizes: savings bonds or other financial investments, trips, boats, cars, expensive jewellery, household or office products, and so forth. The most popular means of initial contact with the victim is the "cold call," but contact may also be initiated by postcard (most often sweepstakes offers), classified ads, or solicitation booths at malls or fairs. Cheques, credit-card numbers, or money orders are requested to pay for items purchased. In the case of prizes, fees are requested to pay for prize delivery, service charges, or even to purchase items conditional upon winning. Of course, the items ordered or promised are either never delivered or are not of the value originally discussed; toy boats or cars or cheap jewellery may be sent in place of the genuine article.

High-loss victims (who actually are few in number) are enticed into purchasing land, penny stocks, commodities, precious metals or stones, franchises, distributorships, and the like. Payments are made by cheque or wire transfer. Phone Busters estimates that at least one Canadian per week loses more than $50,000, and that entire life savings are sometimes lost. Particularly active in Canada in the past several years has been an English-speaking illegal telemarketing group operating out of Montreal. To avoid detection and prosecution, this group has changed its company name more than 600 times and conducts almost none of its fraud against Quebec residents. As a result of the latter tactic, the majority of victims live elsewhere and bring their complaints to police forces that have no authority in Quebec. Of the more than 6,800 complaints logged by police agencies in Canada in 1994 (1,500 were victims, the rest attempts), only twelve reports to Phone Busters were from Quebec, compared with 3,300 from Ontario, 1,900 from the Prairie provinces, 700 from British Columbia, and 500 from the Atlantic provinces (see Table 10-2).

The elderly are among the preferred targets of such groups. Older people are easily accessible by phone during the day, and are often motivated by the desire to enlarge incomes or nest eggs. Many elderly fail to ask for guarantees and are often too embarrassed to report their victimization to family, friends, or enforcement authorities. Phone Busters estimates that only 5% of all complaints, including attempts, reach the authorities. A U.S. study conducted in 1992 found that 31% of those actually cheated reported their victimization to the authorities.

Large-scale computer and telecommunications fraud, a relatively recent development, has been made possible by the advances in telecommunications technology. Most computer crime, according to the 1993 *Organized Crime Committee Report* (OCCR) prepared by the Canadian Association of Chiefs

Table 10-2   Number of Telemarketing Fraud Attempts and Victims by Province/Territory, January–December 1994

Province	# Attempts	# Victims	Totals
Newfoundland	80	10	90
Prince Edward Island	75	23	98
Nova Scotia	101	12	122
New Brunswick	160	30	190
Quebec	11	1	12
Ontario	2,462	794	3,256
Manitoba	347	97	444
Saskatchewan	295	90	385
Alberta	815	225	1,040
British Columbia	543	164	707
Yukon	3	1	4
Northwest Territories	8	2	10
Unknown	94	360	454
Total telemarketing frauds	5,269	1,543	6,812

Source: Ontario Provincial Police Phone Busters Unit.

of Police, involves the unlawful "obtaining or intercepting of computer services or functions." Computer systems are accessed through public-switched telephone or data communications networks worldwide. A telephone call may be routed from Columbia, for example, through an unprotected voice-mail office system in Canada to Southeast Asia. When the line is left open for a long weekend, a single access can cost tens of thousands of dollars. Losses in excess of $250,000 are not rare according to the above report. Organized crime also employs underground communications networks to share information, not just on compromised mailboxes but also on stolen credit cards and computer access information. Computers are used as well to access profiles of legitimate plastic cardholders; this information is then shared with card counterfeiters. Cellular phones, too, are now vulnerable to the fraudulent avoidance of billing systems through the modification of their computer components. Canadian police estimate that between 60% and 70% of illegal computer cases either escape detection by the victim or are not reported. Internationally reported computer crime is estimated at closer to 5% of the total. The reasons for not reporting to the police include the potential loss of confidence in the victimized business, fear of sanction internally, the length of the investigation process, and doubt about the competence of the authorities.

Counterfeit credit cards and cheques present serious security challenges to the Canadian banking industry. According to the Security Division of the Canadian Bankers Association (CBA), there were about 25 million credit cards in circulation in Canada in 1993, with annual sales volumes exceeding $40 billion. Between November 1992 and October 1993, however, Canadian issuers of Visa and Mastercard lost over $55 million as a result of the fraudulent use of over 55,000 Canadian credit cards. In comparison, bank robbery losses annually in Canada have been between $3.4 million and $4.3 million since 1989–90. Table 10-3 shows that cards involved in fraudulent use in 1992–93 were either stolen (31%), lost (26%), counterfeited or modified (23%), not received by applicants but used (13%), used with respect to the card information rather than the card itself (5%), and falsely applied for and used (1%).

The CBA also reports that the counterfeiting of credit cards is one of the fastest-growing categories of fraud in Canada and around the world. In 1993–94, counterfeit-card activity actually replaced the use of lost cards as the second highest form of credit-card fraud after stolen cards. The use of counterfeit cards rose 11% between 1992 and 1993, compared with an actual drop in the use of lost and stolen cards during this period. Counterfeiting may take several forms: changes to the information on the raised portion of the card, usually through heating and re-embossing; the production of "white plastic" cards with legitimate cardholder information that are then run through credit-card imprinters for fictitious purchases, with the collusion of a

Table 10-3 Percentage Distribution of Credit Cards Used Fraudulently, November 1992–October 1993

Type	Percentage	Total
Lost	25.9	14,379
Stolen	30.5	16,919
Nonreceipts	12.6	6,998
Fraudulent applications	1.3	714
Counterfeit cards	23.4	13,000
No card	4.8	2,655
Other	1.5	810
Total	100.0	55,475

Source: Canadian Bankers Association, Security Division.

Contributors: Royal Bank, CIBC, Bank of Montreal, Bank of Nova Scotia, Toronto Dominion Bank, National Bank, Citibank, Visa Desjardins, Canada Trust, Royal Trust, Credit Union Electronic Transaction Services (CUETS).

merchant or employee; and the production of high-quality forgeries using the latest silk-screening techniques. The latter process is the fastest growing; according to both the CBA and the 1993 *OCCR*, it originates in organized-crime groups from the Asia-Pacific region. The 1993 *OCCR* estimates that between 75% and 90% of all counterfeit credit-card fraud in Canada, and 50% worldwide, comes from this area.

Other categories of credit-card fraud reported on by the CBA include "nonreceipts," that category of card stolen somewhere between the point of mailing and its destination (i.e., in the postal system or from home mailboxes). Because they are not detected immediately as stolen, card losses can be especially high. Further, fraudulent card applications usually involve the impersonation by criminals of creditworthy applicants. Finally, "no card" fraud refers to the use of someone else's card number to make a purchase, generally by telephone or mail. With respect to counterfeit cheque fraud, according to Peat Marwick Thorne (1993), American-based criminal groups, particularly Asian gangs, are using desktop-publishing equipment to reproduce cheques identical to those of large Canadian companies. Fictitious or real names may be used on the cheques to withdraw the contents of corporate accounts. Made out in amounts between $20,000 and $100,000, the cheques clear the bank and are not discovered as fakes until account reconciliation at the end of the month. This practice, begun in the fall of 1992, was already being reported as yielding larger returns than those from bank robberies (Peat Marwick Thorne, 1993).

In 1994, Peat Marwick Thorne (KPMG) conducted a survey of Canada's 1,000 largest companies on the issue of fraud. Responses were received from 210 companies. Sixty-one of these reported being the victims of fraud in 1993, and of the 100 who provided dollar amounts, total losses were $176 million. Given the small sample size, the inability of companies to measure the exact amount of their victimization, and the reluctance to disclose losses, KPMG concluded in its *1994 Fraud Survey Report* that fraud against Canadian businesses is a problem involving billions of dollars in losses annually for the economy. The types of fraud activities companies reported being vulnerable to internally included expense-account padding, unnecessary purchases, kickbacks, conflicts of interest, and cheque forgery and counterfeiting. External vulnerability showed up in false representation (against banks when loans are being applied for), credit-card fraud, cheque fraud, automated-teller-machine fraud, and bribes and secret commissions.

Insurance fraud in Canada has also become a major financial and security preoccupation of the insurance industry. Property and casualty insurers in Canada believe that between 10% and 15% of household, automobile, and commercial insurance claims are fraudulent (Insurance Bureau of Canada, 1994). An estimated $1.3 billion a year must be covered from the premiums of all policyholders. This amount does not include the secondary or hidden costs paid by society when fires set by arsonists must be fought, when medical exams and rehabilitation treatments are taken by people claiming false injuries, and when police and fire investigators are called in. The Insurance Bureau of Canada (1994) also notes the frequent padding of legitimate claims, known as "opportunistic" fraud or claims "build-up."

Governments are also vulnerable to the siphoning of public monies from their treasuries through the fraudulent acts of their own citizenry. An example of this type of crime is social assistance fraud, which is more prevalent during periods of poor economic activity and in areas of the country with high rates of unemployment. Social assistance fraud may involve the theft of cheques, the nondeclaration of income from other sources (a job, workers' compensation, unemployment insurance, etc.), or the use of false identification and addresses. The 1993 OCCR links the practice in many cases to drug addiction and, with respect to the multiple uses of false identification, to some members of the Somalian refugee community. One Quebec case involving $20 million implicated over 200 refugees who were using multiple identities in Montreal, Ottawa, and Toronto.

THE AFTERMATH

The total dollar value of losses incurred by governments, individuals, and businesses in Canada is not known because of the probable high rate of underreporting of fraud. The figures collected by those police departments reporting to the revised UCR survey suggest that fraud ranks third after theft and break and enter on the list of overall property crime losses, and first when average comparisons are made for amounts under $1 million.

Table 10-4 shows that of the 26,065 fraud cases for which dollar values are known, out of the total 113,000 reported cases, total losses were $607.6 million. Credit-card fraud accounted for $400.6 million, other fraud for $110.2 million, and cheques for $96.9 million. In comparison, theft and break-and-enter incidents on the revised UCR database accounted for $3.1 billion and $2.6 billion respectively.

The average dollar losses for fraud under $1 million were $1,897 for cheques, $1,620 for credit cards, and $6,542 for other fraud, with an overall

Table 10-4 Dollar Losses for Selected Property Violations, 1993

Violation Type	Total Incidents	Total Dollar Cost	Average Dollar Cost
Break and enter	106,200	2,633,320,251	24,796
Robbery	13,455	81,032,372	6,022
Theft	284,030	3,118,591,547	10,980
Mischief	88,222	572,396,794	6,488
Fraud total	26,065	607,583,229	23,310
Cheque	15,242	96,808,096	6,351
Credit card	3,624	400,582,672	110,536
Other fraud	7,199	110,192,461	15,307

Source: Revised Uniform Crime Reporting survey, Canadian Centre for Justice Statistics, 1993.

fraud average of $3,140. The averages for break and enter and theft under $1 million were $2,572 and $1,999 respectively. Robbery and mischief came fourth and fifth in the averages at $1,490 and $567 respectively. Forty fraud cases, of the 26,065 above, averaged more than $1 million in losses.

Police clearance rates for fraud are more successful than for any other property crime. As Table 10-5 indicates, 57% of the revised UCR fraud cases were either cleared by charge (46%) or by other means such as police discretion or complainant refusal to support the laying of a charge (11%). The latter may occur when the accused is a first-time young offender or when reimbursement is agreed to. The police clearance rate for all other property crimes in the revised sample was just 15%.

While the Canadian Centre for Justice Statistics (CCJS) does not yet have full national coverage of sentence types for those cases of fraud that end in

Table 10-5 Clearance Status for Selected Property Violations, 1993

Violation Type	Total Violations	Not Cleared %	Cleared by Charge %	Cleared Otherwise %
Fraud	32,472	43	46	11
Theft under $1,000	258,033	84	11	5
Theft over $1,000	101,092	91	7	2
Break and enter	152,753	87	9	4
Other property	140,119	79	17	4

Source: Revised Uniform Crime Reporting survey, Canadian Centre for Justice Statistics, 1993.

findings of guilt, the Adult Criminal Court database contains such information for five jurisdictions: Prince Edward Island, Nova Scotia, Quebec, Saskatchewan, and the Yukon. The median length of prison sentences for cases of fraud/forgery in 1993–94 ranged from a high of 90 days in Quebec and Saskatchewan to a low of 30 days in PEI and Nova Scotia. Median fines levied were between $150 and $250, and median probation terms were between one and two years.

The CCJS database for young offenders is complete nationally and records sentences for four categories of fraud, namely, false pretences, forgery, fraud, and other fraud. The median sentence lengths in 1993–94 for those sent to secure custody ranged between 45 and 60 days depending on the type of offence. The median sentence for open custody was 60 days, while the median probation period was 360 days. Fines ranged between $100 and $200. Again, only 7% of police-reported fraud cases resulted in young offenders being charged.

SUMMARY AND CONCLUSIONS
■ ■ ■

Modern telecommunications systems, worldwide computer-based financial networks, and the ready availability of low-cost technology in our personal and business lives are making Canadians increasingly accessible to the predatory adventures of those who would practise deceit for gain. Our worst enemies are our lapses of caution in using these new utilities, and perhaps even our own gullibility and greed when the opportunity "too good to be true" comes our way. Fraud in Canada in 1993, while not as prevalent in police statistics as it was in the 1980s, was nonetheless a very costly crime. Some sectors and individuals suffered more than others, but in reality we all suffer the high business and social costs required to compensate for, take security measures against, and prosecute this crime.

Cheque fraud is still the most frequently reported type of fraud (50% in 1993), but it is rapidly losing ground to other types of fraud, including credit-card fraud, which is growing apace with the increasing use of this form of credit purchasing. In 1993, female participation rates were higher for fraud than for other types of crime, including property crime in general; in contrast, youth participation rates were significantly lower for fraud than for property crime. Most fraud incidents involved only one action, with credit cards being used more often in multiple actions. Most fraud targeted commercial/corporate establishments in 1993, with nonprofit organizations coming second.

Underreporting to the authorities is a characteristic behaviour in many victims of fraud, both personal and commercial. The most commonly obtained property stolen in 1993 was Canadian currency, followed by securities, credit cards, and consumables. Police clearance rates for fraud in 1993 were more successful than for any other property crime. However, some types of fraud, including telecommunications, telemarketing, and petty insurance fraud, are difficult to prosecute.

THEFT

11

by Dianne Hendrick

The majority of crime that is reported to police in Canada is a form of theft. Dianne Hendrick begins this chapter by introducing the reader to the various categories of theft. Drawing upon GSS data, she goes on to discuss victimization rates and the risk factors associated with theft of household property. Her examination of theft incidents and court dispositions is based on data from the UCR survey, the Youth Court Survey, and the Adult Criminal Court Survey. Particular attention is given to the problem of youth crime and the response of the justice system to young offenders.

This chapter draws upon Uniform Crime Reporting (UCR) data, both aggregate and incident-based, as they relate to the crime of theft. The trends examined focus to a large extent on the period from 1986 to 1993 because of legislative changes that were made to the maximum dollar amounts in 1985. At that time, the minor theft ceiling for the value of property stolen was raised from $200 to $1,000.

DEFINITIONS

The definition of a theft incident used in the UCR survey is based on the appropriate sections of the *Criminal Code*. The theft offences, listed in Table 11-1, are grouped into two categories based on the value of the goods stolen, that is, theft of goods valued at $1,000 or less and theft of goods valued over $1,000.

According to the UCR scoring rules, an incident refers to a set of connected events that are reported by the police. Theft incidents are those in which the most serious component of the crime is theft. In this chapter, incidents refer to cases that the police have determined to be valid following a preliminary investigation. *Excluded from the discussion are all thefts of motor vehicles from both the aggregate and incident-based survey data.* (Motor-vehicle theft is discussed as a separate crime in Chapter 12.) The aggregate survey data are considered a census of reported crime and are used for all historical comparisons, whereas the incident-based data provide more detailed characteristics for one year—1993—for approximately 32% of the national volume. As discussed in Chapter 2, the incident-based data are not considered to be representative of any single geographic area.

PRECURSORS

Cohen and Felson (1979) argue that changes in the way we live has substantially altered levels of target suitability and guardianship of property. The period following World War II has seen dramatic changes in the nature of the labour force, moving people from home to work locations. Changing

Table 11-1 Types of Criminal Code Offences Defined as Theft

RSC 1985	Description of Offence
356	Theft from mail
338	Theft of cattle
334a	Theft of property valued at more than $1,000
334b	Theft of property valued at less than $1,000
332	Theft—misappropriation of funds
331	Theft by person with power of attorney
330	Theft by person required to account
329	Theft by spouse
328	Theft by/from person with special property/interest
327	Possess device to obtain telecommunications service
326	Theft of telecommunications service/electricity/gas
324	Theft by bailee of things seized
323	Theft of oysters
322	Theft with intent to deposit/deprive

Source: Canadian Centre for Justice Statistics, 1995.

patterns in leisure, including longer vacation periods, have also added to the time people spend away from home. At the same time, there has been "a revolution in small durable product design" (Cohen and Felson, 1979:500). A general increase in the standard of living combined with technological advances led to the production of a wide range of lightweight, durable consumer goods. Demand for tape recorders, television sets, and stereo equipment increased, as it later did for products like home computers, compact disc players, and VCRs (Felson, 1994). These changes, according to Cohen and Felson, created greater opportunities for direct-contact predatory crimes. The rates of property crimes increased as theft focused on highly desirable durable consumer goods that were easy to steal, easy to carry, and easy to sell or use.

Several researchers have pointed out that popular images of the calculating, highly specialized, and rational property offender may be exaggerated. According to Cromwell, Olson, and Avary (1991), much of what we know about such offenders comes from interviews with offenders or ex-offenders who may engage in "rational reconstruction." In other words, in recalling their crimes, they suggest that far more planning took place than was actually the case. While it is sometimes said that the professional seeks opportunities for crime, Cromwell and his colleagues maintain that these offenders do not so much seek opportunities as develop a special sensitivity to the opportunities they happen to encounter. Data on theft incidents generally uncover large numbers of crimes that point to amateurish offenders with little technical knowledge or experience (Felson, 1994). Property crimes such as theft and break and enter (irrespective of the level of professionalism of the offender) are motivated by instrumental needs (Bennett and Wright, 1984). These crimes do not reflect expressive needs like anger or revenge, but are prompted by a desire on the part of the offender to obtain the property of the victim.

THE EVENT

In 1993, 886,617 incidents of theft accounted for 55% of the property crime in Canada.[1] Theft of goods valued at $1,000 or less ("theft under") represented 87% of these thefts. Of the 768,859 "theft under" incidents in 1993, 41% were thefts from motor vehicles. Shoplifting accounted for 13% of "theft under," followed by bicycles (12%), and "other thefts under" (34%). Similarly, the majority of theft of goods valued over $1,000 ("theft over") were thefts from motor vehicles, accounting for 49% of the 117,758 "theft over" incidents in 1993. As expected, bicycles (5%) and shoplifting (2%) accounted for small proportions of "theft over," whereas "other thefts over" represented 44% of "theft over" incidents.

Almost three-quarters of the nation's "theft under" incidents were located in three provinces: Ontario (36%), British Columbia (21%), and Quebec (17%). A similar pattern was indicated for "theft over" incidents, with Ontario accounting for 42%, Quebec for 20%, and British Columbia for 19%.

As Table 11-2 indicates, in 1993 there were 2,674 "theft under" incidents for every 100,000 Canadians, while the rate of "theft over" incidents was substantially lower at 410 per 100,000 population. Provincial rates of "theft under" ranged from 1,410 per 100,000 population in Newfoundland to 4,654 per 100,000 population in British Columbia. Rates of "theft over" ranged from 112 to 628 per 100,000 population in Newfoundland and British Columbia respectively.

Total incidents of theft rose markedly during the early 1980s, increasing from a rate of 2,826 per 100,000 population in 1979 to 3,436 per 100,000 population in 1982. Rates of theft fluctuated slightly throughout the remainder of the decade, followed by a notable increase in the early 1990s. From 1989 to 1991, the rate of theft incidents rose from 3,083 to 3,492 per

Table 11-2 Rates per 100,000 Population of Theft Incidents, 1993*

	Theft Under	*Theft Over*	*Total Theft*
Newfoundland	1,410	112	1,522
Prince Edward Island	2,220	164	2,384
Nova Scotia	2,434	202	2,635
New Brunswick	1,812	168	1,980
Quebec	1,835	332	2,167
Ontario	2,594	461	3,055
Manitoba	2,961	299	3,260
Saskatchewan	2,836	352	3,188
Alberta	3,055	402	3,457
British Columbia	4,654	628	5,282
Yukon	4,325	622	4,947
Northwest Territories	3,084	404	3,488
Canada	2,674	410	3,084

* All counts in this chapter exclude auto theft.

Source: Uniform Crime Reporting survey, Canadian Centre for Justice Statistics, 1993.

Table 11-3 Rates per 100,000 Population of Theft Incidents, Canada, 1986–1993

	Theft Under	Theft Over	Total Theft
1986	2,951	260	3,211
1987	2,985	270	3,255
1988	2,887	298	3,184
1989	2,765	318	3,083
1990	2,875	366	3,240
1991	3,074	418	3,492 ·
1992	2,896	422	3,318
1993	2,674	410	3,084

Source: Uniform Crime Reporting survey, Canadian Centre for Justice Statistics, 1993.

100,000 population (see Table 11-3). The rates have declined moderately since 1991 to the earlier 1989 level. In summary, the rate of total theft incidents increased from 2,826 per 100,000 population in 1979 to 3,084 per 100,000 population in 1993, representing an average annual increase of 1%.

According to the General Social Survey (GSS), young persons aged 15–24 were three times more likely than adults aged 45–64 to be a victim of theft of personal property (93 per 1,000 pop. vs. 29 per 1,000 pop.). Overall, males and females were equally likely to be victims of this crime (51 per 1,000). However, young females aged 15–24 were more likely than males of the same age to be victimized (98 per 1,000 vs. 89 per 1,000), as were women aged 25–44 compared with men of this age (65 per 1,000 vs. 56 per 1,000). Although the overall rate of victimization was lower for rural residents (36 per 1,000) compared with urban residents (57 per 1,000), young persons in rural areas were substantially more likely than other age groups in rural areas to be victims of theft of personal property (74 per 1,000). Young persons in urban areas were also much more likely to be victims (97 per 1,000).

The risk of being a victim of theft of personal property increased with income and education. Persons with an income level of $60,000 or above were more than twice as likely to be victimized (73 per 1,000), compared with those earning between $15,000 and $30,000 (39 per 1,000). Persons with post-secondary education had the highest rate of theft of personal property (66 per 1,000), compared with those with some secondary education (40 per 1,000); persons with less than some secondary education had the lowest rates of victimization.

Single people were much more likely than married people to be victims of theft of personal property. In addition, single females were more likely than single men to be victimized (94 per 1,000 vs. 79 per 1,000). The number of evening activities outside of the home was related to risk, such that as the number of activities increased, so did the risk of theft. Consistent with these findings were those that identified a person's main activity. The highest victimization rate was indicated for "student" (101 per 1,000), compared with "working at job" (60 per 1,000) and "keeping house" (23 per 1,000).

Many of the variables related to theft of personal property were also important risk factors for theft of household property. Income, education, and urban/rural characteristics showed similar patterns of relationships. Victimization rates were greater for high-income earners, the well educated, and those living in urban areas. The risk of theft of household property also increased with the size of the household. Five-person households were most at risk (91 per 1,000 households), compared with one-person households (27 per 1,000). Persons living in semidetached dwellings, row houses, or a duplex were most at risk (82 per 1,000), compared with those in single homes (50 per 1,000) or low-rise apartments (33 per 1,000). Those who owned their residence were at slightly greater risk than those who rented (51 per 1,000 vs. 47 per 1,000).

In summary, young persons (who are often out in the evening), singles (especially women), high-income earners, well-educated persons, those living in urban areas, and homeowners are most at risk of being targets of theft. Somewhat surprising was the finding that larger households were at greater risk of theft of personal property given the other variables associated with high risk.

Theft incidents were most prevalent during the summer months. Theft incidents peaked during the month of August and dipped to their lowest levels in February. Most theft incidents occurred in commercial or corporate places, in parking lots, on the streets or in open areas, and in residences. A large proportion of "theft over" incidents recorded in the 1993 Revised UCR survey occurred in parking lots (30%), on the streets (25%), in residences (23%), and in commercial establishments (19%). "Theft under" incidents more often occurred in commercial establishments (26%) and parking lots (23%), while incidents were as likely to have occurred on the streets as in residences (22% each). Although motor-vehicle theft is excluded from the analysis, theft of goods stolen from motor vehicles is included, which may account for the large proportion of theft incidents in parking lots and on the street. In contrast, schools were identified as the location for only 1% of "theft over" incidents and 3% of "theft under" incidents.

Most items stolen were household articles. In the "theft over" incidents recorded in the 1993 Revised UCR survey, 57% of the items stolen were household articles, 17% were personal accessories, and 7% were currency or stocks. Household articles include stereos, televisions, appliances, tools, and alcohol. Furs, clothing, perfume, and jewellery are included in personal accessories. Vehicle accessories and office equipment represented 5% each, and bicycles and identification papers (including passports and driver's licences) 3% each. In "theft under" incidents as well, items stolen were more often household articles (39%), personal accessories (17%), and currency or stocks (13%). In these incidents, bicycles were the next most common item stolen (11%), followed by vehicle accessories (9%) and identification papers (7%). Less than 1% of the items reported as stolen in theft incidents were guns.

In "theft under" incidents, two-thirds of items stolen were valued at $500 or less, while in "theft over" incidents nine in ten items stolen ranged in value from just over $1,000 to $10,000. The dollar value refers to the total value of all property stolen in the incident, because more than one item may be stolen and the police report the total dollar loss per incident when providing information.

THE AFTERMATH

A relatively small number of theft incidents are solved by police. In 1993, 13% of "theft under" incidents and 7% of "theft over" incidents were cleared by charge, while 7% of "theft under" incidents and 3% of "theft over" incidents were cleared otherwise.

In 1993, 116,332 persons were charged with theft, and 93% of this number with "theft under." Adults accounted for 71% of persons charged. Similar proportions of youths (95%) and adults (92%) were charged with "theft under." Two-thirds of persons charged with "theft under" are male. Females represented about one-third of persons charged with "theft under," compared with 17% of persons charged with "theft over."

Although the number of youths charged accounts for about one-third of persons charged, the crime may be described as a youth crime given the number of young people in Canada. The rate of young persons charged is more than four times the adult rate for "theft under" and more than twice the rate for "theft over." In 1993, there were 1,397 youths charged with "theft under" for every 100,000 youths, compared with a rate of 348 per 100,000 adults. The rate for "theft over" was 74 per 100,000 youths, compared with 31 for every 100,000 adults. However, the enormity of these differences must be tempered with the knowledge that the population of adults includes a large component that are known to be less active in crime.

In 1993, Quebec had the lowest rate of persons charged with theft (268 per 100,000 population), while Alberta had the highest (597 per 100,000 population). Influencing the number of youths charged in Quebec are the provincial directors, who are responsible for the protection of youths under the province's social welfare legislation. The provincial director in each region evaluates the cases of youths that have been brought to their attention by the Crown (Substitut du procureur général), even though the police have sufficient evidence to lay a charge. Only in the most serious cases does the Crown choose to proceed immediately with charges. Pursuant to the *Young Offenders Act*, a provincial director has the authority to make recommendations, which result in one of three actions: diverting the youth to an alternative measures program[2] (representing 48% of those referred for evaluation in 1993, and stated as "cleared otherwise" in the police statistics); charging the youth (representing 32% of those referred in 1993); or discharging the youth from further intervention by the justice system (representing 20% of those referred in 1993).[3] Consequently, only a small proportion of those youths in

Table 11-4   Rates per 100,000 Population of Youths and Adults Charged in Theft Incidents, by Province, 1993

	Youths			Adults			Total Persons Charged		
	Theft Under	Theft Over	Total	Theft Under	Theft Over	Total	Theft Under	Theft Over	Total
Newfoundland	1,553	62	1,615	425	32	457	467	30	496
Prince Edward Island	1,119	68	1,186	227	30	257	266	28	294
Nova Scotia	1,893	54	1,947	447	26	473	493	24	517
New Brunswick	1,204	83	1,286	314	25	340	341	26	368
Quebec	651	47	698	243	33	276	239	29	268
Ontario	1,363	67	1,430	309	27	336	340	26	365
Manitoba	2,118	108	2,226	371	31	402	452	32	483
Saskatchewan	2,015	127	2,142	455	39	494	513	40	553
Alberta	2,022	105	2,127	530	41	571	558	39	597
British Columbia	2,018	98	2,116	481	34	515	523	34	556
Yukon	2,040	120	2,160	450	35	485	484	34	519
Northwest Territories	1,424	182	1,606	444	72	515	424	64	488
Canada	1,397	74	1,471	348	31	379	375	30	405

Source: Uniform Crime Reporting survey, Canadian Centre for Justice Statistics, 1993.

Quebec who are eligible to be charged are in fact charged. In contrast, similar cases in other jurisdictions may result in the laying of charges. In Alberta, the police decide independently how to proceed with the case, in accordance with established policy and procedures. Since 1986, the difference in charge rates between Quebec and Alberta has been increasing, although rates in both provinces have declined markedly since 1991.

As Table 11-5 shows, the rate of youths charged with "theft over" fluctuated notably in the years between 1986 (75 per 100,000 youths) and 1993 (74 per 100,000 youths), representing a 1% average annual increase. The rate of youths charged with "theft under" declined during this period from 1,604 per 100,000 youths in 1986 to 1,397 per 100,000 youths in 1993, with an average annual decline of 2%.

In 1993, there were two males under age 12 charged with "theft under" for every female youth charged. However, females represent a growing proportion of youths charged because, in 1986, the ratio was three males charged for every female. "Theft over" among youths is more predominately male, with six males charged for every female in 1993. The number of females charged has risen at a faster rate since 1986 compared with males (5% vs. 1% average annual increase). In 1986, 189 females and 1,504 males were charged, compared with 229 females and 1,487 males in 1993. From 1986 to 1993, the rate of adults charged with "theft over" declined slightly from 33 to 31 per 100,000 adults, with an average annual decrease of 1%. The rate of adults charged with "theft under" decreased from 424 to 348 per 100,000 adults during this period, with an average annual decline of 3%.

Table 11-5   Rates per 100,000 Population of Youths and Adults Charged in Theft Incidents, Canada, 1986–1993

	Youths Charged			Adults Charged			Total Persons Charged		
	Theft Under	Theft Over	Total	Theft Under	Theft Over	Total	Theft Under	Theft Over	Total
1986	1,604	75	1,678	424	33	457	455	31	486
1987	1,554	56	1,610	432	29	461	455	27	482
1988	1,553	64	1,617	418	32	451	443	30	473
1989	1,655	77	1,732	398	33	431	435	31	466
1990	1,801	81	1,881	404	34	438	450	32	482
1991	1,890	91	1,980	427	36	462	474	34	508
1992	1,632	83	1,715	405	33	438	437	32	469
1993	1,397	74	1,471	348	31	379	375	30	405

Source: Uniform Crime Reporting survey, Canadian Centre for Justice Statistics, 1993.

The 1993 Revised UCR survey reported that children (under age 12) and youths (aged 12–17) accounted for 29% of accused in theft incidents. Nearly all of the 715 accused children were in "theft under" incidents.[4] Specific results for theft by age and gender are presented in Table 11-6.

Sentencing data on youths and adults found guilty of theft is collected by two CCJS surveys. The Youth Court Survey (YCS) collects data on young persons appearing before all youth courts. Case counts do not directly correspond to UCR incident or person counts due to variations in the survey definitions, time lags between the surveys, and the different procedures (used by the police, the Crown, and other players in the system) that determine which persons appear in court.[5]

In 1993–94, there were 24,480 cases heard in youth courts where the most significant charge in the case was theft. "Theft under" accounted for 78% of cases heard, "theft over" for 15%, "theft unspecified" for 6%, and "theft other" for less than 1%. As expected, males were the majority of accused (74%), and accounted for 71% of "theft under" incidents. Only four theft cases—all "theft over"—were transferred to adult court. Sixty-four percent of theft cases resulted in a guilty finding, while 26% of cases were withdrawn. Only 1% of theft cases ended in a finding of not guilty, while 3% were dismissed and 6% were stayed. As Table 11-7 indicates, probation (43%), community service orders (17%), open custody (14%), secure custody (8%), fines (7%), and absolute discharges (6%) represented the major-

Table 11-6 Proportion of Males and Females Accused in Theft Incidents by Age, 1993

	Theft Over		Theft Under	
	Male %	Female %	Male %	Female %
under 12	0.49	0	1.66	1.26
12–14	3.55	3.75	9.93	12.19
15–17	15.99	8.75	19.04	14.7
18–20	20.69	9.99	14.58	8.8
21–23	11.37	10.53	7.44	6.23
24–26	10.45	10.35	6.43	6.74
27–29	8.47	11.79	7.13	7.93
30–32	6.47	9.28	6.86	7.81
33–34	3.35	3.93	4.23	4.6
over 34	18.77	31.25	22.38	29.57
unknown	0.39	0.36	0.32	0.19

Source: Revised Uniform Crime Reporting survey, Canadian Centre for Justice Statistics, 1993.

Table 11-7 Proportion of Theft Cases Heard in Youth Court by Duration of the Most Serious Disposition, 1993–1994

		Disposition Length						Total cases 100%	Median no. of days
		<1 month %	1–3 months %	4–6 months %	7–12 months %	13–24 months %	>24 months %		
Secure Custody	Theft over	17	44	20	15	3	0	544	90.0
	Theft under	35	45	13	5	1	0	629	30.0
	Theft unspecified	29	52	13	5	2	0	56	37.5
	Theft other	38	13	25	25	0	0	8	90.5
Open Custody	Theft over	11	46	26	14	3	0	641	90.0
	Theft under	24	55	15	5	1	0	1,407	42.0
	Theft unspecified	14	61	21	4	0	0	148	60.0
	Theft other	8	54	23	15	0	0	13	60.0
Probation	Theft over	0	2	17	58	23	0	1,059	360.0
	Theft under	0	6	33	48	12	0	5,164	270.0
	Theft unspecified	0	4	31	55	10	0	404	270.0
	Theft other	0	7	28	44	21	0	43	360.0

		Fine amount				Total cases 100%	Median fine
		<$50 %	$50–$100 %	$101–$500 %	$500 %		
Fine	Theft over	0	33	63	4	51	$200.00
	Theft under	12	51	38	0	1,065	$100.00
	Theft unspecified	18	61	18	2	44	$62.50
	Theft other	0	0	0	0	0	0

Source: Youth Court survey, Canadian Centre for Justice Statistics, 1993–94.

ity of dispositions assigned by the court for theft cases with a guilty finding in 1993–94. These proportions are based on the most serious disposition ordered in a case, although more than one type may be ordered (e.g., a case with a custody and probation order is common but included only in the custody count).

Young offenders in "theft over" cases were more likely to be ordered to serve a term of secure custody than offenders in other types of theft cases; 20% of "theft over" cases led to secure custody. The median sentence length ordered for secure custody was three months for "theft over" and "theft other" cases, just over one month for "theft unspecified" cases, and one month for "theft under" cases. A quarter of "theft over" cases led to open custody, with a median sentence of three months, compared with a median sentence length in open custody of two months for "theft unspecified" and "theft other" cases and 1.5 months for "theft under" cases. About one-half of cases resulted in probation. A one-year term of probation was the median sentence for "theft over" and "theft other" cases (nine months was ordered for "theft under" and "theft unspecified" cases).

The case characteristics component of the Adult Criminal Court Survey (ACCS) collects information from provincial/territorial courts in five jurisdictions (see Table 11-8). The sentencing information is subject to similar cautions as those described for the youth court data.[6] The types of sentences ordered in a case are not categorized by the most serious disposition (unlike YCS counts), so the sentence types are not mutually exclusive. "Theft over" cases with a conviction were more likely than other types of theft to result in a prison term, whether federal or provincial/territorial. A term of imprisonment was ordered in 82% of "theft over" cases with a conviction in PEI and the Yukon, about 50% of the cases in Nova Scotia and Quebec, and 45% in Saskatchewan. Terms of imprisonment were shorter and ordered much less frequently for other types of theft cases. Probation was ordered for at least one-half of the "theft over" cases with a conviction in all jurisdictions.

Table 11-8 Duration of Sentences for Theft Cases Heard in Adult Court, by Most Serious Charge and Most Serious Disposition, 1993

	Sentence Type	Theft Over Median no. of days/$ fine	Theft Under Median no. of days/$ fine	Theft Other Median no. of days/$ fine
Prince Edward Island	Prison	90	30	60
	Probation	730	360	540
	Fine	$1,125	$400	0
Nova Scotia	Prison	120	30	30
	Probation	540	360	365
	Fine	$350	$124	$150
Quebec	Prison	180	60	90
	Probation	730	365	365
	Fine	$300	$100	$100
Saskatchewan	Prison	165	60	60
	Probation	365	240	36
	Fine	$500	$175	$200
Yukon	Prison	60	15	60
	Probation	730	180	180
	Fine	$600	$100	0

Source: Adult Criminal Court survey, Canadian Centre for Justice Statistics, 1993.

Orders to make restitution or pay compensation were more common in the Yukon (46%) and Nova Scotia (25%) than other jurisdictions.

SUMMARY AND CONCLUSIONS
■ ■ ■

Persons who are most at risk of being a victim of theft are the young, the single, the urbanite, the well-educated, the high-income earner, and the home-owner. Most thefts involve goods valued at less than $1,000 and go unsolved. Although car theft was excluded from the analysis, a large proportion of "theft over" incidents occur in parking lots or on the streets. "Theft under" incidents most often occur in commercial establishments and parking lots. The persons accused in incidents of theft are typically male, and one-third of accused are youths aged 12–17. With respect to dispositions, in 1993–94 about half the cases of "theft over" with a finding of guilt in youth court were ordered one year of probation, whereas "theft under" cases received nine months of probation. Youths in "theft under" cases were seldom ordered a term of custody, while those in "theft over" cases were more likely to serve a term in custody of three months. In adult court, "theft over" cases with a conviction were more likely than other types of theft to result in a prison term; the length of sentence varied by jurisdiction.

NOTES

[1] The research file of 1993 Revised UCR survey results includes approximately 296,000 theft incidents, excluding motor-vehicle theft.

[2] These programs are discussed in Chapter 2.

[3] In 1993, 14,206 youths were referred for assessment in Quebec, as reported in the annual report of the Ministry of Public Security, *Statistiques 1993*.

[4] The research file of 1993 Revised UCR survey results contains approximately 50,000 accused involved in theft incidents (excluding motor-vehicle theft), 72% of whom were male.

[5] To illustrate some definitional variations, the UCR categories of "theft over" and "theft under" refer to fourteen *Criminal Code* offences, whereas these categories refer to a single offence in the YCS classification scheme; the residual offences are included in "theft other" in the YCS. The YCS category "theft other" includes, for example, theft from mail, theft of credit card. In the UCR classification, theft of goods with an unspecified value falls within "theft under" rather than a separate category. For further information, see the CCJS publication *Youth Court Statistics,* 1993–94, Cat. No. 85-522.

[6] Unlike YCS data, the adult court data (case characteristics component) are collected on a calendar-year basis; however, the classification scheme used in both court surveys is quite

similar, and the definition of the case is identical. Note that "theft unspecified" is included in "theft other." For further information, see the CCJS publication *Adult Criminal Court Statistics, 1993*, Cat. No. 85-214.

Property
Crime

MOTOR-VEHICLE CRIMES

by Peter Morrison

In this chapter, Peter Morrison dispels the notion that motor-vehicle crimes are "victimless" crimes. Not only do these crimes have considerable economic costs, but activities such as joyriding can have potentially deadly consequences. This chapter discusses incident and offender characteristics as they relate to the three components of motor-vehicle crime—namely, theft of a vehicle, theft from a vehicle, and automotive vandalism. Comparative data on international and provincial motor-vehicle crime are presented. Morrison concludes the chapter with a discussion of crime-prevention strategies and measures, ranging from improved vehicle safety features to neighbourhood antitheft programs to broadly based public policy initiatives.

Motor vehicles are the most widely used form of transportation in Canada. Among OECD countries, Canada was second only to the United States in total motor-vehicle (personal use and commercial) ownership rates in 1991: 622 vehicles for every 1,000 Canadians, compared with 761 for every 1,000 Americans (Silver, 1994). The significance of motor vehicles is demonstrated by Statistics Canada's 1992 Family Expenditure Survey, which reported that of the $55 billion spent by households on transportation, 92%, or more than $51 billion, was spent on the purchase and maintenance of motor vehicles. According to the General Social Survey (GSS), one in ten households owning a motor vehicle was a victim of a motor-vehicle crime in 1993. This included not only the theft of a vehicle[1] or its parts, but also motor-vehicle vandalism.

Although motor-vehicle crimes maintain an image of being victimless (individuals are usually reimbursed by insurance companies and therefore assume little direct cost for their stolen vehicles), they contribute to rising insurance rates and increased costs to the criminal justice system. Moreover, the perception of motor-vehicle crime as victimless may need revisiting in light of recent increases in violent carjackings and the involvement of stolen vehicles in high-speed police chases, drive-by shootings, accidents, and a practice known as "ramraiding," in which a stolen vehicle is used to smash into and loot commercial premises.

Motor-vehicle crimes account for a considerable proportion of the annual crime volume each year. For instance, nearly one in five *Criminal Code* offences reported to the police in 1993 involved the theft of a motor vehicle or theft of property from a vehicle. In 1993, one of every 100 registered motor vehicles was reported stolen, and automotive parts or personal property were stolen from two of every 100 vehicles. According to the 1993 GSS, losses from motor-vehicle thefts, property thefts from motor vehicles, and vandalism amounted to $1.6 billion.[2] This figure excludes the cost of police investigations and the economic cost of days lost from work. In sharp contrast, the Canadian Bankers Association reported $55 million in losses from credit-card fraud during the 1993 fiscal year, while the Insurance Bureau of Canada reported that annual losses from bank robberies averaged about $3.5 million.

Although the problem of motor-vehicle crime is not new, there continues to be a lack of research on the subject. In their analysis of auto thefts, Clarke and Harris (1992) were unable to locate a single academic book on auto theft published in the English-speaking world in the last twenty years, despite the fact that "theft of vehicles is perhaps the best reported of all property crimes, while the offenders most usually involved, juveniles, are among the most accessible groups for study" (2). This chapter examines data drawn from police records and victimization surveys in order to provide a comprehensive picture of the circumstances surrounding motor-vehicle crimes.

DEFINITIONS

For the purpose of this report, a motor vehicle is defined as an automobile, truck, van, bus, recreational vehicle, tractor-trailer, motorcycle, construction/farm equipment or other motorized land vehicle, go-cart, dune buggy, or snowmobile. Airplanes and boats are excluded from the discussion.

Theft of a motor vehicle consists of stealing a motor vehicle or taking it without permission. *Theft from* a motor vehicle includes the theft of automotive accessories (e.g., tires, hubcaps, engines) as well as personal property located within the vehicle (stereo, clothes, purse/wallet, tools, etc.).

Automotive *vandalism* refers to the willful destruction or damage of a motor vehicle. Examples of automotive vandalism include the spray painting of a car or the deliberate breaking of antennas or headlights. These definitions include both completed and attempted thefts and vandalisms.

PRECURSORS

Who commits motor vehicle crimes? Existing literature indicates a strong relationship between young males and motor vehicle crimes throughout Western Europe and North America (Light, Nee, and Ingham, 1993; Houghton, 1992; Webb and Laycock, 1992; Spencer, 1992; Morrison and Ogrodnick, 1994). Canadian evidence supports these findings in that the vast majority of motor vehicle crimes in which charges are laid are committed by young men. Table 12-1 indicates that in 1993 youths aged 12–17 represented over one-half of those charged with motor vehicle theft, one-third of those charged with theft from motor vehicles, and nearly one-quarter of those charged with automotive vandalism. For people aged 18–25, the percentages of those charged were 30% (motor vehicle theft), 44% (theft from motor vehicles), and 35% (vehicle vandalisms).

Most of those accused of a motor vehicle crime who were "cleared otherwise" were under 18. In 1993, 40% of all motor vehicle vandalisms cleared otherwise involved accused who were 12–17, while 16% involved accused who were under 12. These figures may indicate that young offenders involved in motor vehicle crimes are dealt with through avenues other than the formal criminal justice system. For example, the accused's parents may be informed or the accused may be warned or asked to pay restitution for damages. Because children under 12 cannot be charged with a criminal offence, the cleared-otherwise category is the only available mechanism to measure the criminal activity of this group.

A number of theories have been put forward to explain the motivations for involvement in motor vehicle crimes. According to McCaghy, Giordano, and Henson (1977), a contributory factor in this crime is the symbolism

Table 12-1 Age of Persons Accused of Motor-Vehicle Crimes, 1993[1]

Age of Accused	Theft of Motor Vehicle		Theft from Motor Vehicle		Motor-Vehicle Vandalism	
	Charged	Cleared Otherwise	Charged	Cleared Otherwise	Charged	Cleared Otherwise
	%	%	%	%	%	%
11 and under	...	1	...	1	—	16
12–17	51	49	33	45	22	40
18–25	30	25	44	37	35	18
26–35	13	17	15	11	25	12
36–49	4	4	8	4	15	9
50–64	1	1	—	—	2	2
65 and over	—	0	—	—	1	2
Unknown	—	4	—	1	—	1
Total	100	100	100	100	100	100

... Figures not appropriate or not applicable.

— Amount too small to be expressed.

[1] The unit of count for this table is persons charged or cleared otherwise for each type of incident. Percentages may not add to 100 due to rounding.

Source: Revised Uniform Crime Reporting survey, Canadian Centre for Justice Statistics, 1993.

attached to the motor vehicle within our society—a symbolism reinforced by the media's glamorization of the motor vehicle and all it is supposed to represent. As far as joyriding is concerned, they maintain, the car is stolen not for what it does, but for the status it confers on its possessor. Other studies have suggested that initial involvement in motor vehicle crime centred on peer influence, the desire to drive or to make money, or boredom (Cooper, 1989; Foster, 1990; Light, Nee, and Ingham, 1993).

Light, Nee, and Ingham (1993) found that most car-theft offenders identify increased maturity and responsibility, not legal sanctions, as the main reason for the cessation of car-theft activities. This seems to support the premise that boredom or the need for excitement are motivating factors in early incentives to commit motor vehicle crimes, a trait characteristic of younger age groups and likely to weaken with maturity. On the other hand, studies have indicated that those who progressed into a long-term car-theft career cited the potential for financial reward and their subsequent dependence on this income as the primary reason for continued involvement in the auto-theft activity (Cooper, 1989; Parker, 1974; Light, Nee, Ingham, 1993).

Frustrated police maintain that the *Young Offenders Act* fails to serve as a deterrent and gives teenagers a licence to steal cars with little to fear if apprehended. This attitude of invincibility by offenders is motivated by a perception that motor vehicle offences are not a serious form of crime. Light, Nee, and Ingham (1993) found that the majority of offenders did not weigh the risks of being apprehended or consider the punishment they would receive if caught. Furthermore, the sanctions attached to motor vehicle crimes, whether fines, probation, or serving a custodial sentence, did not appear to deter a significant number of offenders from committing these offences.

According to Karmen (1979), if we are to understand the conditions that promote motor vehicle crime, we must focus not only on offenders and victims but also on an automobile industry that designs and produces cars that are easily damaged, expensive to repair, and vulnerable to theft because of inadequate security features. Questions have been raised as to whether manufacturers have a vested interest in not designing theft-proof cars, since they profit directly from theft and vandalism in the form of increased sales. In addition, the extra cost to consumers of theft-resistant vehicles serves as a deterrent to manufacturers concerned with declining sales (Brill, 1982), although the 1988 British Crime Survey found that 64% of consumers would be willing to pay higher purchase prices for effective security features (Clarke, 1991).

A number of recent studies have underlined the importance of offender characteristics in attempting to explain auto crime. For instance, unemployment, inadequate schooling, and poor leisure facilities have all been cited as contributing factors (McCullough and Schmidt, 1990; Spencer, 1992). For Briggs (1991), social deprivation in the form of inadequate opportunities for excitement and status is another explanation. However, motorists must accept some responsibility for their misfortunes. According to the 1991 Motor Vehicle Theft Survey (see Figure 12-1), where the security of the vehicle was known at the time of the motor vehicle theft, 23% of vehicles were not locked, 20% had keys left inside, and 2% were left running. These figures may actually be higher because victims of vehicle theft may be reluctant to report their own negligence for fear of jeopardizing their insurance coverage.

It is not known whether motor vehicle theft is inhibited by anti-theft devices such as alarm systems or by etching the vehicle identification number (VIN) on vehicle windows. Theoretically, VIN etching allows stolen parts to be identified and thus renders them undesirable for the resale trade. Organized thieves, however, are able to remove or alter VINs. According to Clarke and Harris (1992), many of these security measures are of doubtful utility to a majority of motorists because they increase the risks for those who do not, or cannot, take advantage of them.

Figure 12-1 Security of Vehicle at Time of Theft[1]

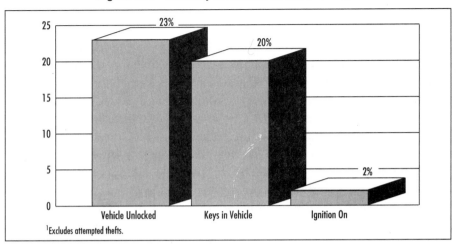

¹Excludes attempted thefts.

Source: Motor Vehicle Theft survey, Canadian Centre for Justice Statistics, 1991.

Property
Crime

According to Spencer (1992) and Light, Nee, and Ingham (1993), high-performance cars were a popular target among young car thieves, as were cars that could be stripped of parts and easily sold. Other vehicles were susceptible to theft due to the high interchangeability of their parts. The Vehicle Information Centre of Canada reports that the most popular two-door car models stolen in 1992–93 were the Mustang Cobra GT, Volkswagen Golf, and Honda Civic (see Table 12-2). Among four-door models, the Volkswagen Golf, Plymouth Sundance, and Dodge Shadow were the most popular targets among thieves. In comparison, the best claim records reported among two-door models were the Buick Regal, Mercury Cougar, and Oldsmobile Cutlass Supreme, while the Mercury Sable, Oldsmobile Ninety-Eight, and Buick Century recorded the lowest theft rates among four-door models.

THE EVENT

Two versions of the UCR survey are running concurrently. The older UCR survey measures the level of criminal activity that comes to the attention of all police forces in Canada. The "revised" UCR survey provides detailed information on the characteristics of an incident, and basic data on victims and accused. In 1993, eighty police forces reported to the revised UCR survey. These forces accounted for approximately 32% of all criminal incidents

Table 12-2 Car-Theft Claim Frequency, 1992–1993[1]

Best Claim Experience			Worst Claim Experience		
Make	Model	Claim Frequency[2]	Make	Model	Claim Frequency[2]
2-Door Models					
Buick	Regal	31	Ford	Mustang Cobra GT	1,221
Mercury	Cougar	31	Volkswagen	Golf	627
Oldsmobile	Cutlass Supreme	39	Honda	Civic	404
Mercury	Topaz	45	Ford	Mustang L(X)	384
Ford	Tempo	48	Acura	Integra	212
Chevrolet	Lumina	52	Dodge/Plymouth	Colt	198
4-Door Models					
Mercury	Sable	20	Volkswagen	Golf	456
Oldsmobile	Ninety-Eight	20	Plymouth	Sundance	184
Buick	Century	21	Dodge	Shadow	180
Chrysler	Fifth Avenue	28	Honda	Civic	174
Pontiac	Bonneville	29	Volkswagen	Jetta	140
Mercury	Grand Marquis	30	Acura	Integra	139

Note: The ranking of claim frequencies is expressed in relative terms, with 100 representing the average in each category. This means that a result of 122 is 22% above the average and a result of 87 is 13% below the average.

[1] Excludes data for British Columbia and Saskatchewan. Theft claim frequency rates are not presented for multipurpose vehicles, passenger vans, and station wagons.

[2] Claim frequency refers to how often a theft claim is presented to an insurance company in comparison to the total number of vehicles insured for theft.

Source: *Car Theft, 1992–93 Models,* Vehicle Information Centre of Canada, 1993.

---

reported to the police. The CCJS also completed a special study on motor vehicle theft that was funded by the Insurance Crime Prevention Bureau of Canada. The purpose of the Motor Vehicle Theft Survey was to provide data on the conditions surrounding motor vehicle theft. Twenty-six large police forces across Canada were asked to complete a form for each motor vehicle stolen during the months of July, August, and September 1991.

According to the Revised UCR survey, radios/stereos were stolen in 28% of thefts from motor vehicles in 1993 (see Figure 12-2). Other items stolen included vehicle accessories such as hubcaps or tires (16%), personal items such as clothing or luggage (16%), currency or identification such as credit cards (11%), and machinery and tools (6%). While firearms accounted for less than 1% of all property stolen, approximately 1,112 firearms were taken from motor vehicles. In her study of young offenders and car crime, Spencer (1992) reports that the primary reason offenders steal property from motor vehicles is to make money.

Figure 12-2 Type of Property Stolen from Motor Vehicles, 1993

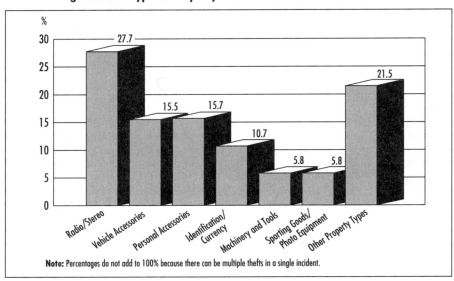

Note: Percentages do not add to 100% because there can be multiple thefts in a single incident.

Source: Revised Uniform Crime Reporting survey, Canadian Centre for Justice Statistics, 1993.

Motor vehicle crime has become a national and international problem, and appears to be escalating at an alarming rate. In recent years, several countries have conducted criminal victimization surveys. Unfortunately, it has not always been possible to use the findings to make detailed comparisons of national crime levels between countries because of different methodological frameworks. In 1989, the first international victimization survey was conducted in fourteen countries. This survey, which used a standard interview questionnaire to ensure comparable results, collected data on eleven types of victimization occurring in 1988. A second survey, conducted in 1992 (the 1992 and 1989 surveys cover crime in the previous year), expanded the number of countries covered to twenty and the number of victimization categories to twelve. For those countries that participated in both cycles of the International Crime Survey, an average of proportions of victimization for both 1988 and 1991 is computed. These numbers are presented in Table 12-3.

The risk of having a motor vehicle stolen was highest in England (2.8%), Australia (2.7%), New Zealand (2.7%), Italy (2.7%), and France (2.4%). Of the twenty countries surveyed, Canada ranked eleventh, with 1.1% of all motor vehicle owners having experienced a motor vehicle theft. The risk of victimization in the United States was more than twice that in Canada.

Table 12-3 Proportion of Car Owners Victimized, 1988 and/or 1991

Year(s)	Theft of Cars/ Joyriding	%	Theft from Cars	%	Car Vandalism	%
(88+91)	England	2.8	Spain	9.9	Canada	9.2
(99+91)	Australia	2.7	USA	8.1	Australia	9.1
(88+91)	New Zealand	2.7	Canada	7.2	Netherlands	8.9
(91)	Italy	2.7	England	7.1	England	8.7
(88)	France	2.4	Italy	7.0	W. Germany	8.7
(88+91)	USA	2.3	New Zealand	6.9	USA	8.5
(91)	Sweden	1.7	Australia	6.7	New Zealand	8.0
(88)	N. Ireland	1.6	Netherlands	6.0	Italy	7.6
(88)	Spain	1.3	France	6.0	Scotland	6.5
(88)	Norway	1.1	Scotland	5.4	Belgium	6.4
(88+91)	Canada	1.1	Poland	5.4	France	6.4
(88+91)	Belgium	1.0	W. Germany	4.7	Spain	6.3
(88)	Scotland	0.8	Czechoslovakia	4.4	Poland	4.9
(88+91)	Japan	0.7	N. Ireland	4.0	Finland	4.8
(91)	Czechoslovakia	0.7	Sweden	3.9	Norway	4.6
(88+91)	Finland	0.6	Belgium	3.3	Sweden	4.6
(91)	Poland	0.6	Norway	2.8	N. Ireland	4.4
(88+91)	Netherlands	0.4	Finland	2.8	Switzerland	4.1
(88)	W. Germany	0.4	Switzerland	1.9	Czechoslovakia	3.7
(88)	Switzerland	0.4	Japan	1.5	Japan	2.7

Source: Jan J.M. van Dijk and Pat Mayhew (1992), *Criminal Victimization in the Industrialized World: Key Findings of the 1989 and 1992 International Crime Surveys,* Netherlands Ministry of Justice.

For thefts from vehicles, Spain (9.9%) and the United States (8.1%) ranked first and second, while Canada (7.2%) ranked third. Vandalism to motor vehicles was most common in Canada (9.2%), followed by Australia (9.1%), Netherlands (8.9%), and England (8.7%). The United States experienced less vehicle vandalism than Canada, ranking sixth overall (8.5%).

Figure 12-3 compares Canada and U.S. motor vehicle crime rates for the period 1980–93. (The fact that the two countries share a similar definition of motor vehicle theft facilitates such a comparison.) Since 1980, the motor vehicle theft rate has been consistently lower in Canada than in the United States. However, the Canadian rate has continued to rise in recent years, whereas the American rate has remained relatively stable. In Canada, the rate increased to 8.9 per 1,000 registered motor vehicles in 1993 from 5.5 in 1988. The rate in the United States was about 8.2 per 1,000 throughout this period.

According to police-reported data, the rate for property thefts from motor vehicles, including both parts and personal property in the vehicle, has

Figure 12-3 Motor-Vehicle Crimes, Canada and the United States, 1980–1993

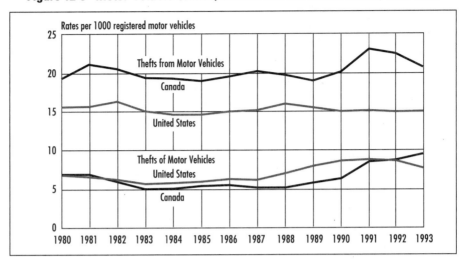

Source: Uniform Crime Reporting survey, Canadian Centre for Justice Statistics, 1993; and Uniform Crime Reporting survey, United States, Federal Bureau of Investigation, 1993.

been considerably higher in Canada for each year since 1980. The Canadian rate increased to 21.1 per 1,000 registered motor vehicles in 1993 from 19.0 per 1,000 in 1980. The American rate was relatively stable throughout the period. In 1993, for example, it was 14.8 per 1,000 vehicles.

According to the UCR survey, 156,811 motor vehicles were stolen in Canada in 1993, the highest annual total recorded since 1961, the year in which comparable statistics were first collected. The rate of theft remained relatively unchanged during the 1980s, before beginning to rise in the 1990s (see Table 12-4).

Among the provinces, owners of motor vehicles in Quebec were the most likely to have had a vehicle stolen during 1993 (see Figure 12-4). That year, 12.9 of every 1,000 registered motor vehicles in that province were stolen. The second highest theft rate was in Manitoba, where 10.1 of every 1,000 vehicles were stolen. The Atlantic provinces reported rates considerably lower than those in central or western Canada, ranging from a high of 2.8 in Prince Edward Island and Nova Scotia to a low of 1.8 in Newfoundland.

British Columbia had the highest provincial rate of property thefts from motor vehicles in 1993, with 35.4 thefts per 1,000 vehicle registrations (see Table 12-5). Ontario (22.3) was the only other province to exceed the national average. As was the case for motor vehicle theft, the Atlantic

Table 12-4   Trends in Motor-Vehicle Crimes, 1980–1993

Year	Motor-Vehicle Registration[1]	Theft of Motor Vehicle	Motor Vehicles Stolen per 1,000 Registrations	% of Motor Vehicles Not Recovered	Theft from Motor Vehicle	Theft from Motor Vehicle, Rate Per 1,000 Registrations
1980	13,717,449	93,928	6.8	19.2	261,021	19.0
1981	13,851,482	96,229	6.9	20.6	289,315	20.9
1982	14,310,717	86,997	6.1	21.9	292,453	20.4
1983	14,620,648	75,988	5.2	22.7	283,357	19.4
1984	14,405,972	76,613	5.3	25.8	281,497	19.5
1985	14,818,625	82,250	5.6	27.3	283,307	19.1
1986	15,114,993	85,585	5.7	26.7	297,502	19.7
1987	15,864,388	87,061	5.5	27.5	318,308	20.1
1988	16,336,261	89,454	5.5	23.4	322,517	19.7
1989	16,719,529	100,208	6.0	26.1	318,573	19.1
1990	16,981,130	114,082	6.7	26.8	352,675	20.8
1991	17,223,039	139,345	8.1	27.4	393,518	22.8
1992	17,412,312	146,801	8.4	27.0	390,887	22.4
1993	17,586,041	156,811	8.9	24.2	370,374	21.1

[1] Source: Motor Vehicle Registrations (Cat. No. 53-219), Transportation Division, Statistics Canada.

Source: Uniform Crime Reporting survey, Canadian Centre for Justice Statistics, 1993.

provinces reported the lowest provincial rates of thefts from vehicles, ranging from 8.1 in New Brunswick to 13.8 in Nova Scotia.

According to the UCR survey, almost two-thirds of all motor vehicles reported stolen in 1993 were automobiles (65%), while 23% were trucks or buses (see Figure 12-5). Five percent of thefts were motorcycles, and 7% were other motor vehicles, such as snowmobiles, tractors, or all-terrain vehicles.

Studies have shown that one of the strongest predictors of motor vehicle theft is the vehicle's location at the time of the offence. Large parking lots and roadside parked cars are the most common sites for motor vehicle crimes (Poyner and Webb, 1987; Saville and Murdie, 1988; Morrison, 1991; Light, Nee, and Ingham, 1993; Morrison and Ogrodnick, 1994). According to the Revised UCR survey, 52% of all motor vehicle thefts, 48% of thefts from vehicles, and 47% of vandalisms took place in parking lots in 1993 (see Table 12-6). Streets, roads, and highways were the second most common location of motor vehicle crimes, with 27% of motor vehicle thefts, 34% of thefts from motor vehicles, and 37% of vandalisms occurring there. Twenty-one percent of motor vehicle thefts, 16% of thefts from motor vehicles, and 14% of vandalisms occurred at a residential location, such as the owner's driveway. The fact that parking lots are prime sites for motor vehicle thefts is

Figure 12-4 Motor-Vehicle Theft Rates by Province, 1993

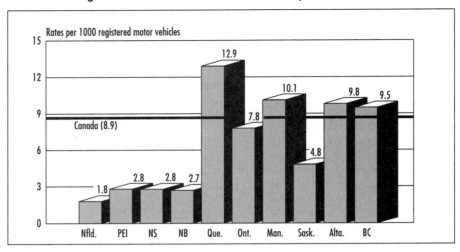

Source: Uniform Crime Reporting survey, Canadian Centre for Justice Statistics, 1993.

Property
Crime

Table 12-5 Motor-Vehicle Crimes by Province/Territory, 1993

Province/ Territory	Motor-Vehicle Registration[1]	Theft of Motor Vehicle	Motor Vehicles Stolen per 1,000 Registrations	% of Motor Vehicles Not Recovered	Theft from Motor Vehicle	Theft from Motor Vehicle, Rate Per 1,000 Registrations
Newfoundland	309,921	572	1.8	9.4	2,576	8.3
Prince Edward Island	90,537	258	2.8	31.3	1,012	11.2
Nova Scotia	625,812	1,777	2.8	25.0	8,660	13.8
New Brunswick	510,454	1,372	2.7	28.8	4,138	8.1
Quebec	3,705,902	47,965	12.9	38.6	54,370	14.7
Ontario	6,231,948	48,703	7.8	24.3	139,141	22.3
Manitoba	787,184	7,932	10.1	10.7	16,248	20.6
Saskatchewan	699,870	3,375	4.8	25.3	11,047	15.8
Alberta	1,910,612	18,718	9.8	17.4	38,346	20.1
British Columbia	2,659,642	25,291	9.5	9.52	94,242	35.4
Yukon	27,436	312	11.4	36.9	376	13.7
Northwest Territories	26,723	536	20.1	26.1	218	8.2
Canada	17,586,041	156,811	8.9	24.2	370,374	21.1

[1] Source: Motor Vehicle Registrations (Cat. No. 53-219), Transportation Division, Statistics Canada.

Source: Uniform Crime Reporting survey, Canadian Centre for Justice Statistics, 1993.

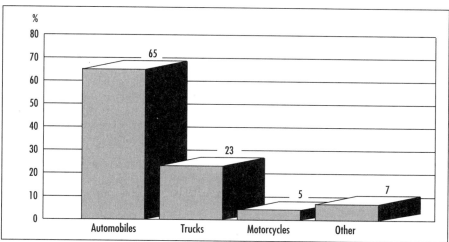

Figure 12-5 Type of Motor Vehicle Stolen, 1993

Source: Uniform Crime Reporting survey, Canadian Centre for Justice Statistics, 1993.

not surprising given that a large number of potential targets are available at any one time in a publicly accessible location and generally left unprotected for considerable lengths of time. While improved security measures such as lighting and patrols might reduce the number of thefts in one parking lot, the likelihood is that these thefts will be displaced to unprotected lots. Brantingham and Brantingham (1984) maintain, however, that offenders may be willing to walk only short distances to locate an unprotected parking lot.

There is some research evidence that motor vehicle crimes are more likely to take place during the night (Ogrodnick and Paiement, 1992; Morrison, 1991; Harlow, 1988; Hope, 1987). Morrison (1991) found that three-quarters of motor vehicle thefts and vandalisms occurred between 6 p.m. and 8 a.m. Furthermore, Ogrodnick and Paiement (1992) found that the likelihood of a vehicle being stolen did not increase during the weekend.

Previous research has identified how offenders marvel at the fact that most vehicles can be entered and driven away in a matter of seconds with minimal risk of police detection (Light, Nee, and Ingham, 1993; Clarke and Harris, 1992). Figure 12-6 indicates that the two most common techniques for gaining access to motor vehicles were using the keys (43%) (keys may have been stolen, duplicated, or left in the vehicle) and disabling the ignition

Table 12-6 Motor-Vehicle Crimes[1] by Location of Incident, 1993

Location of Incident	Theft of Motor Vehicle	Theft from Motor Vehicle	Motor-Vehicle Vandalism
Total No.	24,113	138,911	82,459
Residential[2]	21%	16%	14%
Parking lots[3]	52%	48%	47%
Streets, roads, highways [4]	27%	34%	37%
Other	1%	2%	2%
Unknown	—	1%	1%
Total motor-vehicle violations	100%	100%	100%
Average dollar value of thefts[5]	$5,351	$912	...
Average dollar value of damages[5]	$1,201	$302	$538

... figures not appropriate or not applicable

[1] A single criminal incident may contain multiple motor-vehicle violations. Percentages may not add to 100 due to rounding.

[2] Includes single homes, apartment units, and commercial residences.

[3] Includes commercial and public parking lots.

[4] Includes open areas, schools, public institutions, and public transportation.

[5] Average dollar stolen/damaged calculated on the number of known incidents. Total excludes incidents where the dollar value was unknown.

Source: Uniform Crime Reporting survey, Canadian Centre for Justice Statistics, Statistics Canada, 1993.

lock cylinder (42%). The vehicle steering lock was the focus of attack in 10% of cases, while a tow truck was used to remove vehicles in 1% of cases. For the remaining 3%, other means such as hot wiring or pushing were used.

Motor vehicles are stolen for a variety of reasons. According to the 1991 Motor Vehicle Theft Survey, joyriding was the most common reason (76%) in cases where the purpose of the theft was known (see Figure 12-7). Joyriding is typically committed by amateur thieves who usually abandon the vehicle shortly after its disappearance. Stolen motor vehicles are also often used for various criminal activities (e.g., as getaway cars during robberies or for the transportation of drugs). Figure 12-7 shows that 14% of stolen vehicles were used to commit other criminal offences or to escape from authorities. A further 7% of these vehicles were stolen for the purpose of disassembly and resale of parts. Stolen vehicles can often net double their original value when parts are sold on the black market. The increasing cost of vehicle replacement parts has no doubt contributed to the growth in auto theft for parts.

Another type of vehicle theft involves owners who fraudulently report their vehicle as stolen. In 1991, 2% of vehicle thefts were linked to owners attempting to defraud insurance companies. The remaining 1% of stolen vehicles were resold. This activity usually involves professional thieves who

Figure 12-6   Method of Motor-Vehicle Theft

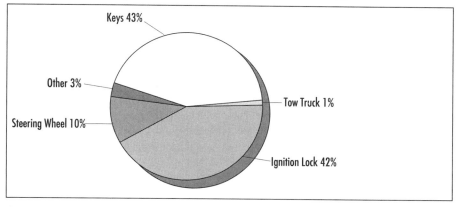

Source: Motor Vehicle Theft survey, Canadian Centre for Justice Statistics, 1991.

operate in organized rings and target specific vehicles for theft and resale. The resale figure may be higher given the difficulty of detecting this particular crime.

THE AFTERMATH

Since 1980, the proportion of unrecovered vehicles has been increasing, rising to 24% in 1993 from 19% in 1980 (see Table 12-4). However. over the last 10 years, the proportion of motor vehicles not recovered has averaged 26%. Among the provinces, Quebec had the highest proportion of motor vehicles not recovered at 39% in 1993, while Newfoundland (9%) and British Columbia (10%) had the lowest proportion of motor vehicles not recovered (see Table 12-5). According to the Motor Vehicle Theft Survey, vans (79%) and cars (72%) were the most likely to be recovered, while snowmobiles (30%) and trailers (23%) were least likely. In light of recent public concern about violent crime, motor vehicle crimes overall may be drawing less attention from police, which would account for declining recovery rates. Another consideration is that we are witnessing the increasing involvement of more skilled offenders (Clarke and Harris, 1992).

Of motor vehicles recovered, 42% were located within 24 hours of being stolen. Over three-quarters (79%) of recovered stolen vehicles were found locally (within the police jurisdiction where the theft occurred). Although most of the stolen vehicles that are recovered are returned to their owners

Figure 12-7   Purpose of Motor-Vehicle Theft

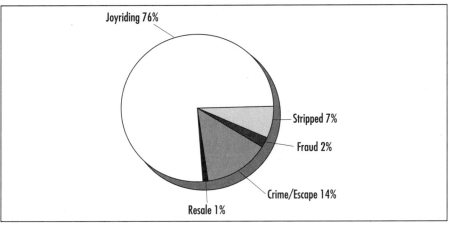

Joyriding 76%

Stripped 7%

Fraud 2%

Crime/Escape 14%

Resale 1%

Source: Motor Vehicle Theft survey, Canadian Centre for Justice Statistics, 1991.

within two days, they are seldom returned in their original condition. Most stolen vehicles (55%) were found damaged upon recovery. Of these, 67% had been involved in an accident, 21% had parts or accessories missing, 8% were totally destroyed and rendered unusable, and almost 4% were completely disassembled. The high proportion of vehicles reported to have been involved in an accident is consistent with the findings of other researchers (see Light, Nee, and Ingham, 1993; Spencer, 1992). The high risk of being involved in an accident appears to stem from the excitement of driving at high speeds and is not viewed by the offender as a deterrent. Light, Nee, and Ingham (1993) characterize offenders' perception of their criminal activity as "youthful feelings of immortality, a belief that it [an accident] will never happen to me, and a high degree of confidence, perhaps misplaced, in driving ability" (44).

Motor vehicle vandalism represented 63% of all motor vehicle crime reported to the 1993 GSS. In addition, motor vehicles were the most common target in vandalisms, representing 56% of such incidents. According to the GSS, the total dollar value of property stolen during motor vehicle thefts amounted to $907 million in 1993, with another $112 million in losses from motor vehicle parts. motor vehicle vandalism accounted for an additional $572 million in losses. More than 60% of all motor vehicle crime resulted in losses of under $500. A further 30% of incidents resulted in losses in excess of $1,000. These dollar values represented the worth of all property stolen/damaged during the commission of a motor-vehicle crime, regardless of whether or not the items were recovered, repaired, or replaced.

The average loss from a motor vehicle theft in 1993 was $5,351, compared with $912 for thefts of accessories or property from vehicles (see Table 12-6). Damages to a stolen motor vehicle averaged $1,201, while damages averaged $302 when the violation involved the theft of property from the vehicle and $538 when a motor vehicle was vandalized. Generally, such losses are not paid for directly by victims of car crimes, but rather are covered by insurance. In 1992, Canadian households paid nearly $8 billion in automotive insurance premiums of which nearly $450 million was for theft coverage.

An average of nine out of 10 motor-vehicle crimes were unsolved by the police in 1993. Theft of property from motor vehicles ranked highest at 95% unsolved, followed by vandalism of motor vehicles (93%) and theft of motor vehicles (85%). In 5% of cases, a motor vehicle reported stolen was "cleared otherwise." The most common reason for a vehicle theft case to be cleared otherwise (44%) was that the police or Crown attorney declined to lay charges. This is often because the owner reported a vehicle stolen only to learn that a relative or acquaintance had borrowed it without permission. When an incident involving a theft from a motor vehicle or vandalism was cleared otherwise (3% and 2% respectively), the primary reason given was that the accused was already involved in other criminal incidents.

Attempts to reduce the conditions that produce crime are an important part of modern crime prevention. In recent years, cooperative efforts between police and the general public have resulted in the implementation of crime-prevention programs that aim to minimize the risk of motor vehicle and other types of crime. Law-enforcement officials and insurance agencies advocate the coordination of educational, enforcement, and engineering efforts as the best means of reducing motor vehicle crime. Drivers can also take simple preventative measures to reduce the likelihood of their vehicle being stolen, such as locking vehicle doors, not leaving keys in the ignition or hidden elsewhere in the vehicle, and not leaving registration, licence, and proof of insurance in the car. A variety of antitheft security products are also available, ranging from steering wheel and transmission locks to electronic car alarms, but further research is required to assess the relative effectiveness of these security devices.

Most major police forces across Canada have initiated antitheft programs. Residents who enrol are given a highly visible sticker to attach to the side or rear window of their car. The sticker alerts patrolling officers to vehicles not usually driven between the hours of midnight and 6 a.m.—the time period when most people are not driving their vehicles—and authorizes them to stop the vehicle during this period and request identification. A similar program in New York City found that of the 28,000 vehicles registered in the program, only 39 were reported stolen.

Public assistance in helping police combat crime is often dependent on the level of community awareness. In today's world of high technology, police forces use computers and telephone networks to simultaneously inform entire neighbourhoods of increases in criminal activity. One such program calls on residents to register their telephone number with their local police force; the number is then entered into an automated database. If a neighbourhood experiences an outbreak of motor vehicle crimes, all residents enlisted in the program receive a recorded telephone message from the police informing them of the occurrences. This program not only heightens public awareness of crime in a specific neighbourhood but also enlists the public's help in detecting and reporting suspicious activities to the police. Strategies that can be used to combat motor vehicle theft include upgrading the physical security features of vehicles and their parts, improving police training programs with respect to the identification of stolen vehicles and their components, curtailing the export of stolen vehicles, and devising a means for cross-checking scrapped vehicles against their registrations (Ogrodnick and Paiement, 1992).

Previous studies have demonstrated that there is a link between automotive design and theft rates (Karmen, 1981). While manufacturers have yet to produce a theft-proof vehicle, they have been working with police and insurance companies to design more sophisticated security systems. One deterrent system called "pass-key" consists of a pellet containing a unique code that is embedded in the ignition key. If a person attempts to start the vehicle with either the wrong key or a key with the correct cut but the wrong code, the fuel system shuts down (Ogrodnick and Paiement, 1992).

In Quebec, which has the highest motor-vehicle theft and nonrecovery rates in Canada, the government has reacted by implementing legislation to combat motor vehicle theft. In September 1987, the *Highway Safety Code* was amended to regulate all individuals selling motor vehicles and used automobile parts in that province. Moreover, recycling plant owners must now maintain a detailed record of vehicles and parts in stock, including their origin and destination. Dealers failing to record every transaction are subject to penalties.

SUMMARY AND CONCLUSIONS
■ ■ ■

The high costs of motor vehicle crimes are escalating the need to find solutions to a growing national problem. Increases in car thefts at gunpoint, more frequent reportings of high-speed chases between police and offenders, and vehicle accidents resulting in serious injury and fatalities to both offenders and innocent bystanders is slowly challenging the popular image of motor vehicle crime as victimless. There is an immediate need for additional research to guide policy initiatives and address the current lack of theoretical analysis of this crime. Better information is required about the conditions that draw young offenders into committing motor vehicle crimes and about the circumstances that foster car-theft careers among adults. Little is known about the relevant effects of improved parking lot security, the deterrent effect of antitheft devices and automobile designs on motor vehicle theft rates, and the growing market for stolen automotive parts. Future research endeavours must also assess the degree of responsibility to be borne by automobile manufacturers, who profit a second time from sales attributed to theft, but whose poor design and security features contributed to the theft in the first place.

Effective prevention programs will require a diversified approach that considers motivational factors such as juvenile boredom, the need for risk and status attainment, inadequate schooling, unemployment, peer pressure, and the recognition that car theft is a means to financial gain. Criminological analysis must consider an offender mindset that trivializes the seriousness of motor vehicle crime and underestimates the likelihood of getting caught or receiving a custodial sentence when apprehended, as well as the apparent failure of sanctions such as fines, probation, or incarceration to reduce recidivism rates. Without detailed knowledge of the extent and nature of motor vehicle crime, it will be difficult to develop successful solutions to this thriving social problem. Effective countermeasures aimed at reducing motor vehicle crime will require a cooperative effort on the part of vehicle owners, the police, federal and provincial regulatory agencies, vehicle manufacturers, and insurance companies.

NOTES

[1] This amount represents the total value of all property stolen or damaged (e.g. breaking garage door in addition to stealing car), regardless of whether or not the property was recovered, replaced, or repaired.

PART V

This section examines two special topic areas, drugs and youth. Illicit drug activity and youth criminality have been the focus of intense public scrutiny over the last few years. Drug crimes have captured public attention through the daily media reports of drug busts, new forms of heroine, drug violence, and gang involvement in drugs. The similar exposure given to youth crime has sparked calls in recent years for a toughening of legal sanctions against young offenders. Chapter 13 provides an extensive review of the nature and extent of illicit drug activity in Canada and the response of the criminal justice system to this crime. Chapter 14 examines juvenile crime in Canada, focusing particular attention on risk factors, offender characteristics, and sentencing patterns.

SPECIAL TOPICS—
DRUGS AND YOUTH

ILLICIT DRUGS

by Lee Wolff and Valerie Pottie Bunge

Drug crimes fall into the category of special prescribed acts that are prohibited by law. Wolff and Pottie Bunge begin this chapter with a brief discussion of the criminalization of drugs in Canada in the early 20th century. They next examine legal definitions of drug crime and drug crime trends since the 1960s. The response of the Canadian court system to this type of crime is addressed in the chapter's concluding section. The authors draw upon studies and national surveys, but take care to emphasize the limitations of each as a source of information on illicit drug activity.

People have been "getting high" for thousands of years—eating opium and marijuana, chewing the coca leaf, consuming the potions of various "medicine men," drinking alcohol, and inhaling tobacco (Boyd, 1991). However, it was not until 1908, when the manufacture and sale of smoking-opium was prohibited, that Canada's crusade against drugs began.

Historical research reveals that, between 1870 and 1908, Chinese merchants with a "Chinese-white" customer base manufactured black tar opium in Vancouver, Victoria, and New Westminster, while "white" pharmacies sold opiate products as patent medicines (Boyd, 1991). It was within this context that Canada's drug control policy was first developed. In 1908, the sale and manufacture of Chinese smoking-opium became prohibited, putting Chinese manufacturers out of business. Patent-medicine companies, however, could continue to sell opiated liquids.

Boyd (1991) suggests that the criminalization of Chinese smoking-opium was, in part, racially motivated. Mackenzie King introduced the first drug legislation in the aftermath of Vancouver's anti-Asiatic riot in 1907. At that time, Vancouver residents rallied to support a ban on Chinese immigration. An ensuing riot resulted in the loss of many Asian businesses. King was sent to Vancouver to assess the damage and compensate the Asian community for its losses. It was within this context that he advocated criminalizing the manufacture and sale of smoking-opium.

Three years later, cocaine joined the ranks of prohibited drugs. In 1911, King told the House of Commons that doctors believed cocaine to be more dangerous than morphine and that continued use of the drug would lead to "the seduction of our daughters and the demoralization of our young men" (Boyd, 1991). He also argued that the offence of possessing illegal drugs was necessary to enforce laws against opium and cocaine. In 1923, marijuana was added to the list of illegal drugs with a simple statement in the House of Commons: "There is a new drug in the schedule." There was no debate. According to Boyd (1991), marijuana had been associated with Mexican immigrants and black jazz musicians, and was said to be connected with madness and promiscuity.

While alcohol went through a short period of prohibition in 1918, it was never enforced with the same vigour as the campaigns against opium, cocaine, and marijuana. By the late 1920s, each province had repealed its prohibition legislation. Together, these events set the stage for the line Canadians draw between legal and illegal drugs in contemporary society.

DEFINITIONS

Today, a plethora of drugs are controlled through criminal sanctions. Cocaine, cannabis, heroin, phencyclidine, and opiates, all of which are covered by the *Narcotics Control Act* (*NCA*), tend to carry the most severe penalties. Box 13-1 outlines the penalties attached to possession, trafficking, possession for the purpose of trafficking, cultivation of opium or cannabis, importing or exporting, and "prescription shopping" (obtaining multiple prescriptions by visiting several doctors). The *Food and Drugs Act* (*FDA*) deals with the nonmedical use of drugs. The offences of trafficking, possession for the purpose of trafficking, and prescription shopping apply to controlled drugs (i.e., amphetamines, barbiturates, and other stimulants, and depressants) (see Box 13-2). The offences of trafficking, possession for the purpose of trafficking, and possession apply to restricted drugs such as LSD.

While the crime statistics discussed in this chapter cover *NCA* and *FDA* offences, it is noteworthy that the *Criminal Code* sets out three other illicit drug crimes (see Box 13-3). There are provisions against possessing property or other proceeds of drug crime, and against "laundering" the proceeds of drug crime. It is also illegal to knowingly import, export, manufacture, promote, or sell illicit drug paraphernalia or literature.

PRECURSORS

The relationship between drug use and criminality is not clear. While evidence of an association abounds, it is unclear if this correlation amounts to

BOX 13-1 NARCOTICS CONTROL ACT

Possession: If someone is convicted of possession for the first time, on *summary conviction,* the penalty can be a fine not exceeding $1,000, a prison term not exceeding 6 months, or both. For a subsequent offence, the penalty is a fine not exceeding $2,000, a prison term not exceeding one year, or both. On conviction of an *indictable offence* the penalty cannot exceed a seven-year prison term.

Trafficking: The maximum penalty for someone convicted of this *indictable offence* is life imprisonment.

Possession for the purpose of trafficking: The maximum penalty for someone convicted of this *indictable offence* is life imprisonment.

Cultivation of opium poppy or marijuana: The maximum penalty for someone convicted of this *indictable offence* is a prison term not exceeding seven years.

Importing and exporting: The maximum penalty for someone convicted of this indictable offence is life imprisonment.

Failure to disclose previous prescriptions: The penalty for someone convicted of this *indictable offence* is a prison term not exceeding seven years. The penalty for someone convicted, for the first time, with a *summary offence,* is a fine not exceeding $1,000 or a prison term not exceeding six months. For subsequent summary convictions, the penalty is a fine not exceeding $2,000 or a prison term not exceeding one year.

BOX 13-2 FOOD AND DRUGS ACT

Possession of a restricted drug: The penalty for someone convicted, for the first time, with a *summary offence*, is a fine not exceeding $1,000, a prison term not exceeding six months, or both. For subsequent summary convictions, the penalty is a fine not exceeding $2,000, a prison term not exceeding one year, or both. The penalty for someone convicted with an *indictable offence* is a fine not exceeding $5,000, a prison term not exceeding three years, or both.

Trafficking in restricted drugs: The penalty for someone convicted of a *summary offence* is a prison term not exceeding 18 months. The penalty for someone convicted of an *indictable offence* is a prison term not exceeding ten years.

Possession of a restricted drug for the purposes of trafficking: The penalty for someone convicted of a *summary offence* is a prison term not exceeding 18 months. The penalty for someone convicted of an *indictable offence* is a prison term not exceeding ten years.

Failure to disclose previous prescriptions: The penalty for someone convicted of a *summary offence* for the first time is a fine not exceeding $1,000 or a prison term not exceeding six months. For subsequent summary convictions, the penalty is a fine not exceeding $2,000 or a prison term not exceeding one year. The penalty for someone convicted of an *indictable offence* is a fine not exceeding $5,000 or a prison term not exceeding three years.

Trafficking in controlled drugs: The penalty for someone convicted of a *summary offence* is a prison term not exceeding 18 months. The penalty for someone convicted of an *indictable offence* is a prison term not exceeding ten years.

Possession for the purposes of trafficking: The penalty for someone convicted of a *summary offence* is a prison term not exceeding 18 months. The penalty for someone convicted of an *indictable offence* is a prison term not exceeding ten years.

cause. For example, Fagan (1990) suggests that the ingestion of intoxicants is a direct pharmacological cause of aggression. However, Fagan's review of related studies also shows that people who become aggressive after consumption often have aggressive histories.

On the other hand, a link has been established between heavy drug use and crimes motivated by the need to finance expensive drug habits. Researchers have found that, among high-rate offenders who are also heroin addicts, the frequency of criminal behaviour varies directly with drug use; in other words, when these offenders decrease their drug consumption, they

BOX 13-3 CRIMINAL CODE

Instruments and literature for illicit drug use: No person shall knowingly import into Canada, export from Canada, manufacture, promote, or sell instruments or literature for illicit drug use.

The penalty for someone convicted, for the first time, with a *summary conviction* is a fine not exceeding $100,000, a prison term not exceeding six months, or both. For subsequent offences the penalty is a fine not exceeding $300,000, a prison term not exceeding one year, or both.

Possession of property obtained by certain offences: No person shall possess any property or any proceeds of any property knowing that all or part of the property or of those proceeds was obtained or derived directly or indirectly as a result of (a) the commission in Canada of trafficking, possession for the purpose of trafficking, importing and exporting drugs, and cultivation of opium poppy or marijuana; or (b) an act or omission anywhere that, if it occurred in Canada, would have constituted an offence as listed in section (a) above.

The penalty for someone convicted of an *indictable offence* is a prison term not exceeding ten years, where the value of the subject-matter of the offence exceeds $1,000. If the value of the subject-matter does not exceed $1,000 the person can be dealt with *summarily* (i.e., 6 months in prison or a fine not exceeding $1,000) or be charged with an indictable offence punishable by a prison term not exceeding two years.

Laundering proceeds of certain offences: No person shall use, transfer the possession of, send or deliver to any person or place, transport, transmit, alter, dispose of or otherwise deal with, in any manner and by any means, any property or any proceeds of any property with intent to conceal or convert that property or those proceeds and knowing that all or a part of that property or of those proceeds was obtained by or derived directly or indirectly as a result of: (a) the commission in Canada of trafficking, possession for the purpose of trafficking, importing and exporting drugs, and cultivation of opium poppy or marijuana; or (b) an act or omission anywhere that, if it occurred in Canada, would have constituted an offence as listed in section (a) above.

Someone convicted of an *indictable offence* is liable to a prison term not exceeding ten years or may be dealt with *summarily* (i.e., 6 months in prison or a fine not exceeding $1,000).

221

Illicit Drugs

also typically lessen their rate of criminality (Chaiken and Chaiken, 1990). However, some argue that those who are willing to use violence to support their addiction were typically involved in crime prior to the onset of heroin use (Fry, 1985).

Official drug crime statistics, as measured by the Uniform Crime Reporting (UCR) survey, do not represent a complete count of drug crimes. Since drug offences usually involve consenting parties, they are less likely than other types of crimes to be reported to the police. Consequently, drug offences that come to the attention of the police are, for the most part, those that the police detect on their own. As well, the UCR survey classifies each offence by the most serious violation within a criminal incident. This means that if, for example, a violent crime and a drug crime are committed within the same incident, the incident is classified as a violent crime and the drug crime is not counted. Changes in drug crime rates over time should also be interpreted with caution. Trends may not reflect changes in drug use, but rather, changing priorities of police departments.

DRUG CRIME TRENDS

The last decade has witnessed significant shifts in the nature of drug crime. Supply offences (in particular, trafficking) account for an increasing proportion of drug crimes, while possession offences make up a declining majority. Also, cocaine-related drug crimes are much more prevalent than they were a decade ago, while the proportion of drug crimes involving cannabis has gone down significantly. These changes do not necessarily reflect trends in illicit drug use, but rather the increased focus of law enforcement on more serious offences and more dangerous drugs.

Drug crimes have historically accounted for fewer than 3% of all offences reported by the police. While this proportion has remained relatively steady over the years, the number of drug crimes per 100,000 people is now considerably higher than it was at the beginning of the 1960s, when national figures were first tabulated. In 1993, drug crimes numbered 56,811 or 198 per 100,000 people (see Figure 13-1). By contrast, the rate in 1962 was just 5 per 100,000 people.

Shifts in enforcement policies over the years have directed attention away from cannabis and toward drugs seen as more harmful to the community, such as cocaine and its derivative, crack. These substances have been involved in an increasing proportion of all drug crimes over the past seventeen years. In 1993, trafficking in cocaine constituted over one-third of all trafficking offences, up sharply from just 4% in 1977 (see Figure 13-2). Similarly, almost one-third of importation offences involved cocaine in 1993,

Figure 13-1 Drug Crime Rate, 1962–1993

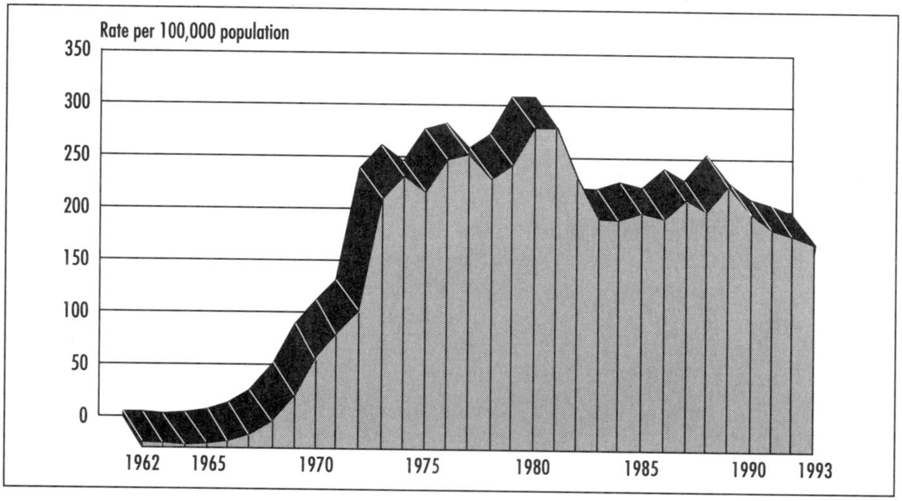

Rate per 100,000 population

Source: Uniform Crime Reporting survey, Canadian Centre for Justice Statistics, 1993.

compared with about one-fifth in 1977. Cocaine possession, although still relatively uncommon, accounted for close to one-fifth of all possession offences in 1993; the proportion was almost nonexistent in 1977.

Over the same period, the proportion of crimes involving cannabis declined sharply. Nonetheless, such offences still made up the majority of all drug crimes in 1993. That year, 44% of trafficking offences involved cannabis, down from 69% in 1977. Likewise, cannabis importation offences dropped significantly over this time period, as did cannabis-possession offences.

In the early 1980s, the RCMP began targeting drug suppliers (traffickers, importers, and cultivators). Consequently, supply crimes now account for a much larger proportion of drug crimes than they did in the past. Overall, trafficking, importation, and cultivation offences made up more than one-third of drug crimes in 1993, more than double the proportion in 1977 (see Figure 13-3). This increase was due mostly to the rise in trafficking offences, which accounted for 31% of drug crimes in 1993, compared with 16% in 1977. Over the same period, importation and cultivation offences together rose to around 7% of drug crimes in 1993, from just under 2% in 1977.

Despite the large increases in supply offences, however, possession offences dominate. In 1993, these offences accounted for 60% of drug crimes—considerably down nevertheless from 82% in 1977. The downturn

Figure 13-2 Cocaine and Cannabis as a Proportion of Trafficking Offences, Canada, 1977–1993

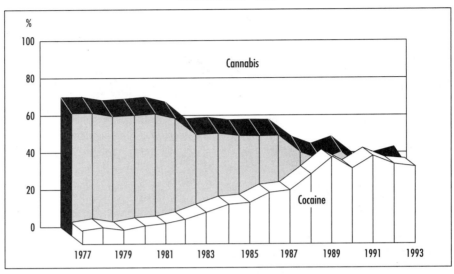

Source: Uniform Crime Reporting survey, Canadian Centre for Justice Statistics, 1993.

in possession offences is no doubt a reflection of shifting police priorities. However, it also parallels shifts that are occurring in the nature and extent of illicit drug use. While most Canadians take drugs in one form or another, illicit drug use is relatively uncommon and has become even less so over time. In 1993, a very small minority of respondents to a national survey reported illicit drug use in the previous year. Among Canadians aged 15 and over, about 866,000 said that they had used cannabis at least once in the past year, representing 4% of the population (see Figure 13-4). For the most

DOMESTIC MARIJUANA INCREASING

Cultivation offences, although still a small proportion of overall drug crimes, have more than quadrupled in number since the late 1980s. In 1993, there were 2,797 such offences, compared with 676 in 1986. The proportion of domestic marijuana on the market also more than doubled over roughly the same period. According to the RCMP, an estimated 25% of the market share was produced in Canada in 1991, compared with just 10% in 1986. This increase is largely attributed to advancements in hydroponic and other sophisticated indoor cultivation techniques, which make it possible to grow crops year-round in any part of the country.

Source: National Drug Intelligence Estimate. Ottawa: RCMP, 1993.

Figure 13-3   Possession[1] and Supply Offences as a Proportion of Drug Crimes, Canada, 1977–1993

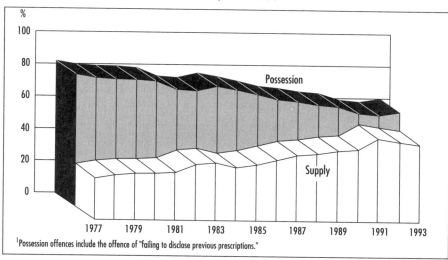

[1]Possession offences include the offence of "failing to disclose previous prescriptions."

Source: Uniform Crime Reporting survey, Canadian Centre for Justice Statistics, 1993.

MOST ILLICIT DRUGS IMPORTED

Most cultivated substances, such as cannabis, coca, and opium, are produced in other countries and smuggled into Canada. According to the RCMP, Colombia was Canada's primary cocaine supplier in 1991, accounting for an estimated 65% of the market. Other principal source countries were Peru (15%) and Brazil (10%). The heroin that reaches Canada is produced mostly in the developing countries of Asia. In 1992, Southeast Asia (42%) and Southwest Asia (38%) supplied most of Canada's illicit heroin.

Unlike cocaine and heroin, a significant share of Canada's marijuana market is produced domestically. In 1991, domestically grown marijuana accounted for 25% of the market share; the remainder originated in Jamaica (20%), Thailand/Southeast Asia (20%), Mexico (15%), Colombia (10%), Trinidad/Tobago (5%), and the United States (5%). Pakistan, Afghanistan, and India supplied 70% of the hashish market in 1991; the remainder originated in Lebanon. Almost all liquid hashish originated in Jamaica, although 10% was produced domestically.

part, use was relatively infrequent. An even smaller proportion had reportedly used either LSD, speed, or heroin and cocaine or crack.

The proportion of adult Canadians reporting cannabis use in 1993 was about one-third of the 1980 level. The 1993 rate (4%) is slightly lower than

Figure 13-4 Population Aged 15 and Over Reporting Illicit Drug Use, Canada, 1993

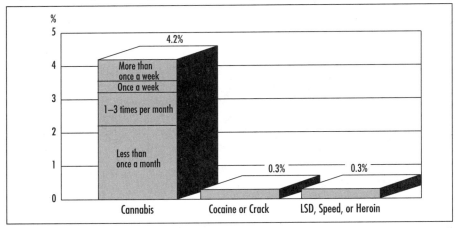

Source: General Social Survey, Statistics Canada, 1993.

*Special
Topics—
Drugs and
Youth*

PROFILE OF CANNABIS USERS

- In the year preceding the 1993 GSS survey, respondents within the 25–34 age group were most likely to have indulged. Younger Canadians (20–24) were also relatively frequent users, while use among older Canadians (45 plus) was virtually nonexistent.

- About two-thirds of users were single, while only one-third were married.

- Men were twice as likely as women to have used cannabis: 69% of users were men compared with 31% who were women. Men were also more likely than women to be frequent users. While 11% of cannabis users reporting weekly consumption were men, just 4% were women.

- Cannabis users tend to fall within relatively high income brackets. Those reporting a middle or upper-middle income were five times as likely to report using cannabis as those in the lower income brackets (54% compared to 10%).

- Those with relatively high levels of education are also more likely to use cannabis. Almost two-thirds of users had at least some post-secondary university education.

- While the demographic profile of alcohol users differs from that of cannabis users, users of both substances tend to have relatively high levels of educational attainment and income.

Source: General Social Survey, Statistics Canada, 1993.

the 1989 (6%) and 1985 (5%) rates, and substantially lower than the rate in 1980 (12%). Furthermore, data available from Ontario students reveals significant long-term declines in cannabis use between 1979 and 1993, from 32% to 13% of respondents (see Figure 13-5).

While statistics are less comprehensive for illicit drugs other than cannabis, available data suggest that the use of LSD, speed, or heroin and cocaine or crack is not rising. In the case of LSD, speed, or heroin, reported use rates were about the same in 1989 and 1993 (0.4% and 0.3% respectively). In the case of cocaine or crack, use rates were actually lower in 1993 than in 1989 (0.3% versus 1.4%). Also, studies of Ontario students reveal a gradual drop in rates of reported cocaine use between 1979 and 1993, from 5.1% to 1.5% of respondents.

While national surveys have been used to measure the number of people who use illicit drugs, other relevant information is lacking, for example, information regarding dosages, temporal patterns of use, and situational features of consumption. Given that very few people report illicit drug use, national samples are typically not large enough to yield reliable estimates beyond prevalence estimates.

Figure 13-5   Ontario Students in Grades 7, 9, 11, and 13 Reporting Cannabis and Cocaine Use, 1977–1993

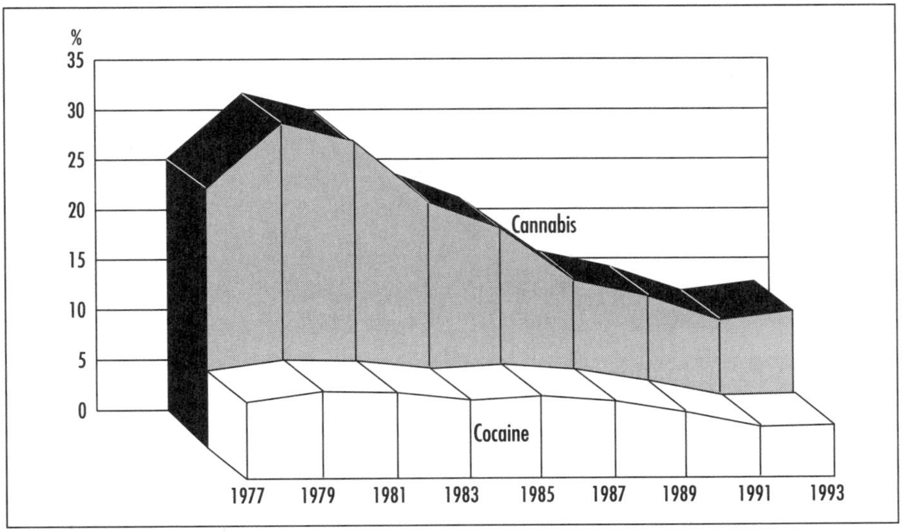

Source: Ontario Student Drug Survey, 1977–1993, Addiction Research Foundation.

Table 13-1 Profile of Cannabis and Alcohol Users[1]

		Cannabis		Alcohol
GENDER	Male	69%	Male	53%
	Female	31%	Female	47%
AGE	15–17 yrs	9%	15–17 yrs	4%
	18–19 yrs	12%	18–19 yrs	4%
	20–24 yrs	21%	20–24 yrs	11%
	25–34 yrs	39%	25–34 yrs	24%
	35–44 yrs	15%	35–44 yrs	23%
	45–54 yrs	4%	45–54 yrs	15%
	55–64 yrs	1%	55–64 yrs	10%
	65–74 yrs	0%	65–74 yrs	7%
	75+	0%	75+	2%
MARITAL STATUS	Single	59%	Single	27%
	Married/common-law	35%	Married/common-law	62%
	Divorced/separated	6%	Divorced/separated	6%
	Widowed	0%	Widowed	4%
INCOME	Lowest	6%	Lowest	4%
	Lower middle	5%	Lower middle	6%
	Middle	24%	Middle	20%
	Upper middle	30%	Upper middle	32%
	Highest	12%	Highest	14%
EDUCATION	Completed university	33%	Completed university	40%
	Some post-secondary	30%	Some post-secondary	18%
	Secondary	12%	Secondary	17%
	Less than secondary	25%	Less than secondary	25%
EMPLOYMENT STATUS	Professional	4%	Professional	9%
	Semiprofessional	13%	Semiprofessional	12%
	Supervisor	3%	Supervisor	3%
	Skilled/farmer	13%	Skilled/farmer	13%
	Semiskilled	15%	Semiskilled	12%
	Unskilled	11%	Unskilled	10%
	Student	27%	Student	12%
	Other	14%	Other	29%

[1] Includes respondents who reported having used cannabis/alcohol at least once in the year preceding the survey.

Note: Columns may not total 100% due to the exclusion of the not stated categories.

Source: General Social Survey, Statistics Canada, 1993.

Crime data are also limited. Illicit drug offences are, for national statistical purposes, considered consensual crimes. This means that much of the information available for crimes "against the person" (e.g., drug consumption, weapons use, and injuries inflicted) is not collected. Of course, we know that this information is highly relevant to the illicit drug trade. Indeed, dealing in illegal drugs is known to involve violence as a means of resolving disputes or as a disciplinary measure. According to Statistics Canada's Homicide Survey, 189 people were known to have been slain in connection with a drug-dealing dispute in the period 1991 to 1993. These murders account for 9% of all people murdered in those years.

THE AFTERMATH

Sample data drawn from selected police departments provide at least some insight into the illicit drug crimes that are reported by the police (Revised UCR survey). For example, sample data reveal that the large majority of those involved in possession and trafficking incidents in 1993 were predominantly male (86%) and had a median age of 27 years. While men were also dominant in importation and cultivation incidents, those involved in these crimes were somewhat older (30 and 31 respectively). Sample data also suggest that the likelihood of being charged in a drug incident varies with the type of crime. In 1993, people involved in possession (90%), trafficking (88%), and importation (82%) incidents were usually charged by the police, while those involved in cultivation incidents were much less likely to be charged (40%).

Court-based data on illicit drug activity are seriously limited by the fact that the most comprehensive data source available at this time excludes incidents involving cannabis, the drug most frequently connected with illicit drug crime (about 60% of all drug incidents in 1993 involved cannabis). However, data available for charges involving other substances provide some perspective on how Canadian courts respond to drug crimes.

For example, in 1992, the Canadian court system disposed of close to 7,000 possession charges (excluding cannabis), two-thirds of which resulted in conviction (Health and Welfare Canada, unpublished data). Fines and prison terms were ordered for about one-half and one-third of these convictions respectively. Close to one-half of all prison terms were for less than one month and almost 90% were for less than six months.

The more serious offences of trafficking and importation generally result in prison sentences. Canadian courts disposed of about 9,000 trafficking charges in 1992 (excluding cannabis); of that number, three-quarters resulted in conviction. Prison terms were ordered over 90% of the time. The most frequent terms were for less than six months (38%) and the vast majority were for less than one year (56%). Importation charges, accounting for about 1% of drug charges, resulted in conviction 65% of the time in 1992. Almost all of these convictions resulted in prison terms of over one year (90%).

SUMMARY AND CONCLUSIONS
■ ■ ■

Public attitudes toward drug use have shifted since the division between "good" and "bad" drugs was created at the turn of the century. For example, a national survey conducted in 1990 indicates that a strong minority (35%) of Canadians believe that the possession of marijuana should not be a criminal offence (Health and Welfare Canada, 1992). Nevertheless, possessing cannabis continues to carry costly criminal sanctions, accounting for close to three-quarters of all possession offences and resulting in numerous charges every year.

At the same time, shifts in attitude have also occurred with respect to the licit substances on the drug menu. That is, Canadians have become much more attuned to the negative effects of the so-called "good" drugs over the years. Canada's 1987 National Drug Strategy, which aims to reduce the harms associated with "substance" abuse generally, is witness to this broadened perspective. It clearly recognizes, for example, the very serious dangers associated with the drugs of choice among Canadians—tobacco and alcohol. Research suggests that about 35,000 Canadians die prematurely each year from tobacco use and another 3,000 to 15,000 suffer alcohol-related deaths (Boyd, 1991). Meanwhile, cannabis, the most commonly used illicit drug, accounts for less than an estimated ten deaths annually.

Given these changes in attitude, it is not surprising that pressures to take stock of our drug-control policies are emerging. For example, Boyd (1991) calls for a thorough examination of Canada's drug-control policy, including the rationale for the substances subject to control under statutes dealing with illicit drugs and nonmedical drug use. This rationale, he argues, should be based on "public health" issues rather than on the "morality" issues that today's policies have inherited from early 20th-century thinking. Perhaps he is right. Even though the effects of some drugs are still not fully known, scientific knowledge has grown considerably over the years, as has our knowledge of the patterns, extent, and consequences of "substance" use generally. Indeed, Canada's policymakers have a wealth of information and experience to draw upon in formulating new approaches to drug control for 21st-century Canadians.

YOUTH CRIME

by Glen Doherty and Paul de Souza

In this chapter, Glen Doherty and Paul de Souza investigate the current state of juvenile crime in Canada. They begin with a review of the principles contained in the Young Offenders Act. *The key risk factors associated with youth criminality are next examined. Following an in-depth examination of offender characteristics, the authors address charging and sentencing patterns for young offenders. Consideration is also given to alternative measures programs and the problems of youth violence and recidivism.*

The introduction of the *Young Offenders Act* (YOA) on April 2, 1984 changed, in many fundamental respects, the organization and delivery of youth justice services in Canada. The *YOA* replaced the *Juvenile Delinquents Act* (*JDA*) and was to serve as a guideline for Canadians regarding the nature, purpose, and effectiveness of juvenile justice. There were criticisms that the *JDA* was not delivering on its promise to control juvenile delinquency by providing young offenders with protection, treatment, and guidance. As well, Canadian society needed protection from their criminal conduct and the young offender needed to be held accountable for his or her behaviour.

The *YOA* is based on the following four key principles that strike a balance between the needs of young people and the interests of society.

1. Young people are responsible for their behaviour and should be held accountable in a manner appropriate to their age and maturity.
2. Society has a right to protection from illegal behaviour and a responsibility to prevent criminal conduct by young people.
3. In view of their special needs, young people may require not only supervision, discipline, and control but also guidance and assistance.
4. Young people have the same rights as adults to due process of law and fair and equal treatment, including the right to participate in deliberations that affect them, the right to the least interference with their freedom that is compatible with the protection of society and their own needs, and the right to be informed of their rights and freedoms.

In addition, the *YOA* holds that while they should be held accountable for their actions, young persons should have special rights and guarantees. The Act allows alternatives to judicial proceedings and limits judicial discretion by clearly defining sentencing options and by setting maximum penalties. It also gives the courts greater control over the application and review of dispositions.

PRECURSORS

Social theories tend to explain the determinants of youth crime in terms of conditions that are often associated with youth who become involved in criminal activity. Whether the youth sets out purposefully to engage in criminal acts, is the unwitting participant in the criminal activities of a peer group, or is simply not cognizant of the consequences of his/her actions, criminal activity is the result. Social scientists and criminologists have attempted to test and document those circumstances and factors that tend to place youth most at risk of involvement in criminal activity. These preconditions or risk factors are the precursors of youth criminality. Although risk factors do not determine the eventual youth involvement in criminal activity, they do increase the likelihood of, or opportunity for, involvement.

Age and gender form two of the most telling of risk factors. Youths aged 12 to 17 are charged with 14% of violent crime and 29% of property crime while constituting only 8% of the total population. Males make up half of the general population but are responsible for 82% of the caseload generated in the youth courts.

Although age and sex are important risk factors associated with youth crime, they are not determinants of youth crime. Causes of youth involvement in crime have been determined to range from family and life experiences through to social and economic factors.

In Canada, being a youth in some aboriginal communities is a strong determinant or factor in potential involvement ostensibly because of the disproportionately high numbers of aboriginal youth in conflict with the law. This factor may, however, reflect economic and social conditions that prevent aboriginal youth from realizing opportunities enjoyed by the rest of Canadians. Aboriginal people constitute approximately 1.5–2% of the Canadian population while making up approximately 8–10% of the federal correctional institution population.

Impoverished and disadvantaged groups would appear to have higher than normal rates of youth involvement in criminal activity. The representation of these groups in correctional facilities may be indicative of an inability to afford quality legal counsel and/or the lack of a supportive home environment. The support of a family that develops sound social values, provides care, and cultivates structure and discipline is a strong positive influence on the development of youth that tends to reduce the risk of criminality. In contrast, marital discord, child abuse, and parental involvement in crime or drug/alcohol abuse pose significant threats to the development of youth, resulting in an increased tendency toward involvement in crime.

The structure of the family is also seen as a factor in youth involvement in criminal activity. Hagan, Simpson, and Gillis's (1987) study of power-control theory maintains that the family structure—patriarchal versus egalitarian—affects the risk of criminal activity. Patriarchal families experienced elevated rates of male youth criminality while egalitarian families had increased levels of female involvement in crime.

Social pressure in the form of cultural differences sets the stage for potential conflict for youths, where differing sets of cultural beliefs and/or values conflict with those of the predominant groups in our society. The effects of peer pressure and need for association with groups provides a strong risk factor for youths, especially if the activities of the group come to focus on criminal activity. Studies show that the bulk of criminal activity involving youths occurs with more than one perpetrator. Brownfield and Thompson (1991) found that "measures of peer involvement in delinquency are strongly and positively associated with self-reported delinquency."

The need to realize social expectations forms another very important factor that may influence the direction of youths and the potential for criminality. The need to be successful in an environment that is devoid of opportunities often leaves youths without another choice. According to the routine activity theory of Cohen and Felson (1979), youths are at high risk of criminal behaviour when they are motivated and a suitable unprotected target presents itself.

Increasingly, youths in conflict with the law are being diagnosed with learning disorders that play significant roles in their introduction to criminality. These youths may lack the self-control needed to curb impulsive behaviour or be blissfully unaware of the potential consequences of their actions (Gottfredson and Hirschi, 1990). Low self-control has its roots in negative influences within the family, schools, and peer groups. Such negative influences may well occur in concert with a learning disorder, such as attention deficit disorder.

THE EVENT

According to the Revised Uniform Crime Reporting (UCR) survey, in 1993, 133,029 youths were charged with federal offences covered in the *Criminal Code*, the *Narcotic Control Act*, the *Food and Drugs Act*, and other federal Acts. Of these youths, 16% were charged with violent offences while the majority (56%) were involved in property crimes. In 1986, only 9% of youths charged with federal offences were charged with violent offences. About one-half (49%) of youths charged with violent offences in 1993 were involved in level 1, or minor, assaults.

PROFILE OF THE YOUNG OFFENDER

In 1993, 8% of the Canadian population were aged 12 to 17. Of all accused in Canada, this age group accounted for 14% of persons accused in violent incidents and 25% of persons accused in property incidents. Young adults aged 18 to 24 (10% of the 1993 population) and adults aged 25 to 34 (17% of the 1993 population) accounted for 22% and 32% respectively of those accused in violent incidents. Males accounted for the majority of persons charged in property and violent incidents as well as incidents of break and enter, theft over $1,000, and theft under $1,000. With respect to particular violent incidents, males accounted for the majority of robberies and sexual- or common-assault incidents.

In 1993–94, approximately eight in ten young offenders were males and one-half of the youth court caseload involved 16- to 17-year-old youths. One-fifth of all cases involved 15-year-old youths while about 26% of all cases involved youths aged 12 to 14. There was a 6% increase in caseload from the previous year for the 12- to 13-year-old age group.

Males appearing in youth court were older than the females. More than half (53%) of males were 16 and 17 years of age compared to 41% of females (see Figure 14-1). Younger youths tended to appear in youth court for different kinds of cases than older youths. Fifty percent of the charges against 12- to 13-year-old youths were for theft under $1,000 (23%), break and enter (14%), and minor assault (13%). These three offences accounted for 42% of the cases involving 14- to 15-year-old youths, and 36% of cases involving 16- to 17-year-old youths. On the other hand, involvement in such offences as failure to appear/comply, the *YOA* offences, possession of stolen goods, theft over $1,000, and drug offences tended to increase with age. Since 1986–87, the population at risk—12 through 17 years of age—has increased by only 3%.

FEMALE YOUNG OFFENDERS

In 1993, the UCR survey reported that a total of 133,029 young persons in Canada were charged by police with federal statute offences. Of this number, 27,423 (21%) were females. Since 1986, the number of female youths charged has increased by 50% (from 18,336 charged in 1986 to 27,423 in

Figure 14-1 Youth Court Cases by Age and Sex of Accused, Canada, 1993–1994

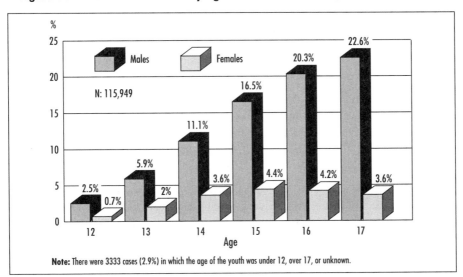

Note: There were 3333 cases (2.9%) in which the age of the youth was under 12, over 17, or unknown.

Source: Paul Souza, "Youth Court Statistics, 1993–94 Highlights," *Juristat Service Bulletin* 15(3), January 1995, p. 4.

1993), far surpassing the 12% increase for male youths (from 94,691 to 105,606 charged).

A comparison of charges against female and male youths in each jurisdiction revealed that the proportion of charges involving young females was below the national average in Quebec and in the Atlantic provinces compared to the proportion of charges in Ontario and in the Prairie provinces. These proportions ranged from 13% in Quebec to 24% in Saskatchewan.

In 1993, female youths were charged with a federal statute offence at a rate of 24 charged per 1,000 female youth population, which is almost four times lower than the male youth rate of 88 charged per 1,000 male youth population. In comparison, the charge rate for adult females (8 charged per 1,000 adult females) is one-third the charge rate for female youths. Quebec had the lowest rate (8 per 1,000 female youths), while Saskatchewan and Manitoba displayed the highest rates (47 and 46 respectively).

In 1993, the majority of the charges against female youths involved theft under $1,000 (40%). Most charges of theft under $1,000 for young females involved shoplifting (87%). Minor assault (12%) was the next most common offence, followed by bail violations (7%) and break and enter (6%). Male youths were also charged most frequently—but to a lesser extent than female youths—with theft under $1,000 (21%).

The number of charges against young females involving minor assault has shown almost a fourfold increase since 1986 (from 968 to 3,386 charges). This compares to a 137% increase in minor assault charges (from 3,031 to 7,188 charges) for male youths.

YOUTH VIOLENCE

There has been a growing concern on the part of Canadians about the apparent rise in violent crime among youth. Although there has been an increase in the reported counts of incidents of youths charged and youth cases processed in the courts, this increase must be considered in the context of decreased societal tolerance for youth violence and public demands for increased police intervention. Changes in the charging practices of police, reluctance on the part of Crown officials to use diversion programs, and the prevalence of "zero tolerance" policies in the schools may well drive the apparent increases in youth violence.

As mentioned earlier, in 1993 youths accounted for 14% of all persons charged with violent offences, up sharply from 11% in 1986. In 1993, youths were charged with 126,932 *Criminal Code* offences, 17% of which were violence-related offences. Of the 21,471 youths charged with violent offences in 1993, 49% were charged with minor assault. Between 1986 and 1993, the number of youths charged with violent offences increased at a faster rate than the number of adults charged with violent offences. There was an annual average increase in the incidents of violence of 13%. The rate of youth charged in violent incidents rose from 408 per 100,000 population in 1986 to 921 per 100,000 population in 1993. The increase in the rate of youth involvement in violent crime has slowed in recent years. Compared to a high of 21% in 1988, the percentage change in the rates of youth involvement in violent crime has decreased to just 6% in 1993 over the previous year.

A comparison of 1988 and 1993 General Social Survey (GSS) results would appear to substantiate the view that increases in the youth crime rate are more a product of better reporting and less tolerance on the part of government, school, and police officials than they are a reflection of actual increases in youth crime.

THE AFTERMATH

YOUTH COURT CASELOAD

According to the Youth Court Survey (YCS), in 1993–94, 115,949 cases involving 212,906 federal statute charges were heard in youth courts. Relative to 1992–93, the youth court caseload remained virtually unchanged in 1993–94. As in previous years, there was an average of two charges per case.

Excluding Ontario and the Northwest Territories,[1] there has been a 25% increase in the youth court caseload since 1986–87 (see Figure 14-2). Much of this caseload increase was due to administrative offences, which include all offences against the administration of justice under the *YOA* and the *Criminal Code*. Excluding these offences, the number of cases heard has increased by 7% since 1986–87.

In 1993–94, there were 59,138 property offence cases, 23,374 violent offence cases, 18,922 other *Criminal Code* offence cases, 11,018 *YOA* offence cases, 3,130 drug offence cases, and 367 cases involving other federal statute offences. Data indicate that the cases heard most often in youth court involved theft under $1,000 (17%), break and enter (13%), offences against the *YOA* (10%), minor assault (9%), and failure to appear/comply (9%) (see Table 14-1).

Figure 14-2 Youth Court Cases by Offence Category, Canada, 1986–1987[1] and 1993–1994

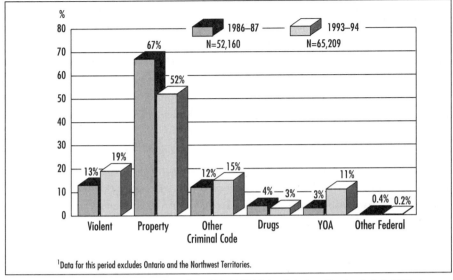

[1]Data for this period excludes Ontario and the Northwest Territories.

Source: Paul de Souza, "Youth Court Statistics, 1993–94 Highlights," *Juristat Service Bulletin* 15(3), January 1995, p. 7.

Compared to 1992–93, the number of property cases has decreased by 5% while the number of cases in all other offence categories has either increased or remained near the same level. Since 1992–93, the number of cases involving violence has increased by 8% (1,721 cases). Two-thirds of this increase (1,137 cases) was due to an increase in minor assault cases. Since 1986–87, both violent offence cases and cases involving administration of justice offences have increased as proportions of overall caseload.

In 1993–94, 78,010 or two-thirds of cases heard in youth courts resulted in a finding of guilt for at least one charge. Proceedings were stayed or withdrawn in 28% of cases, and another 4% resulted in findings of not guilty or dismissal. Few cases were transferred to adult court (94) or to another province/territory (204). Slightly less than half (47%) of all cases transferred to adult court involved violent offences. Manitoba reported half of all cases transferred to adult court.

Cases involving escape custody/unlawfully at large, impaired driving, and break and enter resulted most often in a finding of guilt at 90%, 84%, and 76% respectively. Youth court cases least likely to result in a finding of guilt were failure to appear/comply (55%), aggravated/weapon assault (60%), sexual assault (60%), and theft under $1,000 (62%).

Table 14-1 Cases Heard in Youth Courts by Principal Charge and Age,[1] 1993–1994

Principal Charge[2]	Total Cases	12–13 Years	14–15 Years	16–17 Years
Theft under $1,000	19,481 (17%)	23	18	15
Break and enter	15,643 (13%)	14	14	13
YOA offences	11,018 (10%)	6	9	9
Minor assault	10,854 (9%)	13	10	8
Failure to appear/comply	10,843 (9%)	8	9	9
Possession of stolen goods	7,746 (7%)	5	6	7
Mischief/damage	6,144 (5%)	8	5	5
Theft over $1,000	4,346 (4%)	3	4	4
Aggravated assault/weapon	4,145 (4%)	4	3	4
Drug offences	3,130 (3%)	1	2	4
Weapons/firearms/explosives	2,713 (2%)	2	2	2
Robbery	2,318 (2%)	2	2	2
Escape/unlawfully at large	2,082 (2%)	1	2	2
Fraud/forgery	2,064 (2%)	1	1	2
Sexual assault	1,965 (2%)	3	2	1
Take vehicle without consent	1,583 (1%)	1	2	1
Impaired driving	890 (0.8%)	—[4]	—	1
Other offences[3]	8,984 (8%)	6	7	9
Total offences	115,949 (100%)	12,814 (100%)	41,135 (100%)	58,667 (100%)

[1] There were 3,333 cases (2.9%) in which the age of the youth was under 12, over 17, or unknown.

[2] The principal charge is the most serious charge for a case upon entering the youth court process.

[3] Includes other violent offences (1.2%), other property offences (1.8%), other *Criminal Code* offences (4.4%), and other Federal Statute offences (0.3%).

[4] Percentage too small to be expressed.

Note: Due to rounding, percentages may not always add up to 100%.

Source: Youth Court Survey, 1993–94.

Consistent with the distribution of charges for young persons reported by the UCR survey, female youths represented a relatively small proportion (16%) of the youth court caseload compared to males (84%). The proportion of cases involving female youths has increased slightly from 14% in 1986–87. The Yukon (34%) had the highest proportion of cases involving female youths, followed by Saskatchewan (23%), while Quebec (6%) and Newfoundland (9%) had the lowest.

YOUNG FEMALES IN COURT

In 1993–94, 42% of all female cases heard in youth court involved individuals aged 14–15 at the time of the offence; 41% were aged 16–17 and 14%

were aged 12–13.[2] The largest single age group for male cases was 17 years, compared to 15 years for female cases. Since 1986–87, the proportion of female cases involving 16- to 17-year-old youths has decreased slightly from 49%, while the proportion of 12- to 15-year-old female youths has increased.

Data from the Youth Court Survey indicate that 30% of cases involving females youths were heard for charges against the YOA and offences against the administration of justice (30%), followed by charges of theft under $1,000 (26%). Minor assault (15%) and break and enter (5%) were also fairly common offences heard in youth court for female youths.

In 1993–94, 13,394 cases, or 61% of the total female caseload, resulted in a finding of guilt (including cases in which the accused pleaded guilty). This was very similar to the percentage of cases involving male youths that resulted in a finding of guilt (69%). Stays and withdrawals were a more common outcome in cases involving female youths than in cases involving male youths (35% versus 27%). Dismissals or findings of not guilty occurred in 4% of cases involving both female and male youths.

Among the most common offences heard in youth court for female youths, cases involving minor assault resulted in a guilty verdict (66%) most often, while offences against the administration of justice (59%) and drug offences (56%) were least likely to result in convictions. For cases involving male youths, break-and-enter offences (78%) and drug offences (74%) resulted in convictions more often than other types of offences, while offences against the YOA (69%) and against the administration of justice (62%) were least likely to result in convictions.

Probation was the most common disposition ordered in youth courts for both females and males. In 1993–94, slightly less than half (44%) of all female cases found guilty received a term of probation as the principal disposition, compared to less than half of male cases (38%). The proportion of youths receiving fines was 6% for females and 7% for males. Overall, a smaller proportion of cases involving female youths resulted in a custodial disposition (22.3%), compared to cases involving male youths (35%). Secure custody was ordered in 8.1% of cases involving females (15.5% for males) and open custody was ordered in 14.2% of cases involving females (19.5% for males). Female young offenders received a community service order in 15.7% of cases (12.7% for males), and an absolute discharge was ordered in 5.7% of cases (3% for males).

The offence of theft under $1,000 was the most common offence dealt with in youth court for female youths, and it was selected to illustrate the type of dispositions that female youths receive as compared to male youths. In 1993–94, a custodial disposition was ordered for 9% of all theft under $1,000 convictions involving female youths, compared to 20% of convictions involving male youths. Cases involving young females resulted, on average, in slightly shorter sentence lengths for custody and probation, and smaller fine amounts than cases involving young males. In 1993–94, the average length of custodial sentence for females was two months, compared to three months for males. Probation terms for females were generally shorter (10.5 months) than for males (11.5 months) and average fines for females ($118) were slightly less than those for males ($160).

Cases involving theft under $1,000, minor assault, and break and enter resulted in substantially shorter custodial sentence lengths for female youths. However, for certain other offence types, such as possession of stolen goods and mischief/damage, female youths received slightly longer custodial sentences than did males.

VIOLENT OFFENDERS IN YOUTH COURT

In 1993–94, 23,374 out of a total of 115,949 cases recorded in youth courts involved a violent offence as the principal charge (i.e., the most serious charge for a case upon entering the youth court process). In 1993–94, there were 2.5 times more cases involving a property offence as the most serious charge than cases involving a violence-related offence. In terms of actual charges laid against young persons during the same period, the number of charges for property offences was 3.3 times the number of charges for violent offences.

The majority of violent offence cases processed in youth courts in 1993–94 involved charges for minor assaults (46% of total violent cases), use or possession of weapons, firearms, or explosives (12%), and robbery (10%). Sexual assaults represented 9% of total violent offence cases in 1993–94, while murder and manslaughter represented less than 1% (or 0.2%). Minor assaults posted the largest increase, in real terms, of all violence-related cases between 1986–87 and 1993–94, followed by sexual assaults and robbery. The number of murders and manslaughters fluctuated somewhat, reaching a high of 43 in 1992–93 and falling to 32 in 1993–94. There has not been any significant shift in the relative proportion of various types of violent offence cases over the eight-year period.

The data show that most young persons charged with a violent offence are males (67% in 1993–94) aged 14–17. This profile is consistent with the general profile of young persons charged with a federal offence: in 1993–94, 80% were male and 84% were aged 14–17. In 1993–94, young males aged 14–15 accounted for 27% of the total number of youths charged with violent offences, while those aged 16–17 represented close to 40%.

Of the 22,197 cases in which the most serious charges were for an alleged violent offence, 66% resulted in guilty findings, 26% were stayed or withdrawn, and 7% resulted in not guilty findings or dismissals. A very small proportion (less than 1%) were transferred to adult court; other decisions such as transfers to other jurisdictions or not fit to stand trial were rendered in about 0.2% of the cases. The percentage distribution of types of decisions rendered for violence-related cases changed little over the eight-year period.

Transfer to adult court can have serious consequences for a young offender. The number of violence-related cases transferred to adult court has decreased over the eight years, from 49 in 1986–87 to 44 in 1993–94. The data show that the cases involving serious crimes such as murder and manslaughter are more likely to be transferred to adult court than cases for less serious violent offences such as minor assault and robbery.

Overall, probation with or without accompanying conditions or additional dispositions was the most serious disposition ordered in 45% (6,517 out of 14,381) of the cases with guilty findings involving a violent offence (as the most serious offence) in 1993–94. The distribution of violent cases by other dispositions was open custody (17.7%), secure custody (13.4%), community service orders (13.2%), other dispositions (3.6%), fines (3.4%), and absolute discharge (3.3%). Detention for treatment (in such cases, the young person is admitted to a hospital or some other appropriate facility) represented less than 1% of total dispositions.

Data for 1993–94 indicate that cases involving the more serious types of violent offences resulted in sentences of secure or open custody more often than cases involving less serious offences. Among those resulting in guilty findings, 71% (or twelve of the seventeen cases) with an offence of murder or manslaughter were ordered secure custody and 29% (five of the seventeen cases) were ordered open custody. None of those cases resulted in a term of probation or an absolute discharge in 1993–94. Sixty-three percent of cases with attempted murder offences and almost 63% of cases with the offence of robbery resulted in secure or open custody.

Among the violence-related cases that resulted in guilty findings, and for which secure- or open-custody dispositions were ordered in 1993–94, 17% were for a period of less than one month, 65% for one to six months, 12% for seven to twelve months, 4% for thirteen to 24 months, and 1% for more than 24 months. The incarceration period tended to be longer for the more serious offences: 53% of secure- or open-custody dispositions for murder or manslaughter had a duration exceeding 24 months.

Dispositions of probation with or without accompanying conditions were ordered in 1993–94 mainly for sexual assaults (51% of cases), nonsexual assaults (47%), use or possession of weapons, firearms, and explosives (42%), and "other" violent offences (36%). Over 76% of the probation terms (as the most serious disposition) were for a period of less than one year and about 89% of those were for six months or less.

In 1993–94, the proportion of violence-related cases resulting in secure custody increased with the age of the offender, from 1.3% of cases involving 12-year-old offenders to 32.3% of those involving 17-year-old offenders. This is consistent with the *YOA* stipulation that youths under the age of 14 may not be committed to secure custody except in exceptional circumstances. The number of cases resulting in open custody and absolute discharge did not vary with age, while the proportion of cases resulting in probation supervision or community service orders declined with age.

SENTENCES FOR YOUNG OFFENDERS

In 1993–94, probation was the most significant disposition in 39% of the cases with findings of guilt. In other cases, the most significant dispositions were open custody in 19% of cases, secure custody in 14%, community service orders (CSO) in 13%, and fines in 7% (see Table 14-2). A further 3% of cases resulted in an absolute discharge while 5% resulted in another type of disposition.[3] (see Figure 14-3). The percentage for a CSO appears low because, in most cases, CSOs are used as a condition of probation or in conjunction with a more significant disposition. In fact, 27% of all cases resulting in a conviction included a CSO.

A case may result in more than one disposition for a young offender. Similar to 1992–93, 68% of all cases with guilty findings involved one disposition, 25% resulted in two dispositions, and 5% involved three or more dispositions. For those cases resulting in multiple dispositions, the most frequent combinations included probation and community service (13%), open custody and probation (5%), and secure custody and probation (3%).

CUSTODIAL DISPOSITIONS

In 1993–94, secure- and open-custody orders were the most significant dispositions in 33% of 78,010 cases resulting in convictions across Canada. Custody was the most common disposition ordered in the cases involving

Table 14-2   Cases Heard in Youth Courts with Guilty Findings by Principal Charge and Most Serious Disposition, 1993–1994

Offence Type	Total Guilty Findings	Secure Custody	Open Custody	Probation Services	Fine/ Discharge	Community Service	Absolute Discharge	Other[1]
Violent offences	14,381	13%	18%	45%	3%	13%	3%	5%
Minor assault	7,347	9	14	48	5	17	4	3
Other violent	7,034	19	21	43	2	10	2	3
Property offences	40,253	12	17	44	5	15	4	3
Break and enter	11,330	18	22	45	1	11	1	2
Theft under $1,000	11,807	5	12	44	9	19	7	4
Possession of stolen goods	6,273	14	20	38	5	16	3	4
Mischief/damage	4,352	7	11	48	5	17	6	6
Other property	6,491	13	18	44	4	14	3	4
Other offences	23,376	19	22	27	12	10	3	7
Total	78,010	14	19	39	7	13	3	8

[1] Includes essays, apologies, etc.

Source: Youth Court survey, Canadian Centre for Justice Statistics, 1993–94.

offences such as murder/manslaughter (100% of seventeen cases), escape from custody/being unlawfully at large (90% of 1,915 cases), and importing/exporting drugs (89% of eighteen cases).

The proportion of cases in the jurisdictions with custodial disposition orders ranged from 26% in Manitoba to 43% in Prince Edward Island. The use of custody was consistent with the previous year, with the exception of the Yukon and the Northwest Territories, which have greater variability from year to year due to smaller caseloads.

Under the *YOA*, youth courts may sentence a youth found guilty of an offence to open or secure custody for a maximum of three years.[4] Of the 25,602 cases resulting in a custodial disposition, 24% were sentenced to less than one month in custody, a further 48% from one to three months, 18% from four to six months, and 10% for more than six months. Murder/manslaughter cases had the highest median sentence length of two years and four months, followed by attempted murder at one year. Break and enter and theft under $1,000, the two most common cases, resulted in median sentence lengths of 90 and 30 days respectively.

The proportion of cases resulting in a custodial disposition of three months or less increased from 55% in 1986–87 to 65% in 1993–94. The proportion of cases resulting in a custodial disposition of more than six months decreased from 19% in 1986–87 to 13% in 1993–94. This trend is consistent for both open and secure custody.[5] When Ontario and the NWT

Figure 14-3 Youth Court Cases by Most Significant Decision and Most Significant Disposition, Canada, 1993–1994

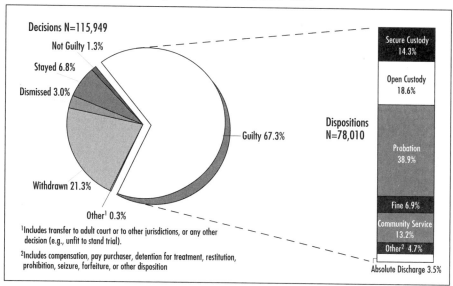

Decisions N=115,949
Not Guilty 1.3%
Stayed 6.8%
Dismissed 3.0%
Guilty 67.3%
Dispositions N=78,010
Withdrawn 21.3%
Other¹ 0.3%

Secure Custody 14.3%
Open Custody 18.6%
Probation 38.9%
Fine 6.9%
Community Service 13.2%
Other² 4.7%
Absolute Discharge 3.5%

¹Includes transfer to adult court or to other jurisdictions, or any other decision (e.g., unfit to stand trial).

²Includes compensation, pay purchaser, detention for treatment, restitution, prohibition, seizure, forfeiture, or other disposition

Source: Paul de Souza, "Youth Court Statistics, 1993–94 Highlights," *Juristat Service Bulletin* 15(3), January 1995, p. 8.

cases for 1993–94 are included, the proportion of custodial cases resulting in a custodial disposition of three months or less is 72%.

PROBATION

Under the *YOA*, youth courts may sentence a young person found guilty of an offence to a term of probation of up to two years. In 1993–94, a probation order was the most significant disposition for 39% of total cases with a finding of guilt. Of the 30,361 cases resulting in probation as the most significant disposition, 28% were for a period of six months or less, 53% ranged from seven to twelve months, and 19% were for more than twelve months. The median sentence length for a probation disposition was one year.

Probation dispositions were ordered most frequently in cases involving rape/indecent assault (57% of 23 cases), soliciting (54% of 191 cases), sexual assault (52% of 1,048 cases), and taking a motor vehicle without consent (52% of 1,151 cases). Sexual-assault offences had the longest median term of probation at one year and six months. Cases involving break and enter resulted in a median sentence length of one year, while theft under $1,000 cases resulted in a median sentence length of nine months.

Under the *YOA*, a young person found guilty of an offence may receive a fine of up to $1,000. In 1993–94, fines were the most serious disposition for only 5,381 or 7% of the total cases resulting in conviction. In the majority of cases receiving fines, the guilty were ordered to pay amounts of $100 or less (56%), 42% were fined between $101 and $500, and 2% received a fine that was over $500. The average dollar amount for fines was $154.

Fines were ordered most frequently in cases involving the impaired operation of a motor vehicle (55%). Impaired operation of a motor vehicle had one of the highest average fines ($343). The average fine amount imposed for break and enter was $210, while the average amount for theft under $1,000 was $123.

ALTERNATIVE MEASURES

Alternative measures (AM) programs provide young persons with the opportunity to avoid judicial proceedings when dealing with conventions of the law. As stated in Section 4 of the *YOA*, these programs are intended to balance society's right to protection with the special needs of young people in conflict with the law. Community-based programs designed to manage socially unacceptable behaviour rely for their success on the legal commitment and cooperation of the police, the Crown attorneys, defence lawyers, youth court judges, provincial directors, and the community. Although the *YOA* outlines the basic administrative framework and principles of AM, the provinces and territories have considerable discretion in the administration of these programs. Each application of AM reflects the unique circumstances of the alleged offence, the special needs of the young person, and the needs of society.

As indicated earlier, AM are used to divert young persons alleged to have committed a criminal offence away from court proceedings. To assess the extent to which young persons in AM are different from young persons found guilty, an analysis of the age and gender of these young persons, from selected jurisdictions, was undertaken. This section presents a summary of AM activity based on a CCJS survey for the fiscal year 1990–91. The unit of analysis is a case, based on the assumption that a young person cannot participate in AM and be found guilty of a crime in youth court. The case count is unique (i.e., unduplicated).

The majority of cases reaching agreement for AM (65%) involved young persons aged 12 to 15 at the time of the criminal incident. Only 47% of all cases found guilty in youth court involved young persons in the same age group. This pattern was consistent across jurisdictions, with the exception of Prince Edward Island, Nova Scotia, New Brunswick, and Alberta. These provinces reported an average of 27% more AM cases involving young persons aged 12 to 15 than the other provinces for which AM data are available.

The fact that younger persons are being handled through AM is further emphasized by the high rate of AM cases involving young persons aged 12 to 15 as compared to all cases found guilty in youth court. The rate of AM cases is similar across jurisdictions for which AM data are available, with the exception of Manitoba and the Yukon. When controlling for property offences, which account for the majority of all offences in youth court and AM, the distribution of age remained unchanged.

In Manitoba, a considerably higher rate of AM cases was reported per cases found guilty in youth court. One possible explanation for this finding is that Manitoba allows a young person to participate in AM up to three times, while in the other jurisdictions a young person may appear only once. The low rate of AM cases reported in the Yukon is partly attributable to the effect of low case numbers when calculating rates.

Males account for a large proportion of the caseload in AM and in youth court, with a lower proportion found in AM (69%) than in youth court (83%). This difference in proportions was similar in most jurisdictions. The exceptions were British Columbia and Manitoba, which each showed a 17% difference between the proportion of males in youth court and in AM. The Yukon reported the smallest difference.

Females were involved in approximately one-third of all AM cases, but accounted for only one-sixth of all youth court cases found guilty. This proportion varied slightly across jurisdictions.

THE HARD-CORE YOUNG OFFENDER OR RECIDIVIST

A majority (54%) of 1990–91 youth court cases involved first offenders; 18% had one or two convictions in the past, 9% had three or four convictions, and 19% of cases were earlier convicted of five or more offences. Youth court caseloads in Canada are predominantly male—only 16% of cases entering court in 1990–91 were female. Furthermore, males were more likely to be recidivists in every jurisdiction but the Yukon. Youth court cases in Newfoundland, Quebec, and the Yukon involved a slightly smaller proportion of recidivists than cases in other jurisdictions for which recidivism data were available.

Generally speaking, one would expect that the older the young person, the more likely she or he would have a prior record, if only because older age groups have been "at risk" of court referral for a longer time than the youngest group. The findings are in the predicted direction. The youngest age category—the 12- to 13-year-olds—had fewer prior charges resulting in a finding of guilt in their official court histories than persons 14 years and over. Almost three-quarters of the 12- to 13-year-old youths were first offenders, whereas 58% of the 14- to 15-year-old youths and 50% of the 16- to 17-year-old youths had no prior convictions. However, there is a relatively small difference between 14- to 15-year-olds and 16- to 17-year olds in terms of the number of prior convictions.

Recidivists were referred to the youth court for similar types of offences as first offenders. The typical offence for young persons with and without prior convictions is an offence against property—two-thirds of cases involved a property offence. (Note that all *YOA* offences, escape, and unlawfully at large charges were excluded from the CCJS survey figures because only recidivists can be accused of these offences.) There was a slight tendency for both first offenders and those with one or two prior convictions to be charged with theft under $1,000 in larger proportions than recidivists with three or more prior convictions. The latter group was somewhat more likely to be accused of break and enter and "other" property crimes such as possession of stolen property. Violent offences are usually seen as more serious than property crimes; 19% of first offenders and 16% of persons with prior convictions were accused of a violent offence.

There is a strong and consistent relationship between the type of the youth court disposition and the number of prior convictions. In every jurisdiction for which recidivism data are available, the larger the number of prior convictions, the lower the likelihood that the young offender will receive a noncustodial disposition. However, about one-half of the young persons with three or more earlier convictions (i.e., charges resulting in a finding of guilt) received a noncustodial disposition.

Because another factor—the type of offence—may also play a part in dispositions imposed by the youth court, the offence of break and enter was used in the CCJS survey to illustrate more clearly the role of prior convictions in dispositional decision making. Along with theft under $1,000, break and enter is one of the most common offences dealt with by the youth court, and is considered to be one of the most serious property offences. In fiscal year 1990–91, almost one-fifth of youth court cases involved break and enter.

In all jurisdictions for which recidivism data are available, there are substantial differences between first offenders and recidivists with respect to dispositions for break and enter. Depending on the jurisdiction, open custody was the disposition for 4% to 14% of first offenders. One-tenth or less of first offenders were sentenced to secure custody. Although there are large jurisdictional variations in dispositions for break and enter, recidivists are much more likely than first offenders to receive custody: 17% to 34% of recidivists were sentenced to open custody, while 18% to 47% received secure custody.

First offenders sentenced to a custodial term were more likely to have been convicted of a violent offence, when compared to cases with prior convictions. This finding applies to both open and secure custody. Almost 30% of first offenders sentenced to open custody were convicted of a violent offence, compared to 18% of the recidivists. In the case of secure custody, 33% of first offenders but only 20% of recidivists were involved in a violent offence. The difference between first offenders and persons with a prior record is even more pronounced when the typically less serious level 1 assaults are omitted from the violent offence category. First offenders are about twice as likely as recidivists to be sent to custody for the more serious "other violent offences" (26% and 13% respectively).

The CCJS survey revealed that a relatively small proportion (9%) of first offenders received custody, but those that were sentenced to custody were more likely than recidivists to be convicted of violent offences. This factor may contribute to the finding that prior record is not related to the length of custody orders. The sentence length distributions are very similar for first offenders and young persons with a prior record.

The mean number of days received by first offenders and recidivists for violent, property, other *Criminal Code*, drug, and *YOA* offences is shown in the CCJS survey for open and secure custody separately. In open custody, except for a small number of cases involving drug offences, first offenders had similar mean sentences as recidivists. For example, the mean sentence for first offenders convicted of a violent crime was 129 days, and 131 days for recidivists; property offences resulted in 109 days for first offenders, and 108 days for recidivists.

In secure custody, too, there were very few differences in the mean sentences of first offenders and recidivists. The largest difference involved violent offences; first offenders sentenced to secure custody received mean sentences of 184 days, while recidivists were sentenced to 200 days. Also noteworthy is the finding that cases involving violent crimes resulted in much longer secure-custody terms than the other major offence categories.

Summary and Conclusions
■ ■ ■

The data show youth criminal activity as being stable over the last several years, with a slight increase in violent offences (largely resulting from an increase in minor assaults) and a steady decrease in involvement in property crime. As societal concerns about youth crime persist, criminologists and sociologists are debating how best to both treat the young offender and protect youth from becoming involved in criminal activity in the first place. The *YOA* has strengthened the idea that young persons should be accountable for their own actions based on their age and maturity level, as well as put into place requirements relating to supervision, guidance, and assistance for youth.

Age, gender, peer pressure, and poverty are some of the key risk factors recognized by sociologists and criminologists as the precursors of youth criminality. Family and life experiences are also regarded as significant determinants. Family support in the form of care, discipline, and development of social values can serve to deter youth from involvement in crime. In contrast, youth criminality may be encouraged by family situations characterized by marital discord, child abuse, and parental involvement in crime or drug/alcohol abuse. Although the *YOA* seeks to protect society from youth crime and hold young offenders accountable for their own actions, the solutions to this problem must start at the individual and family levels. The justice system should be a solution only of last resort.

Notes

[1] Data on Ontario and the Northwest Territories for the period 1986–87 are not available. In subsequent discussion, all trend analyses involving the base year 1986–87 are made excluding these jurisdictions.

[2] These percentages total 97%. Age was unknown or young person was over age 17 or under age 12 in the remaining 3% of cases.

[3] Figures for "other" dispositions are low since they are among the less serious dispositions and are often used in combination with more serious dispositions. About 25% of all cases resulting in a conviction involved or combined with one "other" disposition. These included restitution (3.0%), prohibition (1.5%), compensation (1.2%), pay purchaser (0.4%), and other dispositions such as essays, apologies, and counselling programs (19.4%).

[4] On May 15, 1992, an amendment to the *Young Offenders Act* and the *Criminal Code* (c.11, S.C. 1992) came into force increasing the maximum sentence imposed in youth courts for murder to five years.

[5] The YCS does not distinguish between consecutive and concurrent sentences. As a result, sentence length in multiple-disposition cases may be underestimated.

PART VI

Criminal events create pressure on the different institutions in society to manage and control crime incidents. In this section, we will examine how the three major crime control agencies—the police, the courts, and correctional services—have changed over time to deal with crime trends in Canada. We will see how the composition and size of police agencies have changed in response to such factors as increases in the general population; how the response of the courts to the criminal event has been driven by principles contained within the governing legislation as well as by procedural realities; and, finally, how corrective service agencies are a product not only of federal and provincial legislation but also of the changing character of the offender population.

OVERVIEW OF
CRIMINAL JUSTICE
FACTS

15 POLICING

by Gail Young

The primary agency in defining crime is the police. Gail Young begins this chapter with a description of how the concept of policing has evolved over time. The history of municipal, provincial, and federal policing in Canada is next discussed, along with the responsibilities of Canadian police forces today. Young concludes the chapter with a statistical analysis of police personnel trends and a brief consideration of policing costs.

The concepts of police and policing are very much a reflection of a society's values and priorities. In Canada, the concepts of police and policing are deeply rooted in the democracies of Western Europe and of Britain in particular. The British tradition, which Canada has adopted, is based upon the principle that every citizen is responsible for keeping the peace. The Statute of Westminster of 1285 established the system of "watch and ward" and the principle of "hue and cry." The men of each town or ward were required to serve on night-time watches and given the authority to arrest during their watch. Citizens were also required to pursue any fugitive whenever the watch raised an alarm, the "hue and cry." These principles still apply on a much reduced scale: citizens are called upon to search for missing persons or to form Neighbourhood Watch programs; news stories still appear of private individuals foiling an illegal act or apprehending a criminal.

The other concept inherent in Canadian policing is accountability. During early British history, communities were charged with the responsibility to enforce the sovereign's peace, but with the signing of the Magna Carta even the sovereign was accountable for his actions, and limits were placed upon his power and those of his officials.

As with many aspects of Canadian government, the Constitution of Canada provides a system of sharing responsibilities and costs among the three levels of government—federal, provincial or territorial, and municipal—and each level of government is vested with certain obligations and powers to meet those responsibilities. The power to identify criminal offences rests solely with the federal government. Provinces are restricted to the enactment of statutes and municipalities to the enactment of bylaws. Enforcement of federal laws and statutes is the responsibility of the Solicitor General of Canada. Enforcement of the *Criminal Code of Canada*, legislation drafted and maintained by the federal government, has been delegated to the provincial and territorial governments. Most provinces, in turn, have enacted legislation that makes it mandatory for municipalities of a certain minimum size to maintain a police force.

The division of responsibility and authority of policing agencies is clearly established, as are the mechanisms for accountability. Military police have no jurisdiction in the civilian community; the armed forces are concerned with issues of national security, not the actions of individual citizens; and the national police force—the Royal Canadian Mounted Police—is empowered only to enforce federal statutes unless authorized by the province or municipality. Each police agency is authorized under specific Acts that outline the extent and limits of that authority and establish a method of accountability.

DEFINITIONS

As society has changed, so has the concept of policing. The *Shorter Oxford English Dictionary* provides the following historical definitions of police:

1. 1716: the regulation, discipline, and control of a community; civil administration; enforcement of law; public order.
2. 1730: the department of government which is concerned with the maintenance of public order and safety and the enforcement of the law.
3. 1800: the civil force to which is entrusted the duty of maintaining public order, enforcing regulations for the prevention and punishment of breaches of the law, and detecting crime.

During this period, the concept of policing evolved from regulating, controlling, and disciplining the population; to a government department responsible for maintaining public order and safety (less punitive and more protective); to a civil force entrusted not only with punishment but with crime prevention and detection.

POLICE AND THE CRIMINAL EVENT

Most police manuals state that the primary functions of the police are: (1) to prevent crime; (2) to detect crime and apprehend offenders; (3) to maintain order in the community; and (4) to protect life and property. These duties in conjunction with legislated divisions of responsibilities, measures of accountability, restrictions placed upon police power, and the definition of actions that are considered criminal combine to determine police involvement in the criminal event. Because policing is a reflection of the values of a society, police involvement in the criminal event is also a reflection of the society that the police serve. Legislated differences at the provincial and municipal levels of government affect police involvement in the criminal event, as do regional values.

The two main police activities in the criminal event have to do with prevention and apprehension. Activities such as education, crime prevention, establishing a presence through patrol, and community policing are aimed at preventing or reducing crime. Involvement in the criminal event may also take the form of proactive policing efforts such as road blocks to identify impaired drivers. Most police involvement in the criminal event occurs after the event, upon receiving a report of the crime. Police efforts are then concentrated upon apprehending the culprits and using several investigative procedures to clear the event.

CANADA'S POLICE FORCES

MUNICIPAL POLICING

Canada's first municipal police forces began during the early 1800s in Upper and Lower Canada, with York hiring its first constable in 1834 and Montreal establishing a police force in 1843. By the turn of the century, most provinces had enacted legislation that required police boards to be formed to oversee the activities of the police and provide a local means of accountability. Today, the principles upon which Canada's municipal police forces were founded remain strong among the almost four hundred independent municipal police agencies and almost two hundred RCMP municipal contract police agencies.

Each province assumes responsibility for its own municipal and provincial policing. Provincial legislation can require that cities and towns, upon reaching a minimum population (between 500 and 5,000, depending upon the province), maintain their own municipal police force. Municipal policing can be provided either by an independent police force or through contract with the provincial police force or another municipal police force. Municipal policing consists of enforcement of the *Criminal Code*, provincial statutes, and municipal bylaws within the boundaries of a municipality or several adjoining municipalities that constitute a region or a metropolitan area.

When providing municipal policing services, municipalities may either form an independent police agency or enter into an agreement with another police agency (another independent municipal police agency or the provincial police force) to meet the policing needs of the community. The Yukon, Northwest Territories, and Newfoundland and Labrador are the only areas in Canada without municipal police forces.

Municipal policing in Newfoundland and Labrador is managed differently than in the other provinces. The Royal Newfoundland Constabulary, which is a provincial police force, provides policing only to the three largest municipalities—St. John's, Corner Brook, and Labrador City—with the costs paid by the provincial government. Because of this arrangement, policing data for Newfoundland are considered as provincial policing personnel and expenditures.

In 1993, there were 579 municipal police forces in Canada, 369 "independent" forces, 13 Ontario Provincial Police (OPP) contract forces, and 197 RCMP contract forces. In total, municipal policing accounted for 62% of all police officers and 55% of all policing expenditures. The 369 independent municipal police forces employed 31,772 officers, or 90% of municipal police officers in Canada, and accounted for 92% of the total municipal policing expenditures. Excluding "integrated" municipal and provincial OPP detachments, thirteen Ontario municipalities contracted with the OPP for a total of 219 officers to provide municipal policing services.

In 1993, the RCMP employed 3,380 officers under contract in 197 municipalities in all provinces except Newfoundland, Quebec, and Ontario. These officers represent 6% of the total number of police officers in Canada in 1993. RCMP municipal policing contract charges are based upon the size of the municipality. In the fiscal year 1993–94, policing contracts in municipalities with a population of under 15,000 were billed 70% of the cost of the contract, while municipalities over 15,000 were billed 90% of the contract cost. This costing formula takes into consideration the costs of providing federal and other RCMP policing duties while also performing municipal policing duties. Of the total number of police officers in Canada in 1993, officers at the municipal level of policing represented 56% of all police officers.

PROVINCIAL POLICING

Provincial policing involves enforcement of the *Criminal Code* and provincial statutes within areas of a province not served by a municipal police force. In some cases, there may be an overlapping of policing boundaries. Provincial police perform traffic duties on major provincial thoroughfares that pass through municipal jurisdictions. Only Ontario (Ontario Provincial Police) and Quebec (Sûreté du Québec) maintain their own provincial forces. Newfoundland maintains a provincial police force, the Royal Newfoundland Constabulary (RNC), which provides policing to the three largest municipalities and contracts with the RCMP for all other policing in the province. For the remaining provinces/territories, provincial level of policing is provided by the RCMP under contract.

In 1993, provincial policing accounted for over one-quarter (28%) of total policing costs, with RCMP contract provincial policing accounting for 41% of these expenditures. The three independent provincial police forces (Royal Newfoundland Constabulary, Sûreté du Québec, and Ontario Provincial Police) accounted for the remaining 59%.

The RCMP provides provincial policing services under contract to eight provinces (Ontario and Quebec are the only provinces without RCMP provincial policing) and the Yukon and Northwest Territories. In the provinces and territories where the RCMP is contracted to provide provincial level policing, the provinces are billed 70% of the total contract costs. As with municipal policing, this costing formula takes into consideration the costs of providing federal and other RCMP policing duties while also performing provincial policing duties. In 1993, the RCMP employed 5,184 police officers, or 9% of all police officers in Canada, to provide provincial policing. Ontario, Quebec, and Newfoundland employed 9,184 or 16% of all police officers in Canada to provide provincial policing.

Newfoundland maintains two provincial police agencies. The Royal Newfoundland Constabulary is a provincial force that provides policing to the three largest municipalities, St. John's, Corner Brook, and Labrador City.

The Royal Canadian Mounted Police, under contract with the province, provides policing to the remaining municipalities and the rural areas.

FEDERAL POLICING

ROYAL CANADIAN MOUNTED POLICE

The RCMP has responsibility in all provinces and territories for enforcing federal statutes and executive orders, for providing protective services, and for airport policing. Canada's earliest national police force, the Mounted Police Force, was created in 1845 under the *"Act for the Better Preservation of the Peace, and the Prevention of Riots and Violent Outrages at and near Public Works, While in Progress of Construction."* It was intended to be a temporary police agency responsible for calming disquiet among workers employed in public construction projects such as the Welland Canal.

Following Confederation, the Dominion Police was formed under close regulation from the central government with responsibility for enforcing federal statutes. In 1873, the North West Mounted Police (NWMP) was formed to police the newly acquired territories purchased from the Hudson's Bay Company. The NWMP briefly became the provincial police agency for Saskatchewan and Alberta following their entry into Confederation. In 1910, both provinces formed their own provincial police forces and the NWMP (later renamed the Royal Northwest Mounted Police) became responsible for enforcing federal statutes in western Canada. In 1919, the Dominion Police and Royal Northwest Mounted Police forces were merged to form the Royal Canadian Mounted Police.

The newly created Royal Canadian Mounted Police (RCMP) was given responsibility for all policing in the Yukon and Northwest Territories and for enforcement of all federal laws with the exception of the *Criminal Code*. Between 1928 and 1932, Saskatchewan, Alberta, Manitoba, Nova Scotia, New Brunswick, and Prince Edward Island disbanded their provincial police forces, passing the responsibility to the RCMP. British Columbia and Newfoundland followed in 1950, leaving only Ontario and Quebec with provincial police forces. Because most provinces allowed municipalities to contract for municipal policing with their provincial police force, many municipalities were empowered to negotiate with the RCMP for municipal policing services. As a result, a police force originally created with very narrow responsibilities has become the largest single police force in Canada, providing policing for rural communities, cities, and provinces. Of Canada's 56,873 police officers in 1993, over one-quarter (15,748) were members of the RCMP. Over half (54%) of the RCMP officers are engaged in providing municipal- and provincial-level services under contract.

CANADIAN SECURITY INTELLIGENCE SERVICE

The Canadian Security Intelligence Service was formed in 1984 when responsibility for security intelligence was transferred from the RCMP. The purpose of CSIS is to gather and analyze information on activities that constitute a threat to the security of Canada and to report the intelligence to the government. Because employees do not have peace officer status, they do not have arrest and seizure powers.

PORTS CANADA

Policing Canada's ports began in 1843 with the River Police in Montreal and Quebec City who were responsible for security on the wharves and enforcement of the *Quarantine Law* as it applied to immigrants. Harbour policing was the responsibility of individual municipalities until 1936 when the National Harbours Board was established to administer and control Canada's ports. Each harbour maintained its own police force until 1968 when they were unified into one force. Harbour police officers have the same authority and responsibilities as other peace officers. Under the *Criminal Code,* their authority extends to within 25 miles of any Ports Canada property. Although they are governed by the Canada Ports Corporation, they are responsible to the attorney general of each province.

RAILWAY POLICE

Each municipality was responsible for policing railway property until 1918 when the *Railway Act* was amended to allow the railway companies to appoint police constables to preserve the peace and security of persons and property within one-quarter of a mile of the railway. The railway police are sworn police officers empowered to enforce all laws within their jurisdiction, including criminal and provincial laws.

POLICING IN CANADA

TRENDS IN POLICE PERSONNEL

Between 1953 and 1994, the composition and size of police agencies changed considerably. During this period, the Police Administration Survey underwent revisions to reflect changing police responsibilities, priorities, and technology. Data are available on the numbers of police officers and civilian employees, the level of policing they provide, and the costs associated with each police force. Although it is possible to identify trends in police strength and costs, the data provide little information on the work that police perform. A call for service is not always the result of a *Criminal Code* offence. Creative or proactive usage of policing resources is also difficult to identify; for example, the number of officers assigned to community policing or Neighbourhood Watch programs is hard to measure, as is the effectiveness of these programs on a national level.

Police personnel include sworn police officers, civilians, and those with specialized training (e.g., special constables who provide services such as airport security and bylaw enforcement). For analytical purposes, police personnel are divided into two categories: sworn police officers and all other personnel. In 1994, police personnel in Canada numbered 74,940 people, three-quarters of whom were police officers (see Figure 15-1). This is the fourth time since 1962 that the year-to-year total personnel figures have shown a decline and the third time that both police personnel and other personnel figures decreased during the same year.

Between 1962 and 1975, there was a 93% increase in the total number of police personnel in Canada; by comparison, the Canadian population in

Figure 15-1 Police Personnel Trends, Canada, 1962–1994

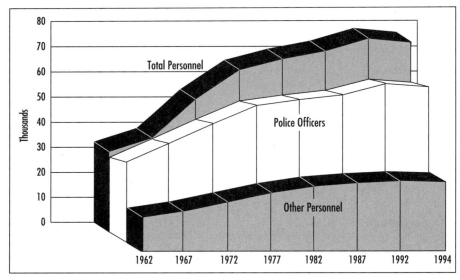

Source: Police Administration survey, Policing Services Program, Canadian Centre for Justice Statistics, 1994.

the same period increased by 25%. Since 1975, the number of police person-nel has increased by 24%, approximately the same rate of increase as the Canadian population (25%) experienced during that period. During the past three years, the number of police personnel has been declining. Since 1962, the "other personnel" category increased more than twice as fast (242%) as the number of sworn police officers (118%). This reduced the police officer to civilian ratio from almost five officers for each civilian in 1962 to almost three officers for each civilian in 1993. This change reflects the reassignment of duties such as dispatch and bylaw enforcement from police officers to civilians and special constables.

The five largest police forces in Canada (Royal Canadian Mounted Police, Sûreté du Québec, Ontario Provincial Police, Metropolitan Toronto, and the Montreal Urban Community) account for 61% of all police officers. A percentage breakdown of police officers by major force is provided in Figure 15-2.

Police officers providing municipal policing services (including RCMP and OPP municipal contracts) accounted for 62% (35,321) of all police offi-cers in Canada. The 14,368 police officers providing provincial policing ser-vices (including RNC policing and RCMP provincial policing contracts) accounted for 25%. RCMP federal police officers accounted for 8% (4,715 officers), while the 2,469 RCMP administrative and law-enforcement service officers accounted for the remaining 4% of police officers.

Figure 15-2 Police Officers by Major Force, Canada, 1993

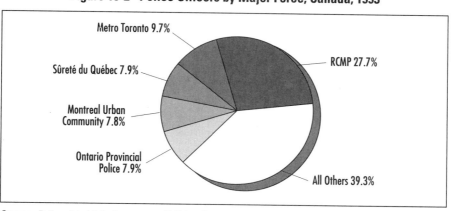

Metro Toronto 9.7%

Sûreté du Québec 7.9%

Montreal Urban Community 7.8%

Ontario Provincial Police 7.9%

RCMP 27.7%

All Others 39.3%

Source: Police Administration survey, Policing Services Program, Canadian Centre for Justice Statistics, 1994.

The ratio of police personnel to general population can provide an indication of real growth or decrease in the size of the police community in relation to that of the general population. As Figure 15-3 illustrates, when placed in context with the population, the increases in the numbers of police personnel are less dramatic than the raw data may suggest.

Between 1962 and 1994, the number of police officers more than doubled, an increase of 114%. When compared to the population to police officer ratio, this was a real increase in police resources, as the ratio fell from 711 Canadians for each police officer in 1962 to 523 Canadians for each police officer in 1994.

Between 1975 and 1985, this ratio increased until it reached 515 people for each officer. Between 1985 and 1991, the ratio declined to 495 Canadians for every officer before increasing in each of 1992 and 1993. In 1994, there were 523 people for each police officer, the highest ratio since 1973.

These rapid increases reflect changes in the demographics of the Canadian population: increased rates of urbanization, which tend to be reflected in higher crime rates and greater need for police presence; a dramatic shift in demographics as baby boomers entered the high crime risk ages (18–24); and a 56% increase in the total Canadian population.

Figure 15-3 Population per Police Officer, Canada, 1962–1994

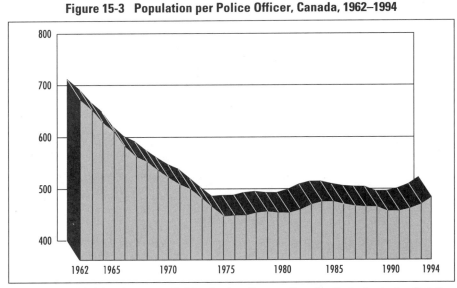

Source: Police Administration survey, Policing Services Program, Canadian Centre for Justice Statistics, 1994.

Between 1962 and 1993, while the number of police officers was growing rapidly, so too was the crime rate. During this period, the number of *Criminal Code* incidents reported to police rose by 431%. This number excludes *Criminal Code* traffic, provincial statute, municipal bylaw, and federal offences, so the crime rate was actually higher. While these officers were responding to more *Criminal Code* incidents, the overall clearance rate remained constant. In 1962, the clearance rate was 37% and in 1993 it was 35%. An incident may be "cleared by charge" or "cleared otherwise." In order to clear an incident otherwise, there must be enough evidence to lay an information (charge), but for a number of reasons (e.g., death of the accused or complainant, an accused under age 12, or departmental discretion), a charge is not laid. The number of criminal incidents per officer for the period 1962–93 is illustrated in Figure 15-4.

POLICE PERSONNEL BY GENDER

As Figure 15-5 shows, policing remains a largely male-dominated field. In 1962, 94% of all police personnel were men. By 1993, this percentage had dropped to 75%. Although female participation in the policing field has risen, the increase has been in specific areas. Women constituted 1% of police officers in 1962 and 9% in 1994. The number of female police officers rose from 168 in 1962 to 5,062 in 1994. Of these women serving as sworn

Figure 15-4 *Criminal Code* **Incidents per Officer, Canada, 1962–1993**

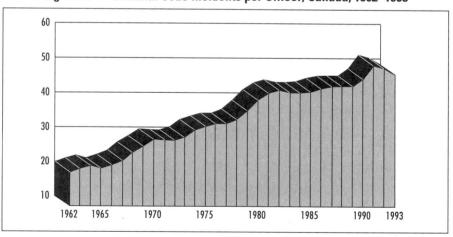

Source: Police Administration survey, Policing Services Program, Canadian Centre for Justice Statistics, 1993.

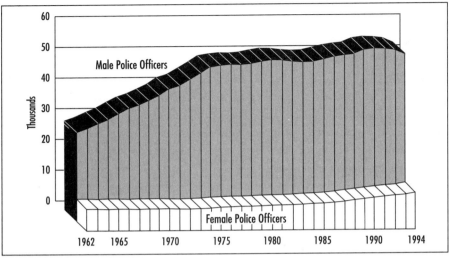

Figure 15-5 Police Officers by Gender, Canada, 1962–1994

Source: Police Administration survey, Policing Services Program, Canadian Centre for Justice Statistics, 1994.

police officers, the majority (93%) hold the rank of constable and fewer than 1% have reached officer status. By contrast, 67% of male police officers hold the rank of constable and 5% serve as officers. Canada's first female chief of police was appointed in November 1994.

The municipal police agencies have been the most responsive in bringing women into the police force. Of Canada's 331 female police officers in 1974, three-quarters (247) were employed by municipal police agencies. The only other police forces to report female officers were the Ontario Provincial Police (provincial policing) and the RCMP (federal policing). By 1992, 56% of women police officers were employed by independent municipal police forces. This is consistent with the distribution of police officers in general.

POLICING BY LEVEL OF POLICE SERVICE

The Canadian Constitution clearly defines responsibilities and authority for legislation pertaining to the conduct of Canadians, while various Acts of Parliament, provincial legislatures, and municipal bylaws define policing responsibilities and authority and the limits to police authority. Each province has legislation that requires communities of a specified minimum size to provide municipal-level policing. This may be done through establishment of a local police force, joining with another municipality, or contracting for policing services with another police agency. Provincial-level policing is responsible for enforcing provincial statutes and the *Criminal Code,* and is usually confined to rural areas and highways. Federal-level policing includes RCMP officers assigned to enforcement of federal statutes, Canadian Police Services, and divisional administration.

Beginning in 1986, the Police Administration Survey defined policing levels as municipal, RCMP municipal, provincial, RCMP provincial, RCMP federal, and RCMP other. It is possible to track the assignment of policing resources by level of policing. From 1986 to 1993, the number of police officers increased by 10% and the proportion of police officers assigned to each level remained proportionately the same. The only change was a slight drop in the number of RCMP officers engaged in administrative and divisional services.

POLICING COSTS

Since 1986, when expenditure data on policing first became available on a national level, policing expenditures increased 56% from $3.7 billion in 1985 to $5.8 billion in 1993. Adjusting for inflation, this represented a 19% increase. The national per capita expenditures increased 39% (or 6.5% after adjusting for inflation) during the same period. During the period from 1986 to 1993, the Canadian population increased 11.5%, settling mostly in urban areas, which tend to have higher crime rates than rural areas. Police operating costs for the years 1985 to 1994 are shown in Figure 15-6.

The distribution of the policing budget has remained fairly constant, with salaries accounting for over three-quarters of expenditures. The distribution of the police dollar among the three levels of policing has also remained constant. In 1993–94, municipal policing, which employs the highest number of officers, accounted for 55% of police expenditures (see Figure 15-7). Provincial policing accounted for 28% and federal policing the remaining 17% of the policing dollar.

SUMMARY AND CONCLUSIONS
■   ■   ■

Policing in Canada involves different kinds of organizations operating at different levels of government authority. Over time, the role and responsibilities of policing agencies have changed due in large part to changes in the task environment, public expectations, and available resources. Policing, however,

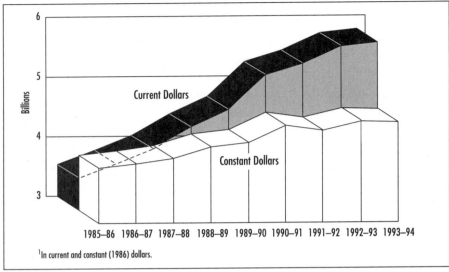

Figure 15-6   Police Operating Costs,[1] Canada, 1985–1986 to 1993–1994

[1]In current and constant (1986) dollars.

Source: Police Administration survey, Policing Services Program, Canadian Centre for Justice Statistics, 1994.

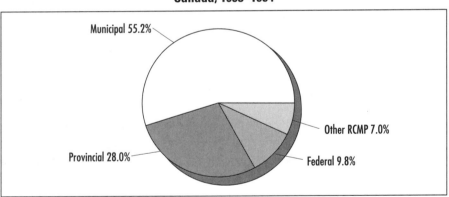

Figure 15-7   Distribution of Policing Costs by Level of Police Service, Canada, 1993–1994

Source: Police Administration survey, Policing Services Program, Canadian Centre for Justice Statistics, 1994.

continues to reflect the needs, values, and priorities of Canadian society as defined by the public through elected officials. Although a statistical survey cannot measure how police officers spend their day or how they use discretion in laying charges, it can measure the costs of providing policing services and through the number of sworn police officers and the number of *Criminal Code* offences, some very general workload measures.

NOTES

[1] In 1993, Canada's population estimates were revised for the year 1971–93, which caused revisions to the ratio of population to police officer.

THE COURTS

by Sandra Besserer and R. Craig Grimes

An important part of the aftermath of crime is the court response, which is affected by a range of factors, including public opinion, legal resources, jurisdiction, and court time. In this chapter, Sandra Besserer and R. Craig Grimes examine the organization and responsibilities of Canadian courts and how the courts work with the police to identify offenders, prosecute these individuals, and direct Corrections Canada in the incarceration of convicted accused sentenced to prison. Data are presented to illustrate the results of criminal prosecution and the costs of operating courts. Knowledge of the technical aspects of court activities is important to an understanding of how crimes are dealt with by the courts, as well as the prospects for deterring these crimes in the future.

When individuals in Canada are charged with a criminal offence or if they become involved in a civil suit, they may be entering into their first—and, in many cases, their only—encounter with the justice system. The courts in Canada play a key role in this system. In fact, they have a dual function. First, they must ensure that other sectors of the system, such as policing and corrections, act in a manner consistent with the law. Second, they must reach a decision on a claim in civil court or on the guilt of the accused in criminal court.

The police have several ways of bringing an individual believed to be involved in a criminal event before the court. The alleged offender may be arrested with a warrant, through the laying of an information, or without a warrant. The power of the police to arrest an individual without a warrant is limited to offences discovered in progress, indictable offences (excluding hybrid offences) already committed, and/or those instances where a warrant is believed to be outstanding. Otherwise, the police or private citizen is obligated to lay an information before the court. The court determines whether or not sufficient evidence exists for the issuance of a summons or an arrest warrant. This protects the accused from undue prosecution and prevents the police from arresting individuals without just cause. If arrested, the accused is tried based on procedural rules outlined for the prosecution of summary conviction or indictable offences. These rules are based on the seriousness of the offences and have been designed to protect the rights of the accused as much as other citizens.

If convicted, the accused faces a variety of sanctions from the court, which may include prison, probation, and/or a fine. The guidelines listed in the governing legislation (such as the *Criminal Code of Canada* or the *Income Tax Act*) include a recommended minimum and/or maximum sentence for the offence. The court is obligated to follow these guidelines in sentencing an accused. Limitations outlined in the governing legislation will also have an impact on how the Correctional Service of Canada administers the incarceration, parole, and probation of the accused.

What follows is a description of the complex principles and structures that govern organization, responsibilities, and procedures as they relate to Canadian criminal and civil courts. Particular attention is given to how the courts work in concert with police to identify and arrest accused individuals, prosecute these individuals, and direct the Correctional Service in the incarceration of convicted accused sentenced to prison. Data are presented to illustrate the results of criminal prosecutions and the costs of operating courts. Data for civil courts are not available.

GOVERNMENT AUTHORITY FOR COURTS

Responsibility for Canada's system of courts is divided between the federal and provincial/territorial governments. The *Constitution Act, 1867* gives the federal government authority to create a general court of appeal for Canada and to establish any additional courts for the better administration of the laws of Canada. Under this authority, Parliament has established the Supreme Court of Canada, the Federal Court of Canada, and the Tax Court of Canada. The Constitution also grants the federal government exclusive authority to enact criminal laws, such as the *Criminal Code*, and to set the procedures to be followed in criminal courts. Finally, Section 96 of the *Act* gives the federal government authority to appoint judges to the superior courts in the provinces and territories. Hence these courts have become known as "Section 96 courts."

Under the Constitution, each province and territory has been made responsible for the creation and administration of courts, both criminal and civil, within its boundaries. Using this authority, each province and territory has structured its court system according to its own needs and resources. As a result, variations exist in the jurisdiction, levels, and names of these courts. The provinces/territories also have responsibility for the administration of justice within their borders. This includes the establishment of procedures to be followed in civil courts.

COURT STRUCTURE AND ORGANIZATION

There are two basic types of courts: trial courts, which try cases; and appellate courts, which hear appeals from decisions in lower courts. Some courts exercise both trial and appeal functions. A second distinction that is made between types of courts is criminal and civil. Civil courts hear cases between private parties (e.g., divorces or child-custody cases). Criminal courts hear cases in which the Crown is prosecuting an individual or corporation for having broken a public law. In Canada, the courts deal with both civil and criminal cases. However, not all civil courts use the same principles when making their judgments. In all provinces and territories except Quebec, the courts apply common-law principles in civil cases, meaning that decisions are based on previous judgments or precedent. In Quebec, civil courts make judgments based on a detailed set of rules contained in the *Quebec Civil Code*.

Canadian courts are organized in a four-tiered structure consisting of federally established courts operating at the national level, and federally and provincially established courts operating at the provincial and territorial level (see Figure 16-1). The Supreme Court of Canada holds the highest position in the Canadian court structure. Below the Supreme Court are the Tax Court and the Federal Court (Trial Division and Appeal Division). All three courts have national authority and are the administrative responsibility of the federal government.

Figure 16-1 Organization of Courts in Canada

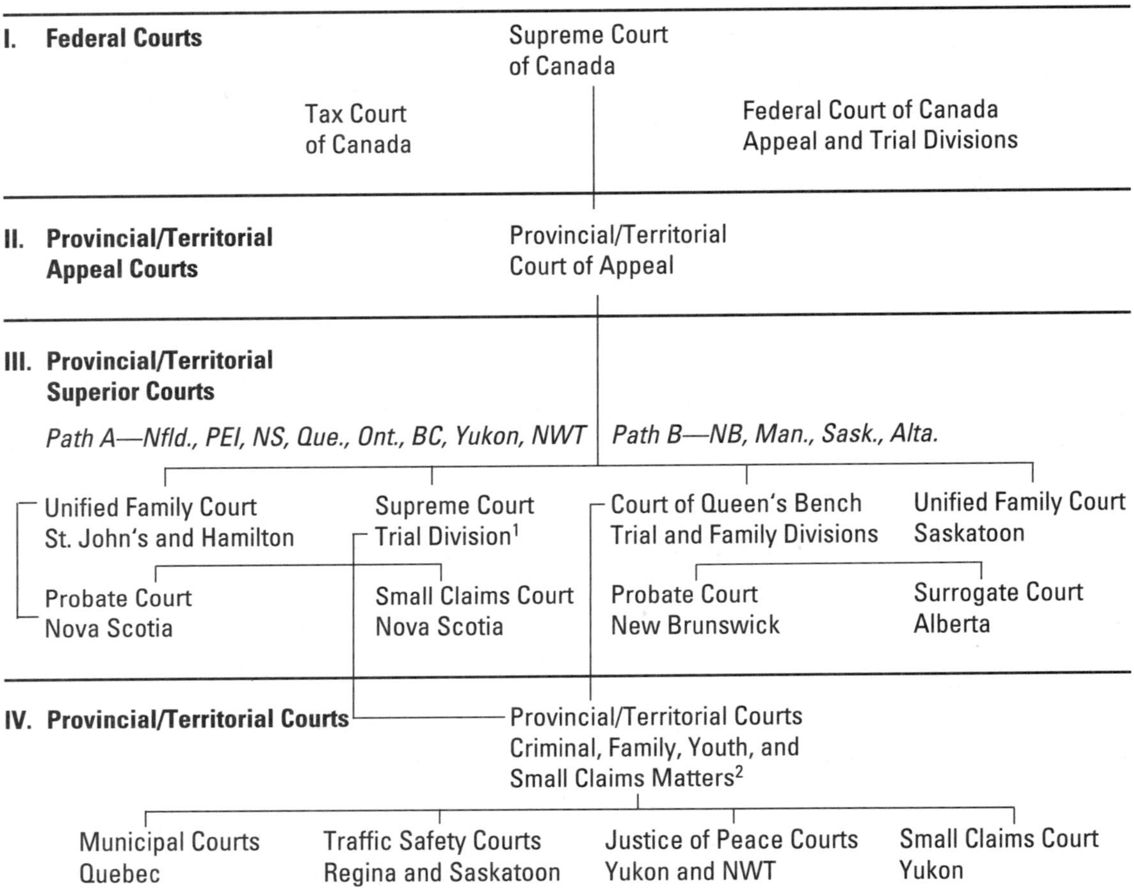

I. Federal Courts

Supreme Court of Canada

Tax Court of Canada

Federal Court of Canada
Appeal and Trial Divisions

II. Provincial/Territorial Appeal Courts

Provincial/Territorial Court of Appeal

III. Provincial/Territorial Superior Courts

Path A—Nfld., PEI, NS, Que., Ont., BC, Yukon, NWT | *Path B—NB, Man., Sask., Alta.*

Unified Family Court
St. John's and Hamilton

Supreme Court
Trial Division[1]

Court of Queen's Bench
Trial and Family Divisions

Unified Family Court
Saskatoon

Probate Court
Nova Scotia

Small Claims Court
Nova Scotia

Probate Court
New Brunswick

Surrogate Court
Alberta

IV. Provincial/Territorial Courts

Provincial/Territorial Courts
Criminal, Family, Youth, and
Small Claims Matters[2]

Municipal Courts
Quebec

Traffic Safety Courts
Regina and Saskatoon

Justice of Peace Courts
Yukon and NWT

Small Claims Court
Yukon

[1] Known as Court of Justice, General Division, in Ontario and the Superior Court in Quebec.

[2] Known as Court of Justice, Provincial Division, in Ontario and the Court of Quebec in Quebec. Small claims matters in PEI, New Brunswick, and Manitoba are heard in Superior Court. In Quebec, family matters are heard in Superior Court, Family Division.

The Courts of Appeal, the highest courts in the provinces and territories, make up the second level. These courts are "Section 96 courts," provincially administered but presided over by federally appointed judges.

The third level consists of provincial/territorial superior courts, which are also Section 96 courts. Superior courts are organized along two general patterns. In New Brunswick, Manitoba, Saskatchewan, and Alberta, the superior court is the Court of Queen's Bench. In all other provinces and territories, the superior court is the Supreme Court, except in Quebec, where it is referred to as the Superior Court of Quebec, and in Ontario, where it is known as the Ontario Court of Justice, General Division. The third level also includes the Unified Family Court in Saskatoon, Saskatchewan, and Family Divisions of the Court of Queen's Bench in New Brunswick and Manitoba. Also at the third level are probate courts in Nova Scotia and New Brunswick, the Small Claims Court in Nova Scotia, and the Surrogate Court in Alberta.

The fourth level of courts is made up of the provincial and territorial courts. At this level, both court administration *and* the appointment of judges are the exclusive responsibility of the provincial and territorial governments. This level of courts also includes the municipally funded provincial court in Halifax; the Family Court in Nova Scotia; the Court of Quebec; municipal courts in Quebec; the Ontario Court of Justice, Provincial Division; Traffic Safety Court in Regina and Saskatoon, Saskatchewan; Justice of the Peace Courts in the Yukon and Northwest Territories; and the Small Claims Court in the Yukon.

As of January 1993, there were 747 permanent court locations in Canada: 23 federal, 14 provincial and territorial courts of appeal, 228 provincial and territorial superior courts, 346 provincial and territorial courts, and 136 municipal courts.

COURT JURISDICTION

FEDERAL COURTS

The Supreme Court of Canada could be considered as the "court of last resort." It is the general appellate court for Canada in both criminal and civil cases. The Court hears appeals from the provincial and territorial courts of appeal and the Federal Court. In most cases, appeals are heard only if leave (permission) is given first. The Supreme Court also has a "reference" jurisdiction, hearing matters referred to it by the Prime Minister or the Cabinet regarding questions relating to the *Constitution Act* and federal or provincial powers and legislation. Canada is the only country with a common law system that has this "reference" function. The judgments of the Supreme Court are final.

The Federal Court is concerned with matters brought against the federal government and its agencies. The Trial Division has jurisdiction in actions involving the Crown or Attorney General of Canada, admiralty proceedings, citizenship appeals, intellectual property disputes, judicial reviews of decisions of federal tribunals, appeals under federal statutes, and claims for relief that are outside the jurisdiction of any other Canadian court. The Appeal Division hears appeals from the Trial Division. It also has jurisdiction to review decisions of federal boards, to determine questions of law referred by federal boards, and to determine constitutional questions referred by the Attorney General of Canada. The Federal Court does not try criminal cases.

The Tax Court of Canada has exclusive jurisdiction to hear references and appeals in several areas. These include matters arising under the *Income Tax Act*, Part III of the *Unemployment Insurance Act*, the *Old Age Security Act*, and the *Canada Pension Plan*.

PROVINCIAL AND TERRITORIAL COURTS OF APPEAL

In the provinces and territories, the Court of Appeal is the general appellate court in each jurisdictional court system. This court may hear any civil or criminal appeal on a decision of any judge in the province or territory. Appeals on less serious matters, such as small claims, may require leave to appeal or may be appealed only to the superior trial court where this right to appeal exists. There are exceptions in Quebec, Ontario, and Alberta where some small claims matters may not be appealed at all.

PROVINCIAL AND TERRITORIAL SUPERIOR COURTS

The superior courts in each jurisdictional court system generally hear more serious matters. These courts have authority in all matters arising in the province or territory except those excluded by statute. Superior courts hear criminal matters under Section 469 of the *Criminal Code* (see Box 16-1) and most indictable offences where an election has been made to superior court. Superior courts also have jurisdiction over matters involving the administration of estates and civil disputes other than those dealt with in small claims court. In Quebec, civil matters beyond the jurisdiction of the Court of Quebec, Small Claims Division ($1,000), are heard in the Court of Quebec, Civil Division, provided they have an upper monetary limit of $15,000.

With respect to family law, the administrative authority over these matters is the responsibility of federally and provincially/territorially constituted courts. Certain subject areas, such as divorce, fall within the exclusive jurisdiction of the federal government and are heard in superior courts. In addition, each province and territory may make its own laws with respect to

Section 469 Offences

The offences listed below are the exclusive jurisdiction of superior criminal courts:

- Treason
- Alarming Her Majesty
- Intimidating Parliament or Legislature
- Inciting mutiny
- Seditious offences
- Piracy
- Piratical acts
- Attempting to commit any of the above offences
- Murder
- Conspiring to commit the above offences
- Being an accessory after the fact to high treason, treason, or murder
- Bribery by the holder of a judicial office

Section 553 Offences

The offences listed below are the exclusive jurisdiction of provincial/territorial courts:

- Theft, other than theft of cattle
- Obtaining money or property on false pretences
- Possession of property obtained, directly or indirectly, from the commission of an indictable offence
- Defrauding the public, or any person, of any item
- Mischief under subsection 430(4) of the *Criminal Code*
- Keeping a gaming or betting house
- Betting, pool-selling, book-making, etc.
- Placing bets
- Offences involving lotteries and games of chance
- Cheating at play
- Keeping a common bawdy-house
- Driving while disqualified
- Fraud in relation to fares
- Counselling, attempts to commit, or being an accessory to any of the offences listed above.

other family matters. As a result, family-related cases encompassing several aspects of family law such as maintenance and custody may be heard in more than one court. In Quebec, however, all family matters are heard in the Superior Court, Family Division.

Unified family courts are presided over by federally appointed judges who may hear matters under both federal and provincial/territorial legislation. This allows family matters to be dealt with in an integrated manner and eliminates the necessity of going before a succession of different courts to settle related matters. Unified family courts exist in Hamilton, St. John's, and Saskatoon. In addition, the Family Section of the Supreme Court Trial Division in Prince Edward Island and the Family Divisions of the Courts of Queen's Bench in New Brunswick and Manitoba are unified family courts.

PROVINCIAL AND TERRITORIAL COURTS

Provincial and territorial courts could be considered the "workhorses" of the criminal justice system. All criminal matters are initiated, and most are heard, in provincial and territorial courts. These courts have absolute jurisdiction over criminal matters listed under Section 553 of the *Criminal Code* (see Box 16-1) and all other criminal matters except those listed in Section 469 of the *Criminal Code*. These courts also have jurisdiction over provincial/territorial statute offences such as traffic matters. There are no jury trials in these courts; all matters are presided over by provincially/territorially appointed judges.

Provincial and territorial courts are designated as youth courts for the purposes of the *Young Offenders Act*. In addition, provincial/territorial courts in Newfoundland, Quebec, Saskatchewan, Alberta, British Columbia, the Yukon, and Northwest Territories hear small claims matters: civil disputes with an upper monetary limit ranging from $1,000 to $5,000. In Quebec, additional civil disputes under the *Code of Civil Procedure* that have an upper monetary limit of $15,000 are heard in the Court of Quebec, Civil Division.

Municipal courts exist throughout Quebec and in Regina and Saskatoon. In Quebec, municipal court judges are provincially appointed and deal with recovery of taxes, municipal bylaw infractions, and matters under the *Highway Code*. In Montreal, Quebec, and Laval, municipal courts also hear summary conviction offences under Part XXVII of the *Criminal Code*. In Saskatchewan, municipal courts deal with parking matters and municipal bylaw infractions.

All criminal trials begin in provincial/territorial court, but where they ultimately end up depends upon the type of offence and elections made by the Crown and the accused. Figure 16-2 provides a summary of the different paths that a criminal trial can take.

Figure 16-2   Overview of Court Procedure in Criminal Cases

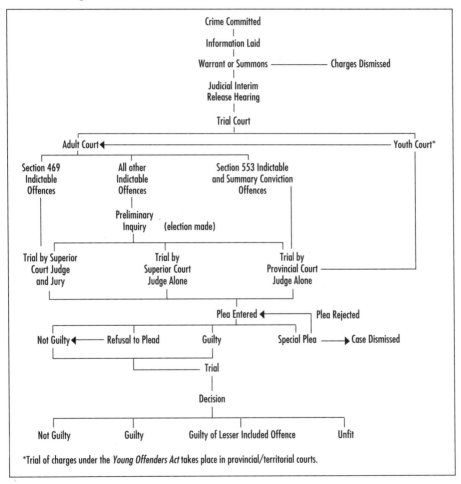

*Trial of charges under the *Young Offenders Act* takes place in provincial/territorial courts.

SUMMARY AND INDICTABLE OFFENCES

Offences are classified as summary conviction offences, indictable offences, or hybrid offences. Summary conviction offences are the least serious type. They can only be tried by a provincial/territorial court judge (without jury). Indictable offences are the most serious offences and can be tried by a superior court judge, a superior court judge and jury, or a provincial/territorial court judge. It is up to the accused to select the mode of trial. Two exceptions to this are offences under Sections 469 and 553 of the *Criminal Code* (see Box 16-1). Hybrid offences are intermediate in terms of seriousness. They can be treated as either summary or indictable offences, a decision that is made by the Crown. (Table 16-1 presents data on the types of charges heard in adult provincial/territorial courts in 1993.)

CASE INITIATION

The initial step in prosecuting a person for a criminal offence is the laying of an "information" before a Justice of the Peace. An information may be laid by the police or a private citizen. The justice hears the allegations of the informant and the testimony of any witnesses. If no case is made, the justice will dismiss the information. Otherwise, a warrant for arrest or a summons to appear will be issued. The summons, which is issued for less serious offences, directs the accused to appear in court or at the police station at a specified time. The first court appearance will take place once the accused has been arrested or ordered to appear. The first appearance is usually a judicial interim release hearing.

JUDICIAL INTERIM RELEASE HEARING

An individual taken into custody for criminal charges must have a judicial interim release hearing, or bail hearing, within 24 hours. The purpose of this hearing is to determine whether the accused should be released pending trial. Accused persons who have been charged with a reverse onus offence (see Box 16-2) must show why they should not be detained. For all other offences, the prosecution must show just cause for the detention by successfully arguing either that detention is necessary to ensure the accused's attendance in court or that it is in the public interest to remand the accused to prevent the commission of additional crimes.

If the justice rules that the prosecution has not shown cause for detention, the accused is released. The following conditions may be imposed on

Table 16-1 Charges by Type and Offence Group, 1993
Adult Provincial/Territorial Court in Selected Provinces

	TOTAL CHARGES No.	Indictable No.	Indictable %	Hybrid Indictable No.	Hybrid Indictable %	Summary No.	Summary %	Hybrid Summary No.	Hybrid Summary %	Unknown No.	Unknown %
PRINCE EDWARD ISLAND											
TOTAL OFFENCES	2,636	457	17.3	346	13.1	306	11.6	1,517	57.5	10	0.4
Criminal Code	2,373	436	18.4	340	14.3	181	7.6	1,407	59.3	9	0.4
Violent offences	370	88	23.8	100	27.0	—	—	182	49.2	—	—
Property offences	747	268	35.9	195	26.1	12	1.6	272	36.4	—	—
Traffic offences	884	2	0.2	26	2.9	—	—	849	96.0	7	0.8
Other *Criminal Code*	372	78	21.0	19	5.1	169	45.4	104	28.0	2	0.5
Other Federal Statutes	263	21	8.0	6	2.3	125	47.5	110	41.8	1	0.4
QUEBEC											
TOTAL OFFENCES	257,030	79,193	30.8	34,059	13.3	31,155	12.1	91,977	35.8	20,646	8.0
Criminal Code	222,856	71,256	32.0	32,782	14.7	24,102	10.8	88,687	39.8	6,029	2.7
Violent offences	30,885	12,571	40.7	9,591	31.1	6	—	8,378	27.1	339	1.1
Property offences	79,567	39,702	49.9	15,949	20.0	967	1.2	21,281	26.7	1,668	2.1
Traffic offences	36,302	350	1.0	982	2.7	71	0.2	34,811	95.9	88	0.2
Other *Criminal Code*	76,102	18,633	24.5	6,260	8.2	23,058	30.3	24,217	31.8	3,934	5.2
Other Federal Statutes	34,174	7,937	23.2	1,277	3.7	7,053	20.6	3,290	9.6	14,617	42.8
SASKATCHEWAN											
TOTAL OFFENCES	58,839	10,881	18.5	5,579	9.5	7,488	12.7	27,265	46.3	7,626	13.0
Criminal Code	55,643	10,187	18.3	5,355	9.6	6,275	11.3	26,507	47.6	7,319	13.2
Violent offences	8,177	2,804	34.3	1,619	19.8	31	0.4	3,105	38.0	618	7.6
Property offences	16,701	6,048	36.2	2,348	14.1	469	2.8	5,890	35.3	1,946	11.7
Traffic offences	14,716	171	1.2	656	4.5	3	—	11,136	75.7	2,750	18.7
Other *Criminal Code*	16,049	1,164	7.3	732	4.6	5,772	36.0	6,376	39.7	2,005	12.5
Other Federal Statutes	3,196	694	21.7	224	7.0	1,213	38.0	758	23.7	307	9.6

TYPE OF CHARGE

Source: Adult Criminal Court survey, Canadian Centre for Justice Statistics, 1993.

---

that release: the deposit of sureties with the justice, limited travel, periodic reporting to a peace officer, no witness contact, or notifying a designated peace officer of changes to place of residence or occupation.

At the interim release hearing, the accused may plead guilty; if he or she does, the justice may make an order for the accused's release pending sentencing by the appropriate court. Judicial interim release offers individuals confronted with criminal charges the opportunity to prepare a defence. More

BOX 16-2   REVERSE ONUS OFFENCES

The offences listed below place the accused in a "reverse onus" position whereby he or she must show just cause why detention is not warranted.

Section 469 (Superior Court Jurisdiction)

- Treason
- Alarming Her Majesty
- Intimidating Parliament or Legislature
- Inciting mutiny
- Seditious offences
- Piracy
- Piratical acts
- Attempting to commit any of the above offences
- Murder
- Conspiring to commit the above offences
- Being an accessory after the fact to high treason, treason, or murder
- Bribery by the holder of a judicial office

Section 515(6) (Provincial Court Jurisdiction)

- Indictable offences committed while released pending appeal
- Indictable offence by non-residents
- Failure to appear while released on bail or released pending appeal
- Crimes committed or conspiracy to commit an offence under Sections 4 and 5 of the *Narcotics Control Act*

important, these hearings protect Canadians from unjustified detention before and during the trial. If the trial is delayed, applications for review of interim release may be made by the prosecution or the accused. Reviews can occur every 30 days for summary offences and every 90 days for indictable offences. Reviews can be unfavourable for an accused—as more evidence is presented, the judge may revoke bail privileges when the evidence suggests the accused is guilty.

FITNESS HEARING

When it is believed that the defendant is mentally ill, the court will remand the defendant into the custody of mental-health professionals for a psychiatric examination. A fitness hearing will take place when this examination indicates that the defendant is not capable of conducting a defence. A defendant found unfit to stand trial is detained in custody until the lieutenant governor of the province permits release. If the defendant is found fit, the trial proceeds.

PRELIMINARY INQUIRY

A preliminary inquiry is held when the accused is charged with an indictable offence that is not the exclusive jurisdiction of provincial or superior court (see Box 16-1). At this hearing, which is held in provincial/territorial court, the accused selects the mode of trial that is desired (i.e., provincial court judge, superior court judge, or superior court judge and jury).

If the accused elects provincial/territorial court, the trial proceeds. However, if superior court is chosen, evidence is presented by the Crown to determine if there is sufficient cause to proceed to trial. The defence need not present any evidence, but it is given the opportunity to hear all the Crown's evidence and question its witnesses. The charges are dismissed if insufficient evidence exists; otherwise, the judge commits the accused for trial in superior court. At any time, the accused has the option of re-electing back to provincial court, which will result in a delay of the process. (Table 16-2 provides data on cases by elapsed time in adult provincial/territorial court in 1993.)

There is an important exception to this preliminary hearing process. The attorney general, or the prosecution with the consent of a judge, may prefer an indictment against the accused, causing the case to proceed directly to trial. This option is rare but important for two reasons. First, if an indictment is preferred, the accused will not have the advantage of cross-examining the Crown's witnesses at the preliminary inquiry. Second, the preferred indictment assumes sufficient evidence exists for trial and removes this delay from the process.

THE CRIMINAL TRIAL

Once the level of court has been determined, the trial can proceed. First, the accused is arraigned to hear the charges and to enter a plea. If the accused pleads guilty, the court will convict. Sentencing takes place either immediately or at a future hearing. Trial of the offence continues if the defendant pleads not guilty or refuses to plead. If an accused has previously been tried for the same charge, he or she may enter one of three special pleas—*autrefois convict* (previously convicted), *autrefois acquit* (previously acquitted), and pardon (previously pardoned by the Queen or prime minister). This is based

Table 16-2 Cases by Elapsed Time, 1993
Adult Provincial/Territorial Court in Selected Provinces and Territories

	TOTAL CASES	ELAPSED TIME FROM FIRST APPEARANCE TO DISPOSITION									
		Single Appearance		Up to 4 weeks		>4 weeks to 8 weeks		>8 weeks to 16 weeks		>16 weeks to 24 weeks	
		No.	%	No.	%	No.	%	No.	%	No.	%
Prince Edward Island	1,616	1,146	70.9	141	8.7	94	5.8	100	6.2	60	3.7
Nova Scotia	17,519	4,834	27.6	2,032	11.6	1,401	8.0	2,477	14.1	2,120	12.1
Quebec	110,565	20,127	18.2	19,551	17.7	10,418	9.4	19,082	17.3	12,233	11.1
Saskatchewan	33,819	10,715	31.7	6,082	18.0	3,301	9.8	4,799	14.2	3,752	11.1
Yukon	1,808	515	28.5	267	14.8	180	10.0	310	17.1	202	11.2

	>24 weeks to 32 weeks		>32 weeks to 52 weeks		>52 weeks (> one year)		MEDIAN TIME (Weeks)	AVERAGE TIME (Weeks)
	#	%	#	%	#	%		
Prince Edward Island	24	1.5	26	1.6	25	1.5	—	5
Nova Scotia	1,695	9.7	1,839	10.5	1,121	6.4	10	18
Quebec	8,635	7.8	10,465	9.5	10,054	9.1	11	22
Saskatchewan	1,806	5.3	1,852	5.5	1,512	4.5	5	14
Yukon	112	6.2	105	5.8	117	6.5	7	17

Source: Adult Criminal Court survey, Canadian Centre for Justice Statistics, 1993.

on the premise that an individual cannot be tried twice for the same offence. If any of these pleas is accepted, the accused is dismissed.

Prosecution of the accused can be terminated at this late stage only if the accused is found unfit to stand trial or successfully raises Charter arguments, or if the Crown withdraws charges. Such events are rare. If a stoppage does take place, it usually occurs as a result of a court-directed stay of proceedings.

A stay may be granted if the court has decided that the proceedings are an abuse of process, or if the court is waiting for some action to be completed. A stayed trial may be restarted at any time up to a period of one year from the day the stay was entered by the court. After one year, the stay becomes final and the trial against the accused may not proceed under the same police-laid information. This does not, however, stop the laying of a new information with identical terms.

Under normal circumstances, the case against the accused is completed when the court reaches a final disposition of found guilty of the offence charged, guilty of an included offence, not guilty of the charged offence, or not guilty on account of insanity. If found not guilty due to insanity, the accused is remanded in custody. If guilty, the accused is sentenced.

SENTENCING

As with trial procedure, sentencing depends on the type of offence. Most offences have maximum sentences and some have minimums. (For data on sentencing patterns in 1993, see Table 16-3.) Individuals convicted of a summary conviction offence are liable to imprisonment for a maximum term of eighteen months and/or a fine of not more than $2,000. If the accused is unable to pay the fine, the court may arrange terms of payment or imprison the accused instead. Imprisonment in default of fine is used only when all attempts to extract fine payment from the accused have failed. If there is no minimum prison term prescribed in the *Criminal Code* and the sentence imposed is less than 90 days, the court can order that the sentence be served intermittently. Corporations convicted of a summary offence are subject to a maximum fine of $25,000.

Most indictable offences carry a maximum sentence of five years in prison. However, some offences carry a maximum term of life imprisonment without eligibility for parole for 25 years. This is the mandatory penalty for high treason, first-degree murder, or second-degree murder when the accused has been previously convicted of murder.

There is no stated fine maximum for indictable offences, and both convicted corporations and individuals may be fined. A fine may be imposed instead of imprisonment for those offences that are punishable by five years or less and have no minimum term of imprisonment. A fine may also be imposed in addition to other sentences.

The court may sentence the accused to a term of probation either in lieu of or in addition to other sentences. Probation consists of one or more restraining conditions that may include the payment of court costs, restitution and compensation, community service, prohibition of driving, professional treatment, or even banishment of the accused from his or her home community. As long as the accused is able to meet the conditions of the probation order, the accused is released from custody.

The above sentencing guidelines may be suspended if the accused has been declared a dangerous offender. Such offenders are subject to indeterminate detention, with parole dependant on periodic reviews of the case.

Sentencing depends more on current charges than on the previous criminal history of the accused. The criminal record is considered in an evaluation

Table 16-3 Charges by Most Serious Sentence and Offence Group, 1993
Adult Provincial/Territorial Court in Selected Provinces and Territories

| | TOTAL CHARGES RESULTING IN CONVICTION | MOST SERIOUS SENTENCE | | | | | | | |
| | | Prison | | Probation | | Fine | | Other | |
	No.	No.	%	No.	%	No.	%	No.	%
PRINCE EDWARD ISLAND									
TOTAL OFFENCES	**1,754**	**1,000**	**57.5**	**316**	**18.0**	**423**	**24.1**	**15**	**0.9**
Criminal Code	**1,530**	**923**	**60.3**	**310**	**20.3**	**284**	**18.6**	**13**	**0.8**
Violent offences	201	113	56.2	63	31.3	20	10.0	5	2.5
Property offences	548	304	55.5	156	28.5	85	15.5	3	0.5
Traffic offences	526	373	70.9	30	5.7	121	23.0	2	0.4
Other *Criminal Code*	255	133	52.2	61	23.9	58	22.7	3	1.2
Other Federal Statutes	**224**	**77**	**34.4**	**6**	**2.7**	**139**	**62.1**	**2**	**0.9**
NOVA SCOTIA									
TOTAL OFFENCES	**16,592**	**4,978**	**30.0**	**3,990**	**24.0**	**7,038**	**42.4**	**586**	**3.5**
Criminal Code	**14,133**	**4,601**	**32.6**	**3,831**	**27.1**	**5,117**	**36.2**	**584**	**4.1**
Violent offences	2,218	831	37.5	919	41.4	367	16.5	101	4.6
Property offences	5,197	1,875	36.1	2,093	40.3	1,112	21.4	117	2.3
Traffic offences	3,497	521	14.9	197	5.6	2,774	79.3	5	0.1
Other *Criminal Code*	3,221	1,374	42.7	622	19.3	864	26.8	361	11.2
Other Federal Statutes	**2,459**	**377**	**15.3**	**159**	**6.5**	**1,921**	**78.1**	**2**	**0.1**
QUEBEC									
TOTAL OFFENCES	**129,876**	**51,787**	**39.9**	**36,661**	**28.2**	**39,738**	**30.6**	**1,690**	**1.3**
Criminal Code	**109,917**	**48,806**	**44.4**	**34,385**	**31.3**	**25,220**	**22.9**	**1,506**	**1.4**
Violent offences	9,599	3,712	38.7	4,631	48.2	991	10.3	265	2.8
Property offences	39,657	18,101	45.6	16,205	40.9	4,648	11.7	703	1.8
Traffic offences	17,535	2,856	16.3	3,876	22.1	10,758	61.4	45	0.3
Other *Criminal Code*	43,126	24,137	56.0	9,673	22.4	8,823	20.5	493	1.1
Other Federal Statutes	**19,959**	**2,981**	**14.9**	**2,276**	**11.4**	**14,518**	**72.7**	**184**	**0.9**
SASKATCHEWAN									
TOTAL OFFENCES	**33,860**	**12,863**	**38.0**	**7,300**	**21.6**	**12,833**	**37.9**	**864**	**2.6**
Criminal Code	**32,026**	**12,389**	**38.7**	**7,128**	**22.3**	**11,686**	**36.5**	**823**	**2.6**
Violent offences	4,137	1,524	36.8	1,593	38.5	900	21.8	120	2.9
Property offences	9,943	4,077	41.0	3,396	34.2	2,012	20.2	458	4.6
Traffic offences	8,183	2,609	31.9	816	10.0	4,749	58.0	9	0.1
Other *Criminal Code*	9,763	4,179	42.8	1,323	13.6	4,025	41.2	236	2.4
Other Federal Statutes	**1834**	**474**	**25.8**	**172**	**9.4**	**1,147**	**62.5**	**41**	**2.2**
YUKON									
TOTAL OFFENCES	**1,414**	**644**	**45.5**	**392**	**27.7**	**364**	**25.7**	**14**	**1.0**
Criminal Code	**1,324**	**620**	**46.8**	**380**	**28.7**	**311**	**23.5**	**13**	**1.0**
Violent offences	277	147	53.1	97	35.0	32	11.6	1	0.4
Property offences	332	128	38.6	172	51.8	32	9.6	—	—
Traffic offences	374	156	41.7	29	7.8	189	50.5	—	—
Other *Criminal Code*	341	189	55.4	82	24.0	58	17.0	12	3.5
Other Federal Statutes	**90**	**24**	**26.7**	**12**	**13.3**	**53**	**58.9**	**1**	**1.1**

Source: Adult Criminal Court survey, Canadian Centre for Justice Statistics, 1993.

of past leniency and whether or not the accused has been free from serious convictions for a substantial period of time. A more serious sentence may be imposed if the accused has not shown any willingness to reform. In any event, the judge must ensure that the sentence handed out is in line with the direction put forward by the *Criminal Code*. The sentence for each charge is determined in isolation, but the total time served may be increased by the judge—after considering the character of the offence and the criminal history or attitude of the accused—through the imposition of consecutive sentences.

APPEALS

The first level of appeal for summary offences is provincial/territorial superior court. Appeals heard in this court can be initiated by the Crown or the defence. An appeal may be made for the following reasons: an error of law has occurred, the court has acted in excess of its jurisdiction, or the court has refused or failed to exercise jurisdiction. The accused may appeal the conviction or the sentence. An appeal must be filed within 30 days of the completion of a case. The superior court, on hearing an appeal, may affirm, reverse, or modify a conviction, or it may order a new trial.

Once the appeal to superior court has taken place, a further appeal may be taken to the provincial/territorial court of appeal. An appeal of a summary conviction to this level can be made only on a question of law. The accused, the Crown, or the Attorney General of Canada may initiate an appeal of this type.

For indictable offences, the first level of appeal is the provincial/territorial court of appeal. Either the Crown or the defence may initiate an appeal. The Crown may appeal against acquittal, on a question of law, or the imposed sentence. The defendant may appeal a conviction or the sentence. An appeal of conviction must be based on a matter of law or fact. The appeal court may order a new trial, modify the sentence, or affirm or reverse the conviction.

The final level of appeal for both summary and indictable offences is the Supreme Court of Canada. An appeal for a summary conviction can be made only over a question of law. For an indictable offence, the defendant may appeal on a question of law or if the court of appeal has reversed the original acquittal. The Crown in an indictable offence case may appeal only on a question of law.

Young persons who at the date of commission of an offence are 12 years of age or more and under 18 years of age are charged under the *Young Offenders Act (YOA)*. (Table 16-4 provides data on the disposition of young offenders by age.) They are dealt with by youth courts, provincial/territorial courts that have special expertise and facilities for dealing with young persons. Youth courts encompass all aspects of court procedure—judicial interim release, fitness, trial, disposition, and review of disposition. The procedures followed in youth court are quite similar to those followed for adult summary conviction offences. One major difference is in the area of sentencing.

The *YOA* recognizes that young offenders have special needs and that they should be held accountable for their actions in a manner commensurate with their age and maturity; in other words, they should not always suffer the same consequences for their behaviour as adults. The *YOA* allows alternatives to judicial proceedings and clearly defines sentencing options, maximum sentences, and application and review of dispositions procedures.

If convicted of an offence under the *YOA*, the youth court judge has the option of fining the accused, issuing a probation order, ordering restitution or compensation for the victim, or ordering the accused to perform community service. The maximum penalties allowed are $1,000 for fines, two years of probation, and community service of 240 hours. The judge may also commit the young offender to custody. The maximum term allowed is five years (three years custody and two years supervision with an option on application to hold the youth for the full five years). If the youth court orders custodial committal, it must specify whether it is to be in a facility designated as "open" or "secure." Open-custody facilities include community residential centres, group homes, child-care institutions, and forest or wilderness camps. Secure-custody facilities are defined as places of secure containment or restraint of young persons. Young offenders held in custody must be kept separate from adults.

The *YOA* requires that the youth court not commit a young person to custody unless it is necessary for the protection of society and done with regard for the age of the young offender, the seriousness of the offence, the circumstances in which it was committed, and the needs and circumstances of the young person. As a result, most of the dispositions given to young offenders are noncustodial.

Parole does not exist in the youth justice system. Instead, the *YOA* makes provision for a review process that features both compulsory and

288

*Overview of
Criminal
Justice Facts*

Table 16-4 Number of Cases Heard by Youth Courts, 1993–1994, by Most Significant Decision, Age, and Sex of the Accused

CANADA Most Significant Decision		TOTAL	<12	12	13	AGE[1] 14	15	16	17	>17	Unknown
TOTAL	T	115,949	46	3,675	9,132	16,977	24,163	28,328	30,335	1,724	1,569
	M	94,057	35	2,840	6,840	12,819	19,081	23,507	26,191	1,508	1,236
	F	21,892	11	835	2,292	4,158	5,082	4,821	4,144	216	333
Transfer to adult court	T	94	—	—	1	2	9	15	60	6	1
	M	94	—	—	1	2	9	15	60	6	1
	F	—	—	—	—	—	—	—	—	—	—
Guilty	T	78,010	21	2,279	6,156	11,620	16,800	19,253	20,410	677	794
	M	64,616	20	1,845	4,732	8,935	13,518	16,328	17,980	605	653
	F	13,394	1	434	1,424	2,685	3,282	2,925	2,430	72	141
Not guilty[2]	T	1,544	1	52	89	209	280	422	473	10	8
	M	1,365	1	40	75	184	245	374	430	8	8
	F	179	—	12	14	25	35	48	43	2	—
Proceedings stayed	T	7,940	4	298	645	1,066	1,513	1,886	2,048	462	18
	M	6,403	3	231	480	795	1,192	1,513	1,755	418	16
	F	1,537	1	67	165	271	321	373	293	44	2
Dismissed	T	3,484	3	117	281	502	646	875	968	35	57
	M	2,794	3	74	193	378	531	715	826	27	47
	F	690	—	43	88	124	115	160	142	8	10
Withdrawn	T	24,644	17	926	1,941	3,556	4,877	5,812	6,303	523	689
	M	18,607	8	647	1,344	2,512	3,559	4,513	5,082	433	509
	F	6,037	9	279	597	1,044	1,318	1,299	1,221	90	180
Transfer to other jurisdiction	T	204	—	3	17	18	29	57	67	11	2
	M	156	—	3	13	11	22	42	52	11	2
	F	48	—	—	4	7	7	15	15	—	—
Other[3]	T	29	—	—	2	4	9	8	6	—	—
	M	22	—	—	2	2	5	7	6	—	—
	F	7	—	—	—	2	4	1	—	—	—

[1] Age at the time the most significant charge was committed.

[2] Includes not guilty by reason of insanity.

[3] Includes unfit to stand trial and other decisions.

T = total   M = male   F = female

Source: Youth Court survey, Canadian Centre for Justice Statistics, 1993–94.

optional reviews and allows for amendments to dispositions should circumstances warrant. Upon review of a custodial disposition, the court may confirm the original disposition, order that the young person be transferred from secure to open custody, or release the young person to probation supervision for a period not to exceed the remainder of the custody sentence. Upon review of a noncustodial disposition, the youth court may confirm the original disposition, terminate the original disposition, vary the disposition, or order any other disposition for any period not exceeding the remainder of the original disposition.

The *YOA* permits the youth court to discharge a young person absolutely in relation to an offence for which there has been a finding of guilt. This disposition is to be used when the court considers it to be in the best interests of the young person and not contrary to the public interest.

COST OF OPERATING COURTS

The five sectors of the justice system—police, courts, legal aid, youth corrections, and adult corrections—spent approximately $9.6 billion on justice services in 1992–93. Canada's court system accounted for 9%, or $867.0 million, of this spending.[1] Provincial and territorial level courts are responsible for the majority of the court spending—93%, or $807.5 million, in 1992–93. A breakdown by type of expenditure shows that salaries make up approximately 75% of total spending and operational costs the balance. Since 1988–89, court operating expenditures have increased an average of 9% per year, or 3.7% per annum when the figures are adjusted for inflation.

SUMMARY AND CONCLUSIONS
■ ■ ■

The courts are an integral part of the Canadian justice system; they are the link between the police and the corrections system. Once the police have identified an accused in a criminal matter, the courts must decide on that person's guilt or innocence, and, if guilty, on the sentence to be served. The corrections system then becomes responsible for monitoring the accused as that sentence is served.

Authority over the courts is shared between the provinces/territories and the federal government. The provinces/territories are responsible for the creation and administration of the courts within their boundaries. Consequently, the organization and structure of courts in Canada varies from province to province.

The federal government has authority to enact criminal laws and to set procedures to be followed in criminal courts. Criminal courts across the country, therefore, utilize a common set of operating principles. Nevertheless, the operation of the courts is by no means simple. The procedures are complex, with many different twists and turns, and there appear to be just as many exceptions as there are rules.

NOTES

[1] Expenditures for courts are collected every second year by the Court Resources, Expenditures and Personnel (REP) Survey, Canadian Centre for Justice Statistics, Statistics Canada. Figures are current to 31 March of survey year. Jurisdictional court systems differ in both the structure and methods by which they provide court services. As a result, court expenditure reporting varies among jurisdictions. Provincial/territorial expenditures include staff and judges appointed by the provinces and expenditures incurred by local court divisions. Also included are superior court judges appointed federally under Section 96 of the *Constitution Act*, and their salaries, benefits, and operational costs paid through the Office of the Commissioner for Federal Judicial Affairs (OCFJA). Federal data include judges, staff, and expenditures of the Supreme Court, the Federal Court, the Court Martial Appeal Court, the Tax Court, and the OCFJA. Excluded from the figures are the costs of prosecution services, expenditures such as occupancy costs paid from central government departments, and administrative services provided through budgets outside courts services.

THE CORRECTIONAL SYSTEM

by Tim Foran and Micheline Reed

In this chapter, Tim Foran and Micheline Reed illustrate how an offender is processed in the aftermath of a criminal event by examining the components, structure, and operations of the Canadian correctional system. Institutional corrections (federal or provincial incarceration) and community corrections (provincial probation and conditional release) are discussed in the context of federal and provincial legislation. The authors also provide extensive data on offender and probationer characteristics. They conclude their review with a brief overview of correctional expenditures.

The theoretical perspective of *The Criminal Event* (Sacco and Kennedy, 1994) stresses that to understand crime one must look at more than the specifics of a criminal incident or a particular type of crime. A comprehensive analysis of the criminal event must examine the precursors of crime, the event itself, and the aftermath. This chapter will focus on one component of the aftermath of the crime—the response of the correctional system.

On a daily basis during 1992–93, an average of 147,960 offenders were under the direct care or supervision of correctional agencies in Canada (see Figure 17-1). Of these, 26,477 were inmates serving custodial sentences; 14,135 (53%) were housed in provincial or territorial facilities, and 12,342 (47%) were in federal

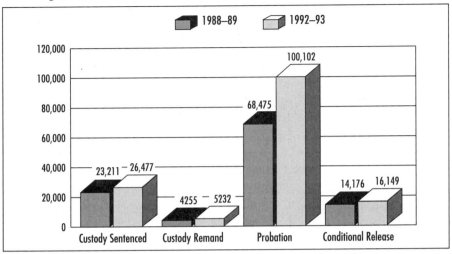

Figure 17-1   Adult Correctional Populations, 1988–1989 and 1992–1993

■ 1988–89   ▨ 1992–93

Source: *Adult Correctional Services in Canada, 1992–93* (Statistical Report), Canadian Centre for Justice Statistics, 1993.

penitentiaries. In addition, there were 5,232 inmates in provincial facilities who were not serving a sentence: 5,111 (98%) were remanded in custody awaiting some judicial action with respect to their cases, while the remaining 121 (2%) were on temporary detention. Remanded inmates represented 26% of the provincial average daily inmate population.

An average of 114,251 offenders (79% of the total) were serving a disposition or part of their sentence under community supervision. Eighty-six percent of these offenders (100,102) were under probation supervision, while 14% (16,149) were in the community, on parole or some other form of conditional release. Since 1988–89, the total correctional caseload (both institutional and community corrections) has risen steadily from 110,117 to 147,960, representing a 34% increase.

This chapter is divided into three main sections. The first, "Institutional Corrections," examines federal and provincial incarceration, focusing particular attention on the various dispositions that are imposed by the courts. In the next section, "Community Corrections," attention shifts to offenders who serve their sentences outside an institution. This section describes in detail the use of provincial probation and conditional release. A brief overview of the cost of maintaining the Canadian correctional system is provided in the third and final section, "Correctional Expenditures."

LEGISLATIVE BACKGROUND

The Parliament of Canada has exclusive jurisdiction over legislation related to criminal matters throughout Canada. The *Criminal Code of Canada* (R.S.C. 1985, c. C-46), which defines criminal offences and sets sanctions and dispositions, is in force in all Canadian jurisdictions. However, the provincial and territorial governments have authority over the actual administration of criminal justice within their respective borders. In addition, the provinces and territories proclaim their own statutes and regulations such as *Highway Traffic Acts* and *Liquor Control Acts*. Each province and territory also has enabling legislation that permits municipalities within its jurisdiction to proclaim and enforce municipal bylaws (e.g., parking control). Band bylaws on reserves are covered by the *Indian Act*, which is federal legislation.

In Canada, all persons who commit an offence after their 18th birthday are processed through the justice system as adults and are subject to the provisions of the *Criminal Code* (CC). Young persons between the ages of 12 and 17 are dealt with under the *Young Offenders Act* (R.S.C. 1985, c. Y-1). The guiding philosophy behind the *Young Offenders Act* is to hold young persons who break the law responsible for their actions and to protect society from illegal behaviour while at the same time protecting the legal rights of young offenders (Hudson, Hornick, and Burrows, 1988). In the *Young Offenders Act*, the principle of responsibility is balanced against the principle of "mitigated accountability whereby ... young persons should not, generally speaking, be held accountable in the same manner aa would adults" (Omer Archambault quoted in Hudson, Hornick, and Burrows, 1988: 1). Children under the age of 12 are not subject to criminal prosecutions in Canada.

The criminal justice system in Canada is administered within four independent sectors—policing services, prosecution (Crown), the courts, and correctional services—each of which the offender is likely to encounter in the aftermath of a criminal event. Policing services have responsibility for law enforcement. In many jurisdictions, such as Ontario, the police are empowered to lay the charges, but in other jurisdictions, such as New Brunswick, Quebec, and British Columbia, the Crown lays the charge. Provincial variations in charging policies affect the proportion of persons charged relative to the number of reported offences. The provincial Crowns prosecute criminal cases before the courts. Offences against the *Food and Drug Act*, the *Narcotics Control Act*, and other federal statutes are prosecuted by federal

Crowns. Correctional services implement the sentences imposed by the courts.

The Canadian correctional system is divided into two distinct administrative sectors. The federal sector is responsible for all offenders serving a sentence of two years or more, while the provincial sector provides custodial services to inmates serving a sentence of less than two years. Federally sentenced inmates awaiting the expiration of the 30-day appeal period are held in provincial facilities prior to being transferred to a federal penitentiary.

COURT-IMPOSED DISPOSITIONS

CUSTODIAL REMANDS

Correctional service agencies are responsible for the administration of court-imposed dispositions, with the exception of fines. In addition, provincial and territorial correctional services are responsible for persons charged with an offence who have been remanded in custody. Typically, a person is remanded in custody pending the arrangement of a judicial interim release hearing, or to ensure that the accused appears in court, or to protect society from the accused (CC, s.515(10)(a),(b)). Under normal circumstances, the onus is on the Crown to show cause why an accused should be remanded in custody. However, if the accused commits an indictable offence while released on judicial interim release for another indictable offence, the onus is on the accused to show cause why he or she should be released (CC, s.515 (6)).

The time an accused spends in jail on remand may be taken into account by the judge when imposing a sentence (CC, s.721 (3)). Thus it is not uncommon for an offender to receive a sentence of "time served." This occurs most often when the accused has spent more time remanded in custody than the judge would normally impose as a sentence.

TEMPORARY DETENTION

A small number of offenders enter correctional institutions on temporary detention status. Temporary detainees are neither remanded nor sentenced. Most temporary detainees are being held for immigration purposes.

CUSTODIAL SENTENCES

Once a finding of guilt has been determined, the actual disposition is at the discretion of the presiding judge (CC, s.717). The *Criminal Code* specifies maximum sentences for most offences and, in some instances, a minimum punishment. In Canada, the maximum sentence is rarely imposed. In most circumstances, the judge will consult with the Crown attorney and the defence counsel in determining the disposition. In some cases, the judge may order a pre-sentence report (PSR) (CC, s.735). The PSR is prepared by a probation officer and is designed to inform the judge about the living and employment circumstances of the accused. In determining the sentence, the judge considers such factors as the degree of harm to the victim and certain characteristics of the accused. In Canada, the use of incarceration is usually limited to very serious offences and to repeat offenders.

It is not uncommon for an offender to be convicted of several offences at the same court sitting. In such cases, the judge may order that the sentences be served consecutively; that is, one after the other (CC, s.717(4)). The use of consecutive sentences can result in an aggregate sentence of greater than two years. Section 731(1) of the *Criminal Code* stipulates that all offenders sentenced to an aggregate sentence of two years or more shall be imprisoned in a penitentiary. In Canada, all penitentiaries are the responsibility of the federal Correctional Service of Canada. All federally sentenced offenders are first admitted to a local provincial or territorial facility to allow the offender to exercise his or her right of appeal of the conviction (CC, s.675 (a)) or the sentence (CC, s. 675 (b)). Normally, a notice of appeal must be filed within 30 days of sentencing. Federally sentenced offenders who waive their right of appeal are transferred to a federal penitentiary to serve the sentence.

Offenders who are sentenced to an aggregate term of imprisonment that is less than two years are the exclusive responsibility of provincial and territorial correctional services. In addition, offenders who are in default of the payment of a fine imposed under either federal or provincial legislation are subject to incarceration to a period of time specified under the relevant legislation. Inmates whose only reason for being in a jail is default of payment of a fine may reduce the time to be served by partial payment of the fine(s) (CC, s.722(2)). The various components of custodial services in Canada are depicted in Figure 17-2.

INSTITUTIONAL CORRECTIONS—A LOOK AT THE DATA

Traditionally, two indicators of the utilization of correctional facilities are used. These are *admissions* and *counts*. Admission data, collected when the offender enters the institution, usually include offence type, sentence length, age, gender, and ethnicity (aboriginal/nonaboriginal).[1] Count data describe only the number of inmates in the institutions at a given instant (i.e., the average daily population in the institutions). Inmates are counted many times

Figure 17-2 Custodial Services in Canada

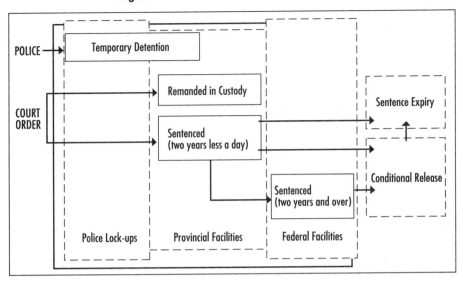

during the day, minimally at every shift change. The counts taken at midnight are used as the indicator of the utilization of the institution. Generally, the provincial and territorial correctional systems cannot provide details about their average daily populations, due to the high turnover of provincial inmates. Therefore, the inmate characteristics presented below are admission data, not count data. Readers should be cautioned not to extrapolate population characteristics from admission data.

ADULT OFFENDER CHARACTERISTICS

Research has found that the likelihood of offender involvement in criminal events is associated with a variety of social characteristics, including age, gender, and minority-group membership (Sacco and Kennedy, 1994). The data presented in this chapter do support the view that the majority of offenders are male. Males accounted for 91% of admissions to provincial/territorial facilities in 1992–93 and 97% of admissions to federal correctional facilities in the same period. Aboriginal peoples are overrepresented in the number of admissions to correctional facilities, constituting only 3.8% of the Canadian population while accounting for 17% of admissions to provincial/territorial institutions and 12% of the admissions to federal facilities.

The popular view that the majority of offenders are in a "target population" under the age of 25 needs to be challenged. This may have been true when baby boomers (those born between 1951 and 1966) were entering the system. By 1991, however, the oldest members of this group were 40 while the youngest were 25. On the basis of demographics, one would expect that the correctional populations would reflect the population at large.

In fact, the data support this hypothesis. In 1984–85, 59% of federally sentenced inmates were at least 25 years of age. By 1992–93, 73% of the federal inmate population was 25 years of age or older. During the same period, the number of federal inmates between 18 and 24 years of age dropped from 35% in 1984–85 to 27% in 1992–93 (see Figure 17-3a). This trend is also evident in provincial/territorial institutions. In 1990–91, 40% of provincial offenders were less than 25 years of age. By 1992–93, only 29% of those admitted to provincial/territorial institutions were under 25. During the same period, admissions of those aged over 25 increased from 60% to 71% (see Figure 17-3b). Clearly, the majority of the correctional population is beyond the "target population" age of under 25.

YOUNG PERSONS IN CUSTODIAL FACILITIES

With respect to young offenders (those aged 12–17), only data that provide the average daily institutional count of young offenders in custody are available.[2] Our discussion of young offenders in custody is preceded by an overview of the limits to the use of secure custody.

The *Young Offenders Act* limits the use of secure custody. Section 24.1(3), which applies to young persons who were 14 years of age at the time the offence was committed, states that a youth may receive custody when

(a) the offence is one for which an adult would be liable to imprisonment for five years or more;

(b) the offence is an offence under section 26 of this Act in relation to a disposition under paragraph 20(1)(j), an offence under section 144 (prison breach) or subsection 145(1) (escape or being at large without excuse) of the *Criminal Code* or an attempt to commit any such offence; or

(c) the offence is an indictable offence and the young person was,

    (i) within twelve months prior to the commission of the offence, found guilty of an offence for which an adult would be liable to imprisonment for five years or more, or adjudged to have committed a delinquency under the *Juvenile Delinquents Act*, chapter J-3 of the Revised Statutes of Canada, 1970, in respect of such offence, or

Figure 17-3a   Age of Admission to Penitentiary, Federal Inmates

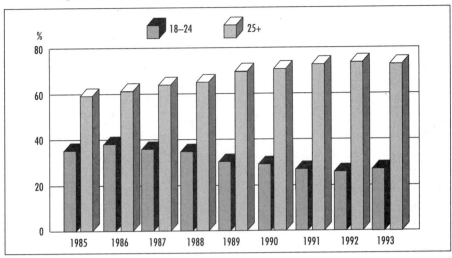

Source: Adult Correctional Services survey for the years 1985 to 1993, Canadian Centre for Justice Statistics, 1993.

Overview of
Criminal
Justice Facts

Figure 17-3b   Age of Admission to Provincial/Territorial Facilities

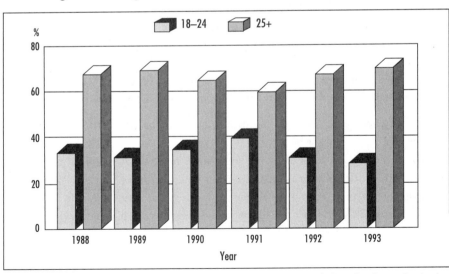

Source: *Adult Correctional Services in Canada, 1992–93* (Statistical Report), Canadian Centre for Justice Statistics, 1993.

(ii) at any time prior to the commission of the offence, committed to secure custody with respect to a previous offence, or committed to custody in a place or facility for the secure containment or restraint of a child, within the meaning of the *Juvenile Delinquents Act* ... with respect to a delinquency under the Act.

The slightly more restrictive Section 24.1(4) applies to young persons who were under the age of 14 years at the time the offence was committed. This section states that a youth may receive custody only when

(a) the offence is one for which an adult would be liable to life imprisonment;

(b) the offence is one for which an adult would be liable to imprisonment for five years or more and the young person was at any time prior to the commission of the offence found guilty of an offence for which an adult would be liable to imprisonment for five years or more or adjudged to have committed a delinquency under the *Juvenile Delinquents Act* ... in respect of such offence; or

(c) the offence is an offence under section 26 of this Act in relation to a disposition under paragraph 20(1)(j), an offence under section 144 (prison breach) or subsection 145(1) (escape or being at large without excuse) of the *Criminal Code* or an attempt to commit any such offence.

The young offender count data are presented by custody status: secure-custody sentenced, open-custody sentenced, and remand.[3] In 1992–93, the total average daily count of young offenders in custodial facilities across Canada was 4,732, an increase of 7% over 1991–92. This number includes young offenders in secure custody (38%), open custody (44%), and remand status (18%).

The number of youths in custodial facilities in Canada has increased over time. As indicated in Table 17-1, in 1992–93, excluding remand, 3,875 youths were held in custody, up 20% from 1988–89. In 1992–93, across Canada, 1,806 youths were held in secure-custody facilities—slightly less than half (47%) of all youths in custody. While the number of youths in secure custody remained consistent between 1988–89 and 1991–92, an increase of 11% was recorded in 1992–93. The number of youths in open custody increased by 17% between 1988–89 and 1992–93.

Between 1988–89 and 1992–93, youth custody rates in Canada have increased very modestly, with approximately 21 youths per 10,000 youth population in custodial facilities in 1992–93. Between 1988–89 and

**Table 17-1 Average Count of Young Offenders by Custody Status,
1988–1989 to 1992–1993**

	Secure Custody	Open Custody	Total	Remand/ Temporary Detention	Actual In[1]	Rate of Incarceration[2]
1988–89	1,555	1,773	3,228	738	3,966	18.5
1989–90	1,655	1,761	3,416	813	4,229	18.8
1990–91	1,693	1,790	3,483	817	4,300	19.0
1991–92	1,633	1,939	3,572	846	4,418	19.3
1992–93	1,806	2,069	3,875	857	4,732	20.5

[1]Actual in counts include secure custody, open custody, and remand/temporary detention.

[2]Rate of incarceration is based on 10,000 youth population.

Source: Corrections Key Indicator Report (August 1994).

1992–93, there was a 16% increase in the total number of youths remanded in custody across Canada.

COMMUNITY CORRECTIONS

Community corrections includes probation and the various forms of conditional release: full parole, day parole, temporary absence, and statutory release. A term of probation is administered provincially. Offenders can receive a probation term up to three years in length. Federal and provincial inmates are eligible for parole and temporary absences. Only federally sentenced inmates are eligible for statutory release.

PROVINCIAL PROBATION

Probation terms are dispositions imposed by the court. Section 737 of the *Criminal Code* stipulates that:

(1) Where an accused is convicted of an offence, the court may, having regard to the age and character of the accused, the nature of the offence and the circumstances surrounding its commission,

    (a) ... suspend the passing of sentence and direct that the accused be released on the conditions prescribed in a probation order;

(2) The following conditions shall be deemed to be prescribed in a probation order, namely, that the accused shall keep the peace and be of good

behaviour and shall appear before the court when required to do so by the court, and, in addition the court may prescribe as conditions in a probation order that the accused shall do any one or more ... things specified in the order ...;

(a) report to and be under the supervision of a probation officer or other person designated by the court.

Section 738(2)(b) further stipulates that "no probation order shall continue in force for more than three years from the date on which the order came into force."

In effect, then, probation is a suspended sentence that may or may not be supervised by a probation officer. Terms of probation that do not stipulate a condition of supervision do not generally come to the attention of correctional authorities. In this chapter, "probation" denotes supervised probation only. Common conditions attached to probation orders are restitution[4] to the victim (*CC*, s.737(2)(e)) and community service orders (CSOs).[5] At present, there is no direct legislative mandate for CSOs. The normal authority used is Section 737(2)(h) of the *Criminal Code*, which stipulates that the offender "comply with such other reasonable conditions as the court considers desirable."

PROVINCIAL PROBATION—A LOOK AT THE DATA

Two indices, intakes and counts, commonly describe the use of probation. Probation intakes denote the number of persons receiving a term of probation. Probation counts are usually taken monthly and are expressed as "month-end counts." As with institutional counts, these month-end counts are used for operational and administrative purposes. Therefore, probation counts are not normally associated with other information about offenders. In 1992–93, 43,364 probationers (excluding Ontario)[6] began a probation disposition under the supervision of a provincial probation service in Canada. On a national level, this represents a 39% increase since 1988–89.

Generally, crime rates vary from east to west in Canada. In order to facilitate comparisons between the jurisdictions, the rate of probation intake per 10,000 adults charged was calculated. The rate per 10,000 adults charged indicates the extent to which probation is used by the courts in each jurisdiction. The highest utilization of probation was in Prince Edward Island (1522), while the lowest was in Quebec (510). The Atlantic provinces tended to have a higher probation utilization rate than the western provinces.

PROBATIONER CHARACTERISTICS

Data on the gender, ethnicity (aboriginal/nonaboriginal), and age of probationers are available from most jurisdictions. These data reflect the status of the probationer on intake. As with institutional admissions, the majority of probationers (85%) were male. On a national level, only 15% of the probationers were female. The percent distribution of females varied from 22% in Alberta to 11% in Quebec. Sixteen percent of the probationers in the 1992–93 probation intake were of aboriginal origin. The distribution of aboriginal probationers varied considerably across jurisdictions, with the western provinces generally having higher proportions of aboriginals than the Atlantic and central provinces. As with the institutional populations, the majority of offenders serving a term of probation are over 25 years of age. In 1992–93, 65% of probationers were at least 25 years old.

NUMBER OF YOUTHS ON PROBATION

The change in the number of youths on probation in Canada between 1988–89 and 1992–93 cannot be calculated due to gaps in the survey coverage. However, in provinces for which data are available, the number of youths on probation has increased. For example, in Newfoundland, the number of youths on probation increased by 20%, from 1,164 youths in 1988–89 to 1,397 youths in 1992–93. In Quebec, the number of youths on probation increased from 2,836 in 1988–89 to 3,214 in 1992–93. Between 1990–91 and 1992–93, the probation counts for young offenders in Ontario increased by 36% (from 11,864 to 16,079). The remainder of the provinces generally recorded gradual increases in the number of youths on probation over the past five years.

CONDITIONAL RELEASE

The planned and gradual release of inmates into the community, through conditional-release mechanisms designed to ensure the protection of society, is an important and often misunderstood aspect of correctional programming. The mechanisms for conditional release used in Canada are described below:

- *Full parole* is a form of conditional release, granted at the discretion of paroling authorities, that allows an offender to serve part of a prison sentence in the community. In all instances, the offender is placed under supervision and is required to abide by conditions designed to reduce the risk of reoffending and to foster reintegration in the community.

- *Day parole* provides offenders with the opportunity to participate in ongoing community-based activities. Ordinarily, the offender resides at a correctional institution or community residence. Offenders are also granted day parole in order to prepare for full parole and statutory release.
- *Temporary absence* allows the offender to leave the institution for specific program purposes. The offender may be either escorted or unescorted on such occasions. These releases can be granted for family visits, medical services, rehabilitative programs, and the like. The new federal correctional legislation includes specific definitions of the reasons for which temporary absences may be granted.
- *Statutory release* applies specifically to federally sentenced inmates. It requires that most federally sentenced offenders serve the final third of their sentence in the community under supervision and under conditions of release similar to those imposed on offenders who are released on full parole.

In November 1992, Bill C-36, the *Corrections and Conditional Release Act* (*CCRA*), came into force, replacing the *Parole Act* and the *Penitentiary Act*. The authority to grant parole is now found in the *CCRA* and the respective provincial legislation. The authority for temporary absences is found in both federal and provincial correctional legislation, and is exercised by correctional authorities in provincial and territorial systems. In the federal system, the responsibility is shared between the National Parole Board (NPB) and the Correctional Service of Canada.

Quebec, Ontario, and British Columbia operate full functioning parole boards that have jurisdiction over all offenders in provincial institutions. The NPB has jurisdiction over all offenders sentenced to federal penitentiaries (those who receive a sentence of two years or more) and offenders held in provincial and territorial correctional institutions where there are no provincial parole boards.

Parole boards are administrative tribunals that have the authority to grant, deny, terminate, or revoke parole in their jurisdiction. The NPB also has the authority to terminate or revoke offenders released on statutory supervision, to detain certain offenders, and to grant unescorted temporary absences for some offenders in penitentiaries.

LEGISLATIVE AUTHORITY OF THE PAROLE BOARDS

The legislative authority of the NPB is currently found in the *CCRA*. The province of Quebec operates the Quebec Board of Parole (Commission québécoise des libérations conditionnelles—CQLC) under the mandate of the federal *CCRA* and the provincial *Act to Promote the Parole of Inmates* (LRQ CL-1.1). The CQLC is responsible for the release of persons in Quebec's correctional facilities who have been sentenced to terms of imprisonment of six months or more.

On October 31, 1991, the Quebec National Assembly enacted Bill 147 amending the *Act to Promote the Parole of Inmates* and the *Act Respecting Probation and Houses of Detention*. Quebec's reform of conditional release came into effect on June 15, 1992. As part of this reform, the CQLC also improved its parole program by adding "parole with close supervision," which is better adapted to the specific needs of some of its clientele.

The Ontario Board of Parole operates under the mandate provided by the federal *CCRA* and the provincial *Ministry of Correctional Services Act*. Under this mandate, the Board considers for conditional release adult offenders who are serving a sentence of less than two years in the province's correctional institutions. Offenders serving sentences of under six months must apply in writing for parole consideration. The British Columbia Board of Parole operates under the authority of the federal *CCRA*, the *Corrections Act* (BC), and the *Parole Act* (BC). In British Columbia, all offenders must apply for parole consideration.

BOARD OF PAROLE PROCESSES

Parole is granted only when a parole board has carefully examined the case and is of the opinion that the offender's release would not represent an undue risk to society and would facilitate reintegration. The continuation of parole is dependent on the behaviour of the offender in the community.

SUPERVISION

While on parole or on statutory release, the offender must conform to a set of release conditions. Some of these conditions are standard while others are determined by the specific needs of the offender. Generally, the inmate must

- remain within the jurisdiction of the Board;
- keep the peace, be of good behaviour, and obey the law;
- report to a parole supervisor and the police as required;
- keep the Board informed about changes of residence or employment; and
- refrain from criminal associates and contacts.

Additional conditions may be imposed. For example, the Board may impose a condition to refrain from possession of firearms, to refrain from the use of alcohol and/or nonprescribed drugs, to reside in a halfway house for a period of time, or to attend a treatment or training program.

CONDITIONAL RELEASE—A LOOK AT THE DATA

FULL-PAROLE DECISIONS

In 1992–93, the NPB and the three provincial parole boards made 21,338 prerelease decisions regarding full parole. Of these decisions, 10,317 (48%) were "parole granted." The grant rate was 57% for provincial offenders and 34% for federal offenders.

FULL-PAROLE OUTCOMES

Because offenders sentenced to terms of imprisonment in provincial institutions are to serve sentences of less than two years, their time on parole is relatively short. Most provincially sentenced offenders will have parole terms of less than one year, with a maximum of sixteen months. Provincial parolees can conclude parole terms either through expiry or revocation. Regular expiry denotes that the parolee successfully concluded the parole term in the community. Revocation means that the parole term was terminated and the offender was returned to a correctional institution. In 1992–93, 6,175 paroles were concluded. The vast majority—5,033 (82%)—were regular expiries, while the remaining 1,142 (18%) were revoked.

Federally sentenced offenders serving longer sentences such as life or indeterminate sentences may, once released, spend the remainder of their lives under parole supervision. To determine parole outcomes for these offenders, information about persons released and supervised over an extended period of time must be used. While the NPB conducts special studies to determine parole outcomes for federal offenders, these data are not collected on a routine basis; therefore, statistics on federal parole outcomes are not reported here.

PERSONS RELEASED ON FULL PAROLE

Supervision of parolees in the community is provided by the appropriate correctional agency. As noted earlier, responsibility for persons granted parole by the NPB rests with the Correctional Service of Canada. Persons released by a provincial board are supervised by probation and parole officers in that particular province.

Figure 17-4 Average Count of Offenders on Full Parole, by Releasing Authority

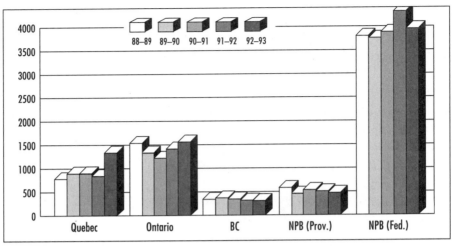

Source: *Adult Correctional Services in Canada, 1992–93* (Statistical Report), Canadian Centre for Justice Statistics, 1993.

Overview of Criminal Justice Facts

On an average day in 1992–93, there were 7,611 offenders under full parole supervision (see Figure 17-4). This represented an increase of 4.3% over 1991-92. Over the five years under review, the number of parolees under full parole supervision in the community increased by 8.9%. Of the 7,611 parolees, 3,193 (41.6%) were released under the jurisdiction of the three provincial boards in Quebec, Ontario, and British Columbia. The remaining 4,418 (58.0%) were released under jurisdiction of the NPB.

FEDERAL DAY PAROLE AND STATUTORY RELEASE DECISIONS

The NPB has authority to grant day parole to offenders under its jurisdiction. In 1992–93, the NPB made 8,516 prerelease decisions regarding day parole. The vast majority of these decisions (7,812 or 92%) concerned federally sentenced inmates. Of the 8,516 total decisions, 5,595 (66%) were "parole granted." As for statutory release, in 1992–93 an average of 2,357 offenders were in the community to serve the final third of their sentence.

CORRECTIONAL EXPENDITURES

Costs associated with the administration of justice are enormous. The price tag for federal correctional services was $859 million in 1992–93, while the

Figure 17-5 Institutional Per Diem Costs, 1992–1993

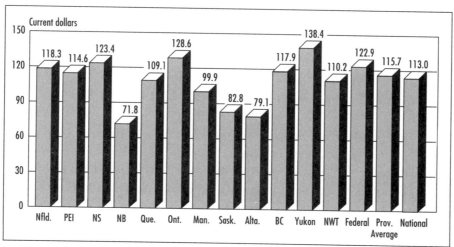

Source: *Adult Correctional Services in Canada, 1992–93* (Statistical Report), Canadian Centre for Justice Statistics, 1993.

provinces spent an additional $1,018 million. In total, the combined cost of federal and provincial corrections was $1.88 billion. The provision of custodial services constituted the bulk of these costs (74%), while the remaining correctional expenses can be attributed to community supervision services (10%), headquarters and central services (13%), and parole boards (3%). In terms of total justice system expenditures in 1992–93, policing services accounted for 60% of justice expenditures, followed by adult correctional services (20%), courts (9%), legal aid (6%), and youth corrections (5%).

Often per diems, or the average daily cost for housing an offender in an institution, are used to describe the cost of corrections. The use of per diems compensates for variations in size and workload among jurisdictions, thereby allowing for more direct comparisons between jurisdictions. In 1992–93, the national per diem cost to house both federal and provincial inmates was $113.00 (see Figure 17-5). Reporting higher per diem costs than the national average were Newfoundland and Labrador ($118.30), Prince Edward Island ($114.60), Nova Scotia ($123.40), Ontario ($128.60), British Columbia ($117.90), the Yukon ($138.40), and the federal correctional system ($122.90). In all other jurisdictions, the cost per inmate ranged from $71.80 in New Brunswick to $110.20 in the Northwest Territories.

It is interesting to note that while 79% of the total correctional population was under some form of community supervision, only 12% of total operating expenditures were allocated to the provision of these services in 1992–93. The largest portion of correctional expenditures (74%) is allocated to custodial services, despite the fact that only 21% of the total correctional population serve their sentence in an institution.

SUMMARY AND CONCLUSIONS
■ ■ ■

In the aftermath of a criminal event, an offender will encounter the police, the courts, and the correctional system. Depending on the seriousness of the crime, offenders will be exposed to either institutional corrections or community corrections. Offenders involved in repeated crimes or serious criminal events are more likely to be sentenced to an institution. Offenders can enter an institution on remand status, as a temporary detainee, or as a sentenced offender. The majority of offenders, however, serve their disposition in the community, on probation. Through various conditional-release mechanisms, offenders also complete their disposition in the community following a period of incarceration. The total cost of maintaining the institutional and community correctional system is substantial ($1.88 billion in 1992–93). An appreciation of the varied and complex components, structure, and operations of the Canadian correctional system will enable readers to better comprehend how an offender is processed through the justice system in the aftermath of a criminal event.

NOTES

[1] Aboriginal/nonaboriginal is the only ethnicity collected on the Adult Corrections Survey (ACS).

[2] The Youth Custody and Community Services (YCCS) survey, still in development, will be able to provide detailed information on the young offender, offences, dispositions, order compliance, youth movements, and reviews. National coverage is expected in 1996–97.

[3] A facility is considered *secure* when youths are detained by security devices, including those that operate with full perimeter security features and/or whose youths are under constant supervision. *Open custody* refers to the minimal use of security devices or perimeter security (i.e., a community residential centre, group home, child-care institution, wilderness camp, or like facility). *Remand* status refers to persons in custody who are awaiting a further court appearance, but who are not currently serving a sentence.

[4] A *restitution order* requires the offender to make restitution for injuries or to pay compensation for loss of or damage to property resulting from the offence.

[5] CSOs are court orders requiring the offender to perform a certain number of hours of volunteer work in the community.

[6] Ontario was not able to provide probation intake data for this period due to updates to the province's offender management system.

REFERENCES

Adlaf, E.M., R.G. Smart, and G.W. Walsh. 1994. *Ontario Student Drug Use Survey*. Toronto: Addiction Research Foundation.

Adler, F., G.O.W. Mueller, and W.S. Laufer. 1991. *Criminology*. New York: McGraw-Hill.

Agnew, R. 1985. "A Revised Strain Theory of Delinquency." *Social Forces* 64(1):151–167.

Allan, B. 1992. "Wife Abuse—The Impact on Children." Ottawa: Health Canada, The National Clearinghouse on Family Violence.

Bala, N. 1991. "An Introduction to Child Protection Problems." In Nicholas Bala, Joseph P. Hornick, and Robin Vogl (eds.), *Canadian Child Welfare Law: Children, State and the Family*. Toronto: Thompson Educational Publishing.

Bayley, D. 1986. "The Tactical Choices of Police Patrol Officers." *Journal of Criminal Justice* 14:329–348.

Bell, D.J. 1987. "The Victim-Offender Relationship: A Determinant Factor in Police Domestic Dispute Dispositions." *Marriage and Family Review* 12(1/2): 87–102.

Bennett, T., and R. Wright. 1984. *Burglars on Burglary*. Brookfield, Vt.: Gower.

Benson, D., C. Charlton, and F. Goodhart. 1992. "Acquaintance Rape on Campus: A Literature Review." *College Health* 40:157–165.

Benson, M.L. 1985. "Denying the Guilty Mind: Accounting for Involvement in a White-Collar Crime." *Criminology* 23(4):583–607.

Birkenmayer, A. 1993. "Parole Decision Making in Canada." *Juristat Service Bulletin* 13(1). Ottawa: Canadian Centre for Justice Statistics.

Blackstone, Sir W. 1771. *Commentaries on the Laws of England*, Book I, Chapter 15.

Black, D. 1970. "Production of Crime Rates." *American Sociological Review* 35:733–747.

Black, D.J. 1983. "Crime as Social Control." *American Sociological Review* 48 (February): 34–45.

Block, R., M. Felson, and C.R. Block. 1984. "Crime Victimization Rates for Incumbents of 246 Occupations." *Sociology and Social Research* 69(3): 442–451.

Bograd, M. 1988. "How Battered Women and Abusive Men Account for Domestic Violence: Excuses, Justifications or Explanations." In G.T. Hotaling, D. Finkelhor, J.T. Kirkpatrick, and M.A. Straus (eds.), *Coping with Family Violence*. Newbury Park, Calif.: Sage.

Boritch, H. 1992. "Gender and Criminal Court Outcomes: An Historical Analysis." *Criminology* 30(3):293–325.

Boyd, N. 1991. *High Society*. Toronto: Key Porter.

Boyd, N., L. Elliot, and B. Gaucher. 1991. "Drug Use and Violence: Rethinking the Connections." *The Journal of Human Justice* 3(1).

Brannigan, A. 1984. *Crimes, Courts and Corrections*. Holt, Rinehart and Winston.

Brantingham, P.J., and P.L. Brantingham. 1984. *Patterns in Crime*. New York: Macmillan.

Briggs, J. 1991. *A Portrait of the Juvenile Joyrider*. Durham: University of Durham.

Brikenmayer, A., M. Reed, and T. Foran. 1994. *Adult Correctional Services in Canada, 1993–94*. Ottawa: Statistics Canada, Cat. No. 95-211.

Brill, H. 1982. "Auto Theft and the Role of Big Business." *Crime and Social Justice* 18:62–68.

Brownfield, D., and K. Thompson. 1991. *Attachment to Peer and Delinquent Behaviour*. *Canadian Journal of Criminology* 33(1):45–60.

Brownmiller, S. 1975. *Against Our Will: Men, Women and Rape*. New York: Simon & Schuster.

Burt, M.R. 1980. "Cultural Myths and Supports for Rape." *Journal of Personality and Social Psychology* 38(2):217–230.

Burt, M.R. 1991. "Rape Myths and Acquaintance Rape." In A. Parrot and L. Bechhofer (eds.), *Acquaintance Rape: The Hidden Crime*. New York: John Wiley & Sons.

Calder, J.D., and J.R. Bauer. "Convenience Store Robberies: Security Measures and Store Robbery Incidents." *Journal of Criminal Justice* 20 (1992):553–566.

Canadian Centre for Justice Statistics. 1995. *Youth Court Statistics 1993–94*. Ottawa: Statistics Canada, Cat. No. 85-522.

Cantor, D., and K.C. Land. 1985. "Unemployment and Crime Rates in the Post-World War II United States: A Theoretical and Empirical analysis." *American Sociological Review* 50 (June):317–332.

Catlin, G., and S. Murray. 1984. *Report on Canadian Victimization Survey Methodological Pretests*. Ottawa: Ministry of the Solicitor General of Canada Secretariat.

Chaiken, J., and M. Chaiken. 1990. "Drugs and Predatory Crime" (pp. 203–240) in M. Tonry and J.Q. Wilson (eds.), *Drugs and Crime*. Chicago: University of Chicago Press.

Check, J., and T. Guloien. 1989. "Reported Proclivity for Coercive Sex Following Repeated Exposure to Sexually Violent Pornography, Nonviolent Dehumaning Pornography, and Erotica." In D. Zillmann and J. Bryant (eds.), *Pornography: Research Advances and Policy Considerations*. Hillsdale, N.J.: Erlbaum.

Check, J., and N. Malamuth. 1985. "An Empirical Assessment of Some Feminist Hypotheses about Rape." *International Journal of Women's Studies* 8(4):414–423.

Clark, L., and D. Lewis. 1977. *Rape: The Price of Coercive Sexuality*. Toronto: The Women's Press.

Clark, S., and D. Hepworth. 1994. "Effects of Reform Legislation on the Processing of Sexual Assault Cases." In J. Roberts and R. Mohr (eds.), *Confronting Sexual Assault: A Decade of Legal and Social Change*. Toronto: University of Toronto Press.

Clarke, R. 1991. *Preventing Vehicle Theft: A Policy Oriented Review of the Literature*. Edinburgh: Scottish Home and Health Department.

Clarke, R.V., and P.M. Harris. 1992. "Auto Theft and Its Prevention." In M. Tonry (ed.), *Crime and Justice: A Review of Research*. Vol. 16. Chicago: University of Chicago Press.

Cohen, L.E., and M. Felson. 1979. "Social Change and Crime Rate Trends: A Routine Activity Approach." *American Sociological Review* 44 (August):588–608.

Collins, J.J., B.G. Cox, and P.A. Langan. 1987. "Job Activities and Personal Crime Victimization: Implications for Theory." *Social Science Research* 16:345–360.

Cooper, B. 1989. *The Management and Prevention of Juvenile Crime Problems*. Crime Prevention Unit Paper No. 20. London: Home Office.

Creechan, J.H., and R. Silverman. 1995. *Canadian Delinquency*. Scarborough, Ont.: Prentice Hall Canada.

Cromwell, P.F., J.N. Olson, and D.W. Avary. 1991. *Breaking and Entering: An Ethnographic Analysis of Burglary*. Newbury Park, Calif.: Sage.

Davis, P.W. 1991. "Stranger Intervention into Child Punishment in Public Places." *Social Problems* 38(2):227–246.

Department of Justice. 1985. *Sexual Assault Legislation in Canada: An Evaluation*. Ottawa: Supply and Services Canada.

Department of Justice. 1993. *Canada's System of Justice*. Ottawa: Supply and Services Canada.

Dobash, R., and R.E. Dobash. 1979. *Violence Against Wives*. New York: The Free Press.

DuWors, R. 1992. "Robbery in Canada." *Juristat Service Bulletin* 12(10). Ottawa: Statistics Canada.

Eliany, M. 1991. "Alcohol and Drug Use." *Canadian Social Trends*. Ottawa: Statistics Canada.

Ericson, R. 1982. *Reproducing Order: A Study of Police Patrol Work*. Toronto: University of Toronto Press.

Fagan, J. 1990. "Intoxication and Aggression" (pp. 241–320) in M. Tonry and J.Q. Wilson (eds.), *Drugs and Crime*. Chicago: University of Chicago Press.

Felson, M. 1987. "Routine Activities and Crime Prevention in the Developing Metropolis." *Criminology* 25(4):911–931.

Felson, M. 1994. *Crime and Everyday Life*. Newbury Park, Calif.: Pine Forge Press.

Felson R.B., W.F. Baccaglini, and S.A. Ribner. 1985. "Accounting for Criminal Violence: A Comparison of Official and Offender Versions of the Crime." *Sociology and Social Research* 70(1):93–101.

Ferraro, K.J., and J.M. Johnson. 1983. "How Women Experience Battering: The Process of Victimization." *Social Problems* 30:325–335.

Finkelhor, D., G.T. Hotaling, and K. Yllo. 1988. *Stopping the Violence: Research Priorities for the Coming Decade*. Newbury Park, Calif.: Sage.

Foran, T. 1992. "Trends in Custodial Counts and Admissions—Provinces and Territories." *Juristat Service Bulletin* 12(9). Ottawa: Canadian Centre for Justice Statistics.

Foster, J. 1990. *Villains: Crime and Community in the Inner City*. London: Routledge.

Frankel-Howard, D. 1989. *Family Violence: A Review of Theoretical and Clinical Literature*. Ottawa: National Health and Welfare.

Fry, L.J. 1985. "Drug Abuse and Crime in a Swedish Birth Cohort." *British Journal of Criminology* 25(1).

Gabor, T., and A. Normandeau. 1989. "Armed Robbery: Highlights of a Canadian Study." *Canadian Police College Journal* 13(4):273–282.

Gabor, T., Baril, M. Cusson, D. Élie, M. Le Blanc, and A. Normandeau. 1987. *Armed Robbery: Cops, Robbers, and Victims.* Springfield, Ill.: Charles Thomas Publishers.

Gartner, R., and A.N. Doob. "Trends in Criminal Victimization: 1988-1993." *Juristat Service Bulletin* 14(13). Ottawa: Canadian Centre for Justice Statistics.

Gelles, R.J., and M.A. Straus. 1990. "The Medical and Psychological Costs of Family Violence." In M.A. Straus and R.J. Gelles (eds.), *Physical Violence in American Families: Risk Factors and Adaptations to Violence in 8,145 Families.* New Brunswick, N.J.: Transaction.

Gelles, R.J., and M.A. Straus. 1988. *Intimate Violence.* New York: Simon & Schuster.

Gottfredson, M.R., and D. Gottfredson. 1988. *Decisionmaking in Criminal Justice.* 2nd ed. New York: Plenum.

Gottfredson, M.R., and T. Hirschi. 1990. *A General Theory of Crime.* Palo Alto, Calif.: Stanford University Press.

Gould, L.C. 1989. "Crime, Criminality, and Criminal Events." A paper presented at the Annual Meetings of the American Society of Criminology.

Gove, W.R., M. Hughes, and M. Geerken. 1985. "Are Uniform Crime Reports a Valid Indicator of the Index Crimes? An Affirmative Answer with Minor Modifications." *Criminology* 23(3):451–501.

Griffiths, C.T., and S.N. Verdun-Jones. 1989. *Canadian Criminal Justice.* Toronto and Vancouver: Butterworths.

Groth, N., and J. Birnbaum. 1979. *Men Who Rape: The Psychology of the Offender.* New York: Plenum.

Hagan, J. 1991. *Disreputable Pleasures: Crime and Deviance in Canada.* Toronto: McGraw-Hill.

Hagan, J., J. Simpson, and A.R. Gillis. 1987. "Class in the Household: A Power-Control Theory of Gender and Delinquency." *American Journal of Sociology* 92:788–816.

Hamilton, B., and J. Coates. 1993. "Perceived Helplessness and Use of Professional Services by Abused Women." *Journal of Family Violence* 8(4):313–325.

Harlow, C.W. 1988. *Motor Vehicle Theft.* Washington, D.C.: U.S. Department of Justice, Bureau of Justice Statistics.

Hartman, D.P., D.M. Gelfand, B. Page, and P. Walder. 1972. "Rates of Bystander Observation and Reporting of Contrived Shoplifting Incidents." *Criminology* (November):247–267.

Hartnagel, T., and W. Lee. 1990. "Urban Crime in Canada." *Canadian Journal of Criminology* 32(4):591–606.

Health and Welfare Canada. 1992. *Alcohol and Other Drug Use by Canadians: A National Alcohol and Other Drugs Survey (1989).* Ottawa: Health and Welfare Canada.

Hewer, P., and A. Birkenmayer. 1994. "Conditional Release Decision-Making in Canada, 1992-93." *Juristat Service Bulletin* 14(2). Ottawa: Canadian Centre for Justice Statistics.

Hilton, N. Zoe. 1992. "Battered Women's Concerns about Their Children Witnessing Wife Assault." *Journal of Interpersonal Violence* 7(1):77–86.

Hope, T. 1987. "Residential Aspects of Autocrime." *Research Bulletin* 23: 28–33. London: Home Office.

Houghton, G. 1992. *Car Theft in England and Wales: The Home Office Car Theft Index*. Crime Prevention Unit Paper No. 33. London: Home Office.

Hudson, J., J.P. Hornick, and B.A. Burrows. 1988. *Justice and the Young Offender in Canada*. Toronto: Wall & Thompson.

Insurance Bureau of Canada. 1994. *Facts of the General Insurance Industry in Canada: 21st Edition*. Toronto.

International Crime Statistics. 1989-1990. International Criminal Police Organization, INTERPOL.

International Association of Credit Card Investigators. 1992. *Credit Card Crime In Canada: Investigation Prosecution*. Toronto.

Jaffe, P.G., E. Hastings, D. Reitzel, and G.W. Austin. 1993. "The Impact of Police Laying Charges." In N.Z. Hilton (ed.), *Legal Responses to Wife Assault: Current Trends and Evaluation*. London: Sage.

Jaffe, P.G., D.A. Wolfe, and S.K. Wilson. 1990. *Children of Battered Women*. Newbury Park, Calif.: Sage.

Johnson, H. 1996. *Dangerous Domains: Violence Against Women in Canada*. Scarborough, Ont.: Nelson Canada.

Karmen, A. 1979. "Victim Facilitation: The Case of Automobile Theft." *Victimology* 4(4):361–370.

Kingsley, B. 1993. *Juristat. Assault in Canada* 13(6). Ottawa: Canadian Centre for Justice Statistics, Statistics Canada.

Karmen, A. 1981. "Auto Theft and Corporate Irresponsibility." *Contemporary Crisis* 5(1): 63–81.

Kempe, C.H., F.N. Silverman, B.F. Steele, W. Droegemueller, and H.K. Silver. 1962. "The Battered Child Syndrome." *Journal of the American Medical Association* 181(1): 17–24.

Kleck, G., and S. Sayles. 1990. "Rape and Resistance." *Social Problems* 37(2):149–162.

Landau, S. F., and D. Fridman. 1993. "The Seasonality of Violent Crime: The Case of Robbery and Homicide in Israel." *Journal of Research in Crime and Delinquency* 30(2):163–191.

Leesti, T. 1994. "Youth Custody in Canada, 1992-93." *Juristat Service Bulletin* 14(11). Ottawa: Canadian Centre for Justice Statistics.

Lejeune, R., and N. Alex. 1973. "On Being Mugged." *Urban Life and Culture* 2(3):259–283.

Levi, K. 1981. "Becoming a Hit Man: Neutralization in a Very Deviant Career." *Urban Life* 10:47–63.

Light, R., C. Nee, and H. Ingham. 1993. *Car Theft: The Offender's Perspective*. Home Office Research Study No. 130. London: Home Office.

Linz, Daniel. 1989. "Exposure to Sexually Explicit Materials and Attitudes Toward Rape: A Comparison of Study Results." *Journal of Sex Research* 26(1):50–84.

Lipset, S.M. 1990. *Continental Divide*. New York: Routledge.

Loftus, E.F. 1979. *Eyewitness Testimony*. Cambridge, Mass.: Harvard University Press.

Loseke, D.R., and S.E. Cahill. 1984. "The Social Construction of Deviance: Experts on Battered Women." *Social Problems* 31(3):296–306.

Luckenbill, D. 1977. "Criminal Homicide as a Situated Transaction." *Social Problems* 25(2):176–186.

Luckenbill, D.F. 1984. "Murder and Assault." In R.F. Meier (ed.), *Major Forms of Crime*. Beverly Hills: Sage.

Lurigio, A.J., and P.A. Resick. 1990. "Healing the Psychological Wounds of Criminal Victimization: Predicting Postcrime Distress and Recovery." In A.J. Lurigio, W.G. Skogan, and R.C. David (eds.), *Victims of Crime: Problems, Policies and Programs*. Newbury Park, Calif.: Sage.

Lynch, J.P. 1987. "Routine Activity and Victimization at Work." *Journal of Quantitative Criminology* 3(4):283–300.

MacLeod, L. 1980. *Wife Battering in Canada: The Vicious Circle*. Ottawa: Canadian Advisory Council on the Status of Women.

MacLeod, L. 1987. *Battered but Not Beaten ... Preventing Wife Battering in Canada*. Ottawa: Canadian Advisory Council on the Status of Women.

Malamuth, N., and J. Briere. 1986. "Sexual Violence in the Media: Indirect Effects on Aggression Against Women." *Journal of Social Issues* 42(3):75–92.

McCaghy, C.H., P. Giordano, and T. Henson. 1977. "Auto Theft: Offender and Offence Characteristics." *Criminology* 15:367–385.

McCullough, D., and T. Schmidt. 1990. "Joyriding in West Belfast." In D. McCullough, D. Schmidt, and B. Lockhart (eds.), *Car Theft in Northern Ireland: Recent Studies on a Persistent Problem*. Belfast: Extern Organization.

Miethe, T.D., and R.F. Meier. 1990. "Opportunity, Choice and Criminal Victimization: A Test of a Theoretical Model." *Journal of Research in Crime and Delinquency* 27(3):243–266.

Miethe, T.D., and R.F. Meier. 1994. *Crime and Its Social Context*. Albany: SUNY Press.

Millar, P.S., and C. Baar. 1981. *Judicial Administration in Canada*. Kingston and Montreal: The Institute of Public Administration of Canada and McGill-Queen's University Press.

Morrison, P. 1991. "Motor Vehicle Theft and Vehicle Vandalism." *Juristat Service Bulletin* 11(2). Ottawa: Canadian Centre for Justice Statistics.

Morrison, P., and L. Ogrodnick. 1994. "Motor Vehicle Crimes." *Canadian Social Trends* 34 (Autumn):21–26.

Normandeau, A. 1968. "Trends and patterns in crime of robbery." Ph.D. diss., University of Pennsylvania, Dept. of Sociology.

Ogrodnick, L., and R. Paiement. 1992. "Motor Vehicle Theft." *Juristat Service Bulletin* 12(12). Ottawa: Canadian Centre for Justice Statistics.

Ontario Social Development Council. 1988. *Y.O.A. Dispositions: Challenges and Choices*. Toronto.

Ouimet, Marc. 1993. "L'Aigle et le Castor: Étude de la Distribution Spatiale de la Criminalité aux États-Unis et au Canada." *Criminologie* 26(2): 85–102.

Parizeau, A., and D. Szabo. *The Canadian Criminal-Justice System*. Toronto: Lexington Books.

Parker, H.J. 1974. *View from the Boys*. Newton Abbot, U.K.: David & Charles.

Peat Marwick Thorne (KPMG). 1993. "Organized Crime Moving to Counterfeit Cheques." *Blue Line Magazine*. June.

Phaneuf, G.F. 1990. "Child Sexual Abuse." Ottawa: The National Clearinghouse on Family Violence.

Plate, T. 1975. *Crime Pays: An Inside Look at Burglars, Car Thieves, Loan Sharks, Hit Men, Fences and Other Professionals in Crime*. New York: Simon & Schuster.

Poyner, B., and B. Webb. 1987. *Successful Crime Prevention: Case Studies*. London: Tavistock Institute of Human Relations.

Reed, M., and A. Birkenmayer. 1994. "Correctional Services in Canada: Highlights for 1992-93." *Juristat Service Bulletin* 14(1). Ottawa: Canadian Centre for Justice Statistics.

Roberts, J. 1994. "Criminal Justice Processing of Sexual Assault Cases." *Juristat Service Bulletin* 14(7). Ottawa: Canadian Centre for Justice Statistics.

Roberts, J., and R. Gebotys. 1992. "Reforming Rape Laws." *Law and Human Behavior* 16(5):555–573.

Roberts, J., and M. Grossman. 1994. "Changing Definitions of Sexual Assault: An Analysis of Police Statistics." In J. Roberts and R. Mohr (eds.), *Confronting Sexual Assault: A Decade of Legal and Social Change*. Toronto: University of Toronto Press.

Rodgers, K. 1994. "The Generational Cycle of Violence." A paper presented at the International Conference "Violence in the Family," Amsterdam, Netherlands, October 13–15, 1994.

Rodgers, K. 1994. "Wife Assault in Canada." *Canadian Social Trends* 34: 2–9. Ottawa: Statistics Canada.

Rodgers, K. and G. MacDonald. 1994. "Canada's Shelters for Abused Women." *Canadian Social Trends* 34:10–14. Ottawa: Statistics Canada.

Roncek, D.W., and M.A. Pravatiner. 1989. "Additional Evidence That Taverns Enhance Nearby Crime." *Sociology and Social Research* 73(4):185–188.

Royal Canadian Mounted Police. 1993. *RCMP National Drug Intelligence Estimate, 1993*. Ottawa: Royal Canadian Mounted Police.

Ruback, R.B., M.S. Greenberg, and D.R. Wescott. 1984. "Social Influence and Crime-Victim Decision Making." *Journal of Social Issues* 40(1):51–76.

Russell, D. 1984. *Sexual Exploitation: Rape, Child Sexual Abuse and Workplace Harrassment*. Beverly Hills: Sage.

Sacco, V.F., and H. Johnson. 1990. *Patterns of Criminal Victimization in Canada*. General Social Survey Analysis Series. Statistics Canada, Cat. No. 11-612E.

Sacco, V.F., and L.W. Kennedy. 1994. *The Criminal Event*. Scarborough, Ont.: Nelson Canada.

Salhany, R.E. 1989. *Canadian Criminal Procedure*. 5th ed. Aurora, Ont.: Canada Law Book Inc.

Saville, G., and R. Murdie. 1988. "The Spatial Analysis of Motor Vehicle Theft: A Case Study of Peel Region, Ontario." *Journal of Police Science and Administration* 16:126–135.

Scheppele, K.L., and P.B. Bart. 1983. "Through Women's Eyes: Defining Danger in the Wake of Sexual Assault." *Journal of Social Issues* 39:63–81.

Schlesinger, Benjamin. 1984. *Child Abuse in Canada*. Toronto: University of Toronto Press.

Scully, D. and J. Marolla. 1984. "Convicted Rapists' Vocabulary of Motive: Excuses and Justifications." *Social Problems* 31(5): 530–544.

Sedlak, A.J. 1988. "The Effects of Personal Experiences with Couple Violence on Calling It 'Battering' and Allocating Blame." In G.T. Hotaling, D. Finkelhor, J.T. Kirkpatrick, and M.A. Straus (eds.), *Coping with Family Violence*. Newbury Park, Calif.: Sage.

Sellin, T. 1938. "Culture Conflict and Crime." *A Report of the Subcommittee on Delinquency of the Committee on Personality and Culture*. Social Science Research Council Bulletin 41.

Sherman, L., P.R. Gartin, and M.E. Buerger. 1989. "Routine Activities and the Criminology of Place." *Criminology* 27(1):27–55.

Shotland, R.L. 1976. "Spontaneous Vigilentism: A Bystander Response to Criminal Behaviour." In H.J. Rosenbaum and D.C. Sederberg (eds.), *Vigilante Politics*. Philadelphia: University of Pennsylvania Press.

Shotland, R.L., and L.I. Goodstein. 1984. "The Role of Bystanders in Crime Control." *Journal of Social Issues* 40(1):9–26.

Shotland, R.L., and M.K. Straw. 1976. "Bystander Response to an Assault: When a Man Attacks a Woman." *Journal of Personality and Social Psychology* 34:990–999.

Silver, C. 1994. "Fire." *Canadian Social Trends* 34 (Autumn):17–20.

Silverman, R.A., and L.W. Kennedy. 1993. *Deadly Deeds: Murder in Canada.* Scarborough, Ont.: Nelson Canada.

Skogan, W. 1986. "Methodological Issues in the Study of Victimization." In E.A. Fattah (ed.), *From Crime Policy to Victim Policy—Reorienting the Justice System.* London: Macmillan.

Skogan, W. 1990. "The National Crime Survey Redesign." *Public Opinion Quarterly* 54:256–272.

Smith, D.A. 1987. "Police Response to Interpersonal Violence: Defining the Parameters of Legal Control." *Social Forces* 65(3):767–782.

Spencer, E. 1992. *Car Crime and Young People on a Sunderland Housing Estate.* Crime Prevention Unit Paper No. 40. London: Home Office.

Statistics Canada. 1992a. *1991 Census—Families: Number, Type and Structure.* Ottawa: Minister of Industry, Science and Technology.

Statistics Canada. 1992b. *The Daily.* Oct. 13.

Statistics Canada. 1992c. "Motor-Vehicle Theft." *Juristat Service Bulletin* 12(12). Ottawa: Canadian Centre for Justice Statistics.

Statistics Canada. 1994. *Canadian Crime Statistics 1993.* Ottawa: Canadian Centre for Justice Statistics.

Steffensmeier, D.J., and R.H. Steffensmeier. 1973. "Who Reports Shoplifters? Research Continuities and Further Developments." *International Journal of Criminology and Penology* 3:79–95.

Stoddart, K. 1991. "It's Easier for the Bulls Now: Official Statistics and Social Change in a Canadian Heroin-Using Community." In R.A. Silverman, J.J. Teevan, and V.F. Sacco (eds.), *Crime in Canadian Society.* 4th ed. Toronto and Vancouver: Butterworths.

Touchette, L. 1994. *Family Violence: Lessons Learned through Project Development.* Ottawa: Department of Justice.

Turner, J. 1993. *Sentencing in Six Adult Criminal Provincial Courts: A Study of Six Canadian Jurisdictions, 1991 and 1992.* Ottawa: Canadian Centre for Justice Statistics.

U.S. Department of Justice. 1993. *Sourcebook of Criminal Justice Statistics.* Washington, D.C.: U.S. Government Printing Office.

van Dijk, J.J.M., and P. Mayhew. 1992. *Criminal Victimization in the Industrial World: Key Findings of the 1989 and 1992 International Crime Surveys.* Netherlands: Ministry of Justice.

Van Stolk, M. 1972. *The Battered Child in Canada.* Toronto: McClelland & Stewart.

Walker, L. 1984. *The Battered Woman Syndrome.* New York: Springer Publishing Company.

Walklate, S. 1989. *Victimology: The Victim and the Criminal Justice System.* London: Unwin Hyman.

Waller, I., and N. Okihiro. 1978. *Burglary: The Victim and the Public.* Toronto: University of Toronto Press.

Waller, I., and R. Weiler. 1984. *Crime Prevention through Social Development.* Ottawa: Canadian Council on Social Development.

Webb, B., and G. Laycock. 1992. *Tackling Car Crime: The Nature and Extent of the Problem.* Crime Prevention Unit Paper No. 34. London: Home Office.

Webb, V.J., and I.H. Marshall. 1989. "Response to Criminal Victimization by Older Americans." *Criminal Justice and Behavior* 16(2):239–258.

Williams, K.R., and R. Hawkins. 1986. "Perceptual Research on General Deterrence: A Critical Review." *Law and Society Review* 20:545–572.

Wilson, J.Q., and R.J. Herrnstein. 1985. *Crime and Human Nature.* New York: Simon & Schuster.

Wilson, M., and M. Daly. 1994. "Spousal Homicide." *Juristat Service Bulletin* 14(8). Ottawa: Canadian Centre for Justice Statistics.

Wilson, M., M. Daly, and C. Wright. 1993. "Uxoricide in Canada: Demographic Risk Patterns." *Canadian Journal of Criminology* 35:263–291.

Wolff, L. 1991. "Drug Crimes," *Canadian Social Trends.* Ottawa: Statistics Canada.

Wolff, L. 1994. "Drug Use and Crime." *Juristat Service Bulletin* 14(6). Ottawa: Canadian Centre for Justice Statistics.

Wolfgang, M. 1958. *Patterns in Criminal Homicide.* Philadelphia: University of Pennsylvania Press.

Wright, C. 1995. "Risk of Personal and Household Victimization: Canada, 1993." *Juristat Service Bulletin* 15(2). Ottawa: Canadian Centre for Justice Statistics.

Wright, C. 1993. *Longitudinal Court Outcome Study of Individuals Accused of Homicide Reported in 1988.* Ottawa: Canadian Centre for Justice Statistics.

Young, G. 1994. "Trends in Justice Spending—1988/89 to 1992/93." *Juristat Service Bulletin* 14(16). Ottawa: Canadian Centre for Justice Statistics.

Ziegenhagen, E.A., and D. Brosnan. 1985. "Victims Responses to Robbery and Crime Control Policy." *Criminology* 23:675–695.

COPYRIGHT ACKNOWLEDGMENTS

To the owner of this book

We hope that you have enjoyed *Crime Counts: A Criminal Event Analysis*, and we would like to know as much about your experiences with this text as you would care to offer. Only through your comments and those of others can we learn how to make this a better text for future readers.

School _____ Your instructor's name _____

Course _____ Was the text required? _____ Recommended? _____

1. What did you like the most about *Crime Counts?*

_____

_____

_____

2. How useful was this text for your course?

_____

_____

_____

3. Do you have any recommendations for ways to improve the next edition of this text?

_____

_____

_____

4. In the space below or in a separate letter, please write any other comments you have about the book. (For example, please feel free to comment on reading level, writing style, terminology, design features, and learning aids.)

_____

_____

_____

_____

Optional

Your name _____ Date _____

May Nelson Canada quote you, either in promotion for *Crime Counts* or in future publishing ventures?

Yes _____ No _____

Thanks!

PLEASE TAPE SHUT. DO NOT STAPLE.

TAPE SHUT

TAPE SHUT

FOLD HERE

MAIL POSTE
Canada Post Corporation
Société canadienne des postes
Postage paid   Port payé
if mailed in Canada si posté au Canada
Business Reply   Réponse d'affaires
0066102399   01

Nelson

0066102399-M1K5G4-BR01

TAPE SHUT

TAPE SHUT

NELSON CANADA
MARKET AND PRODUCT DEVELOPMENT
PO BOX 60225 STN BRM B
TORONTO ON M7Y 2H1